Fifth Edition

Anatomy of a BUSINESS PLAN

A Step-by-Step Guide to Building a Business and Securing Your Company's Future

Linda Pinson

Dearborn™
Trade Publishing
A **Kaplan Professional** Company

Acquisitions Editor: Mary B. Good
Senior Managing Editor: Jack Kiburz
Cover Design: Design Solutions
Interior Design: Eliot House Productions

Published by Dearborn Trade Publishing, a Kaplan Professional Company

Printed in the United States of America

01 02 03 10 9 8 7 6 5 4 3 2 1

Library of Congress Cataloging-in-Publication Data
Pinson, Linda.
    Anatomy of a business plan: a step-by-step guide to building a business and securing your company's future/Linda Pinson—5th ed.
      p.   cm.
    Includes index.
    ISBN 0-7931-4600-3
    1. Business planning. 2. New business enterprises—Planning. I. Title.
HD30.28.P5 2001
658.4'012—dc21   2001002902

DEDICATION

It is with a great deal of pleasure that I dedicate this book to Tom Drewes, the former President of Quality Books, Inc., my mentor and friend. His kindness and encouragement was my inspiration in 1986. Because of his belief in me, my books are now being used in libraries across the nation. Thank you, Tom, for your many years of tireless dedication to independent publishers and for your willingness to share yourself with so many and ask for nothing in return.

ACKNOWLEDGMENTS

During the writing and revising of five editions of *Anatomy of a Business Plan*, it has been my good fortune (and the readers') to have input from many business associates whose expertise in certain areas admittedly exceeds my own. I would like to acknowledge those individuals here.

- **Bernadette Tiernan.** Owner of Tiernan & Associates, in Ridgewood, New Jersey, was instrumental in helping me with the development of our all new "Chapter 5, The Marketing Plan." Bernadette is a marketing professor at Rutgers University and the author of *E-Tailing* and the great new book, *The Hybrid Company* (also published by Dearborn).

- **Dr. Donald R. McCrea.** Director of Executive Education at the University of California, Irvine <www.marketingplan.com> developed the "Product-Market Analysis" on pages 58–61. This is a very valuable tool narrowing your target market to realistic customers. Don is also the developer of my interactive marketing research Web page for **AUTOMATE YOUR BUSINESS PLAN.**

- **John Neal.** CEO of CXO Associates (www.cxoassociates.com) helped me with "Developing an Exit Strategy" on pages 7–11. His company provides executive services to improve the profitability, viability, and shareholder value of client companies. John serves on several for profit and not-for-profit boards and is chairman of the Small Business Committee of the California Chamber of Commerce.

Dearborn would like to acknowledge the works of Small Business Development Centers (SBDCs) around the country for their untiring support of start-ups and small business owners.

TABLE OF CONTENTS

Small Business Books
Business Plan Software

OUT OF YOUR MIND. . .
AND INTO THE MARKETPLACE™

13381 White Sand Drive, Tustin, CA 92780 714-544-0248 FAX: 714-730-1414

AUTOMATE YOUR BUSINESS PLAN
Companion Software to
Anatomy of a Business Plan

2001 version

Version 10.0 for *Windows*®

"We require considerable information to complete loan packages. Anatomy of a Business Plan and Automate Your Business Plan are both assets to any start-up or existing small business. Your financial software program, with its hands-on approach and step-by-step process, lays the groundwork that is mandatory for small businesses."

Paula R.W. Riley, Vice President
CDC Small Business Finance Corp

WHY AUTOMATE YOUR BUSINESS PLAN is the BEST business plan software on the market :

☑ **You can easily create and print your customized winning business plan with this step-by- step program.** Your plan will satisfy your lenders and investors and serve as a guide during the life of your business. You can develop multiple plans concurrently, and parts of one plan can be copied to another through easy cut-and-paste features. An **added bonus** is our special Web page with "hot links" to lots of research sites where you can get marketing, demographic, and financial information.

☑ **We save you 100+ hours with our complete set of pre-formatted and pre-formulated financial spreadsheets.** We help you understand the financial statements, give you filled-in examples. You customize the spreadsheet for your business and input your numbers. We do the calculations for you.

☑ **You do not need any additional software with AUTOMATE YOUR BUSINESS PLAN.** We use our own stand-alone, full-powered word processor and spreadsheet programs. All of our files are also compatible with Microsoft Word Word Perfect, or Lotus. In fact, you have the option within the software to detect and use your own word processor and/or spreadsheet applications. AYBP is also Mac compatible if you PC reader software (such as Virtual PC).

☑ **The SBA, in Washington D.C., chose Anatomy of a Business Plan** (included free with the software) as the basis for its publication MP-32, *How to Write a Business Plan. Anatomy of a Business Plan,* (Ben Franklin Award winner for Best Business Book of the Year), now in its 16th year and 5th edition, has guided over 1,000,000 business owners through the business planning process. It has been used extensively by universities and colleges, SBA BIC Centers, SBDCs, and corporations; is a favorite in libraries throughout the U.S.; and has been translated into several languages including Chinese, Italian, and Spanish.

Free Book

TECHNICAL REQUIREMENTS

Version 10.0 for Windows®
- IBM/PC compatible computer
- Pentium 150+ CPU
- 24MB RAM minimum
- Windows® 95, or later required
- 15MB hard disk space
- PC compatible printer

MAC Users: *If your computer can read PC programs, you can use our software. We also offer pre-formatted and pre-formulated spreadsheets on disk in Excel® for Mac format.*

Automate Your Business Plan 10.0 is a stand-alone program

No other software needed

ORDER BLANK

Please send me:
Automate Your Business Plan with *Anatomy of a Business Plan**
  PC Format: Version 10.0 for Windows

Software & Text Pkg. @ $95*   _____
Mac Spreadsheet Disk @ $50   _____
CA Residents add 7¾% sales tax   _____
Shipping/Handling (USA):
    USPO Priority $7
    2nd Day Air $12   _____
    Next Day Air $21
    Total Amount Enclosed $ _____

* Ask about our discount if you already own the book.

NAME_____
COMPANY_____
ADDRESS_____
CITY_____STATE_____
ZIP_____ TEL (____) _____
___*Please bill my :* __ VISA __ MasterCard __ AMERICAN EXPRESS
Card No:_____
Exp Date:_____ Signature_____
____ *Enclosed is my check payable to:*
OUT OF YOUR MIND...AND INTO THE MARKETPLACE™
13381 White Sand Drive Tustin, CA 92780

Tel: 714-544-0248 EMail: LPinson@aol.com   Home Page: http://www.business-plan.com

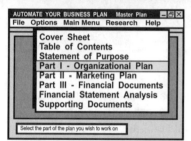
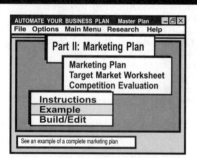
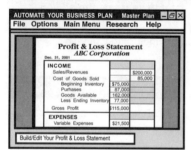

PREFACE

Thank you for choosing *Anatomy of a Business Plan* as the tool to help you write your business plan. I think you will be pleased with the new edition.

"You can run your business by the seat of your pants—but you will probably end up with torn pants." One of the principal reasons for business failure is the lack of an adequate business plan. In today's world, both small and large businesses have come to understand that they need to take the time to evaluate their business potential and map a plan for the future. It is also understood that lenders and investors no longer risk their money on a business unless they have good reason to think that it will be successful (i.e., profitable).

It is the goal of this book to give you a clear, concise, and easy-to-understand process to follow as you develop your business plan. I have been working with business owners for many years and most of them have the same problem—they are experts in their industries, but novices when it comes to business planning. In fact, many times, the prospect of writing a business plan is so formidable that businessowners avoid it until it becomes a requirement for one reason or another.

On the other hand, I am not an expert in your industry, but I can provide you with what I hope is a clear, concise, and easy-to-understand process for writing a business plan. If I am successful, you can follow that process, apply your industry expertise, and write a winning business plan for your company.

Who Is this Book For?

I frequently get asked if *Anatomy of a Business Plan* is appropriate for a big business or a tiny business; a start-up or an existing business; high-tech or low-tech business; a business seeking funding or one looking for an internal planning tool; a product or a service business; a restaurant or a technology business; a sole proprietorship or a corporation; or a division within a company. The answer is that it is the right book for all of the above. No matter who you are, the business planning process is the same.

It is your focus that differs. If you are a smaller business and your business plan is intended only for internal use, your plan may be shorter and you may choose to address only certain issues. On the other hand, if your business is larger and more complex, you will probably need to put key people to work on the development of a more critical business plan that will be in keeping with your company vision. If you need funding, you will have to consider the goals of the lender or investor and address those issues. If you are a new business, you will only have projections. If you are an existing business, you will also have historical information. If you are a pure service business, you have no cost of goods. If you are a product business, you do. If you are high-tech or low-tech, the process is still the same. The variable is how you focus on your specific industry.

The simplification of your business planning task has always been the primary goal of *Anatomy of a Business Plan*. In order to get the most out of the book and to make your job easier, I would suggest that the first thing you do is read the book to give you a general overview of the format and content. After reading, you will be ready to begin working your way through the actual business planning process.

Example Business Plans

In the back of the book (Appendix I, II, and III) you will find three full-length business plan examples that are for three different kinds of business. All three were written by the business owners and/or consultants they worked with. The common tools that they used were *Anatomy of a Business Plan* and its companion software, **AUTOMATE YOUR BUSINESS PLAN**.

- **Marine Art of California.** This start-up product business is owned by Bob Garcia, a sole proprietor dealing in fine art pieces. He is seeking short-time limited partners and plans to recapture 100 percent ownership within four years. A possible one-year history for his business has been added to show what might have happened during his first year.

- **Dayne Landscaping, Inc.** This is a one-year-old landscaping and snow removal (service) business. It is a small corporation, seeking to expand into new territories. Dayne Landscaping, Inc. is planning to seek funding from a traditional lending institution (bank).

- **Wholesale Mobile Homes.com, Inc.** This dot.com bricks and clicks start-up corporation plans to go after $10 million in venture capital. Because the business is more complex and is seeking venture capital, the executive summary and the organizational and marketing plans are researched heavily and written in more detail.

The interesting thing about the three plans is that they were researched and written by three different people. As you read them, you will find that each of these writers (Robert Garcia, Robin Dayne, and Ndaba Mdhlongwa) brings something new and different into the planning process that will prove valuable to you in your own efforts.

Thank you again for choosing *Anatomy of a Business Plan* to help you accomplish your goal. I appreciate your confidence in the book and wish you success in the writing of your business plan!

—Linda Pinson

BUSINESS PLAN CONSIDERATIONS

A well-written business plan will provide a pathway to profit for any new or existing business. Your business plan will also provide the documentation that a lender or investor requires if you find it necessary to seek outside funding sources for your business.

This chapter is designed to give you some background information and guidelines to consider prior to writing your business plan.

Why do you need a business plan? If you need access to additional capital, what does the lender or investor need to know? What are the key words that make your plan more effective? How do you develop an Exit Strategy? Where do the numbers come from in your financial plan? These questions will be addressed in the following pages.

- **Why Do You Need a Business Plan?**

- **What Do Lenders and/or Investors Look For?**

- **The "Key" to Effective Writing**

- **Developing an Exit Strategy**

- **Developing Financial Assumptions**

- **Steps to E-Tailing**

WHY DO YOU NEED A BUSINESS PLAN?

Every business will benefit from the preparation of a carefully written business plan. There are three main purposes for writing that plan. There is an additional benefit if you do business internationally.

1. *To serve as a guide.* The most important reason for writing a business plan is to develop a guide that you will follow throughout the lifetime of your business. The business plan is a blueprint of your business and will provide you with the tools to analyze and implement changes that will make your business more profitable. It will provide detailed information on all aspects of your company's past and current operations, as well as its projections for the next few years. Of course, new business owners have no history and will base the information in their plans on projections developed through current research of the industry. To be of value, your plan must be kept up-to-date. While plans presented to lenders must be bound, you may choose to keep your working copy in a loose-leaf binder. Then you may add current financial statements, updated rate sheets, recent marketing information, and other data as they become available.

2. *As documentation for financing.* A business plan is a requirement if you are planning to seek financing. If you are seeking capital, the business plan details how the desired investment or loan will further the company's goals and increase its profits. Every lender wants to know how you will maintain your cash flow and repay the loan (with interest) on a timely basis. Every investor wants to know how his or her investment will improve the overall net worth of the company and help him to achieve his desired return on investment. You will have to detail how the money will be used and back up your figures with solid information, such as estimates, industry norms, rate sheets, etc. Lenders and investors have access to statistics that are considered normal for various industries, so be sure that your projections are reasonable.

3. *To work in foreign markets.* If you do business internationally, a business plan provides a standard means of evaluating your business potential in a foreign marketplace. More than ever before, world trade is essential to the health of the American economy and to the growth of most U.S. companies. No business today can afford to overlook the potential of international commerce brought about by changes in communications, technology, and transportation. The development of a business plan will demonstrate ways in which your business can compete in this global economy.

Before you begin to write your business plan, remember that one of the principal reasons for business failure is lack of planning. It is an often repeated saying that:

The business that fails to plan, plans to fail.

Take the time to write a clear, concise, and winning business plan. The success of your business depends on it!

WHAT DO LENDERS AND INVESTORS LOOK FOR?

If you are looking for lenders or investors, it is to your advantage to understand the elements that they would most want to see in a well-written business plan. Investors (or venture capitalists) will become equity partners in your company. They will need to justify to themselves that the money they are investing in your company will essentially result in the desired return on their investment. In terms of lenders, remember that bankers are people, too. Just as you will have to present your business plan to them, they will have to present your plan to their bank's loan committee. We all fear rejection. You are afraid of having your loan denied. The loan officer is fearful of presenting your plan to the committee and having it rejected. You can increase your chances of success with lenders and investors by considering the following items. Keep them in mind as you write your plan and review them when your plan has been completed.

1. *What is your credit history?* Provide a credit history that demonstrates that you are a good risk. If you are an existing business, provide information about your payment history. A past bankruptcy or a history of late payments can serve as a "red flag" and send out a warning signal that you may be a bad risk. You will have to prove through a well-prepared Financial Section that you understand all of the costs involved in your business and that you have a complete understanding of cash flow. If you are a new business, your personal financial history will be examined. The owners of the company may be required to submit personal balance sheets listing their assets. Copies of tax returns may also be requested. The lender or investor frequently determines character based on prior business and/or personal financial performance.

2. *What collateral do you have?* What assets do you have and what are you willing to risk for the success of your business? You may be asked to use your home as collateral. You may have money in CDs or other investments that will qualify. The collateral you provide shows your commitment to your company and removes risk on the part of the investor (your new equity partner) or the lender (the bank or whatever institution that is granting your loan request).

3. *Can you meet the lender's or investor's goals?* Lenders and investors want to know that you appreciate their needs and that you have given consideration to your company's ability to fulfill their financial goals.

   • *If you are seeking a lender.* Your lender (banker) wants to know that your company can repay the loan plus interest and, for the period of the loan, maintain a positive cash flow that will allow you to continue to operate your business.

   If the loan is to increase assets, any asset you want to finance must last at least as long as the loan period. For example, you cannot get a five-year, $25,000 loan on a piece of electronic equipment that is expected to become obsolete within two years of the purchase date. The asset should generate the repayment of funds. Show in your Financial Section (specifically in your Cash Flow Projections and Three-Year Projected Income Statement) that the object of the loan will increase sales, increase efficiency, or cut costs and will, in turn, generate added revenue for repayment of the loan plus interest.

If the loan is for working capital, you will need to show how the loan plus interest can be repaid through cash (liquidity), generally during the next year's full operating cycle.

- *If you are seeking an investor.* Venture capitalists and other equity investors will frequently require that you provide them with an exit strategy. They will want to know where the business is ultimately heading. Venture capitalists are most concerned that the company has a high profit potential, that it is competitive, sustainable, and something they understand. They will want to see a financial plan that shows how your company will move toward its goals and produce the desired profit to be distributed to them under a predetermined agreement. As equity partners, investors have a say in how the company is operated. They will want to see a strong management team and will be the hardest to satisfy because they are putting their own funds at risk.

4. **Is there a demand for your product or service?** Be prepared to show evidence that your product or service is well received by your target market (your customers) and that the demand will be sustainable. You can demonstrate demand through a favorable sales history, accounts receivable information, or purchase orders. If you are a new service company or a business with a new product, show customer acceptance through test market results, questionnaire and survey data, and testimonials. To be valid, the responses must come from your target market and not from friends and family. Test market your product and get some evaluations. Ask people who have tried your products or utilized your services to write testimonial letters.

5. **Have you established a proprietary position?** This means you have secured your position in the market in some manner. There is something unique about your business and you have protected this uniqueness in some way. This may be through copyright, trademark, or patent. Include a copy of the document verifying such protection. If you are located in a mall or shopping center, you may be able to work with management to limit competition in some manner. For example, location of competition may be written into the terms of the lease. You may be able to ensure that you will be the only donut shop in a small shopping center or have it specified in the terms of your lease agreement that you will have no direct competition within a given radius of your store. Include a copy of your lease in the Supporting Documents section of your plan and stress any proprietary rights when you write about your location.

6. **Are your projections realistic?** Base your figures on your current market share. Explain your opportunities for growth and demonstrate how you plan to make use of these opportunities. Each industry has its range of accepted financial results and market approaches. The most common error is overstating revenues and understating expenses. Projections that are outside of industry standards will quickly kill the perceived credibility of your

business plan. Examine the annual reports of public companies in your field. Make use of the public library or college library in your area. Read trade journals, business publications, and government and industry reports to determine trends in your business area. Work out a realistic timetable for achieving your goals. Remember that lenders and investors judge your plan and goals in terms of your industry's practices and trends.

7. ***Do you have a strong marketing plan?*** When a lender or an investor is reviewing your business plan, one of the primary areas of focus will be your marketing plan. As you write your marketing plan, you will learn that much of the emphasis is placed on the development of a highly targeted market that can be effectively served by your business—customers who need what you have to offer and who will choose you over your competitors and pay you to solve their problems and fill their needs.

    The lender will make an assessment regarding the logic of your marketing plan and will decide whether it is probable that, during the term of your loan, you will be able to sell to those customers in a volume that is sufficient to repay your loan plus interest.

    An investor (or venture capitalist) will not be looking at your marketing plan solely in terms of your current plans. As a potential equity partner, he or she will also focus on your long-term marketing goals, making a determination as to whether it is likely that the company can continue to increase its market share accordingly and generate the desired return on investment.

THE KEY TO EFFECTIVE WRITING

The text of the business plan must be concise and yet must contain as much information as possible. This sounds like a contradiction, but you can solve this dilemma by using the *key word* approach. Write the following key words on a card and keep it in front of you while you are writing:

Who?	**When?**	**Unique**
What?	**Why?**	**Benefit to the Customer**
Where?	**How?**	**How Much?**

Answer all of the questions asked by the key words in one paragraph at the beginning of each section of your business plan. Then expand on that thesis statement by telling more about each item in the text that follows. Stress any uniqueness and benefit to the customer that may pertain to the section in which you are writing. Examples will be given in the following chapters to give you guidance. Keep in mind, if you are seeking financing, that the lender's or investor's time is limited and your plan is not the only one being reviewed. Often the first paragraph following a heading will be the only area read; therefore, it is very important to include as much pertinent and concise information as possible in that first paragraph.

EFFECTIVE USE OF YOUR TIME

There is no set length to a business plan. The average length seems to be 30 to 40 pages, including the Supporting Documents section. Break the plan down into sections. Set up blocks of time for work with target dates for completion. You may find it effective to spend two evenings per week at the library. You will not be interrupted by the telephone or tempted by the refrigerator or television set. An added bonus is that the reference material you need will be close at hand. It takes discipline, time, and privacy to write an effective business plan.

SUPPORTING DOCUMENTS

You will find it time-saving to compile your list of Supporting Documents while writing the text. For example, while writing about the legal structure of your business, you will realize the need to include a copy of your partnership agreement. Write "partnership agreement" on your list of Supporting Documents. When it comes time to compile that section of your plan, you will already have a listing of necessary documents. As you go along, request any information you do not have, such as credit reports. If you take care of gathering the necessary documents in this manner, the materials you need to complete the Supporting Documents Section will be available when you are ready to assemble it. Remember that you do need to include copies of all of your supporting documents in every copy of your business plan. If a potential lender or investor needs additional information, you can provide copies on demand.

BUSINESS PLAN OUTLINE

With the previous considerations in mind, you will be ready to begin formulating your plan. The pieces of a business plan presented in this book are as follows:

- Cover Sheet
- Table of Contents
- Executive Summary
- The Organizational Plan
- The Marketing Plan
- Financial Documents
- Supporting Documents

Each of the areas of the business planning process is covered in a separate chapter of the book. *Anatomy of a Business Plan* is designed to help you write a complete, concise, and well-organized plan that will guide you and your company toward a profitable future.

The remainder of this chapter addresses three subjects, developing an exit strategy, developing financial assumptions, and steps for e-tailiers, that will help you to focus on your goals and write your business plan more effectively.

· · · · ·

DEVELOPING AN EXIT STRATEGY
START THE RACE WITH THE FINISH LINE IN SIGHT

Before you begin the business planning process, I would like to introduce you to the concept of planning your exit strategy. An exit strategy is not a plan for failure. It is a plan for success. Developing an exit strategy before you write your business plan will enable you to make the best decisions for your business. I think as you read the following pages, you will understand what an exit strategy is and how you can apply it to the business planning process.

It is always good to utilize the talents of experts who specialize in areas that are beyond your specific expertise. With that in mind, I asked John P. Neal to work with me to develop a section on planning an exit strategy. John is the CEO of CXO Associates in Encinitas, California. CXO provides executive services that increase profitability, viability, and shareholder value for client companies. He serves as Chairman of the Small Business Committee of the California Chamber of Commerce.

WHERE IS THE FINISH LINE?

Have you ever seen runners line up for a race not knowing where the finish line is? This would never happen, right? Whether you are starting a new business or expanding a current business, the implication is the same. *Before you begin the race you need to know where you expect to finish.*

Businesses are started for many reasons. Some of the more common reasons include:

- To build a business for yourself instead of for someone else

- To pursue a passion (e.g., "I've always wanted to own a restaurant.")

- To be your own boss and the master of your own time

- To earn money doing what you really like to do (woodworking, quilting, photography, writing, etc.)

- To capitalize on an invention

- To replace income from the loss of a job

- To create net worth (long-term capital appreciation)

It is also inherent in the makeup of entrepreneurs to think early on about future expansion. What new products or services can be added? Can new markets be reached? Can the business use more employees? Can it open more offices?

The list of reasons for start-up and expansion could go on and on. What's really important, though, is to understand that, in all cases, it is critical to develop an *exit (liquidity) strategy*.

DEVELOPING AN EXIT STRATEGY IS THE SECRET

It is a given that professional investors (i.e., venture capitalists) will require a well thought out exit strategy as part of the business plan for any venture in which they plan to invest. However, most entrepreneurs, intent on creating an immediate source of income or just caught up in the excitement of launching or expanding their business, have a habit of over-looking the "finish line." Consequently, they are unprepared for this certain-as-taxes event.

What should your strategy be? Before going any further, you need to understand that there are no right or wrong strategies, only different ones. *Your* strategy should fit *your* goals. The logical place to start is with your long-term goals. The most obvious and often cited goal is retirement. Some entrepreneurs like to develop one business and then leave it to start another venture. You may have other reasons that you foresee will eventually cause you to exit your own business. Whatever your goals may be there are three things that you need to know before you begin to build a better business plan:

1. Where you are headed.

2. When you want to get there.

3. What your business will look like when you arrive.

WHAT ARE SOME OF THE FORMS OF EXIT?

Some of the potential forms of exit include:

- *Selling all or a portion of the business.* It may be possible to sell the business outright to an independent buyer. If this is the case, you will want to maximize the net income of the business and avoid having assets tied up in the business, which you would intend to later keep in your personal possession.

- *Passing the business to a family member.* This can be a good way to transfer value to your heirs in a way that minimizes estate taxes. Proper structuring is important, as well as determining who will run the business.

- *Selling to an Employee Stock Ownership Plan (ESOP).* This can be a valuable vehicle when the new owner group is comprised of key employees in the business. There are certain tax advantages to ESOPs. Existence of the ESOP can also add to the value of the enterprise by giving employees a sense of ownership in the business.

- *Taking the company public.* For those interested in gaining liquidity quickly while having the option to share in future stock appreciation, this might be a good option. The complexities of this form of exit are substantial, as is the demand on management's time leading up to and continuing on after the "event." This option is not for the faint of heart!

- *Liquidation.* In some cases, the best option to gain liquidity may be to simply discontinue conducting business, sell off the business assets, pay off creditors, and keep the proceeds (after taxes, of course). While this is, in some respects, the simplest option, it often yields the least return to the owners because there is little or no value given for the "going concern" or goodwill of the business. This is often the method used when the business value is closely tied to real estate or other productive assets. It is also common for sole proprietor service businesses where income production is dependent solely on the owner practicing his or her skills.

Each of the above involves a variety of considerations. For instance, if you plan to sell, what kind of market can you expect for your type of business? How big might it need to be to achieve optimal value? If you plan to pass it on to a family member, who will that be? How will you train them to run the business? Will whomever you have in mind to succeed you be interested in taking over when you are ready to get out? When will you need to begin the transition? Many of these questions are difficult to answer, but ultimately your successful exit will depend on it.

MAKING DECISIONS BASED ON YOUR EXIT STRATEGY

If you will take the time to think about and answer some of these questions, a clear picture of your business will begin to take form. Three of the major decisions you will be better prepared to make will be those of (1) selecting the source, type, and amount of capital you will need for your business; (2) deciding on the current form of organization, or legal structure, (sole proprietorship, partnership, or corporation) that will best serve your needs; and (3) considering tax issues that will impact your business.

Financing Your Business

Your choice of financing (source of capital) is important and will directly influence your choice of exit. Keep in mind, when considering financing options, not only the ease with which you can raise the funds you require to reach your goals, but the costs of each type of financing in terms of both money and relationships. In the simplest sense, capital is available from four sources: (1) yourself, (2) friends and family, (3) financial institutions, and (4.) the public at large. The monetary cost of each of these options is generally inversely proportional to its personal or "relationship" cost.

- *Yourself (owner financing).* The first question you should ask yourself is, "Do I really need additional financing to meet my goals, or do I just need to manage my cash flow effectively?"

- *Friends and family.* Friends and family can be the easiest, quickest, and least expensive form of financing. However, the emotional or relationship cost can be very high. What if your business fails and you are unable to repay your friends and family? Receiving funds from a traditional lender or a venture capital firm will take far longer, but failure to repay them isn't likely to affect your family gatherings.

- *Financial institutions (debt capital).* In the middle is the traditional bank or finance company. Like the venture capitalist, they want to see a completed business plan before loaning any money to you. However, they don't tend to focus on *your* exit. Instead they focus on *their* exit, which is repayment of the loan when it is due along with interest and other applicable fees. These lenders want to see that management will be able to generate sufficient income and manage cash flow in such a way as to ensure timely repayment. They typically require personal guarantees of the owners and often will require additional collateral, such as a lien on your house or other property, to further ensure repayment.

- *Venture capitalists (equity capital).* Venture capitalists typically invest in opportunities they expect to earn a high compound rate of return on and that will provide an exit (return of their capital along with a return, or profit, on that capital) within five to seven years. They require a complete business plan with a strong exit strategy. Exit in this case, is usually via an Initial Public Offering (IPO) or acquisition by a larger, often public, company. In either case, such an exit typically results in a change of management and loss of control of the entity by the founders. While the venture capital option can be attractive, obviously it is not appropriate under many circumstances.

Dealing with Legal and Tax Issues

It is always a good idea to seek the advice of an experienced corporate attorney and a business accounting professional. Since laws vary from state to state, it is best to choose advisors familiar with the state in which you will operate and live.

The determination of financing needs has a direct bearing on the form of legal structure you will need for your business. Thinking about your exit strategy will provide the basis for determining the form or organization that will best serve your needs as you pursue your goals. If you are a new business and the choice is not clear-cut, your attorney and tax advisor can help you make the best decision. Alternately, if you are a current business that is planning to expand through the use of debt or equity capital, you may be advised that you need to change to a legal structure that will enable you to protect your personal assets and ensure your ability to deal with your lender or investor.

1. *A few of the legal issues you and your advisors need to consider:*
   - *Liability of owners, directors, and officers.* Owners, directors, and officers may become liable for the actions and debts of the company in certain events. Reasonable protection from such liability can be achieved by a combination of effective use of elections and structuring alternatives and supplemented with Directors and Officers (D&O) insurance.
   - *Applicability of state and federal securities laws.* Rules regarding solicitation of investors are complex and require close compliance to avoid civil and criminal penalties.
   - *Rights of minority owners.* Access to books and records and minimum disclosure requirements create obligations requiring strict compliance.
   - *Ease and cost of transfer of ownership.* Depending on your time frame for exit, some legal structures are easier to deal with than others.
   - *Buy-sell agreements among partners or shareholders.* Terms and conditions for buying out a partner/shareholder or their heirs should be spelled out clearly up front to avoid later disputes.

2. *Some of the tax issues to be considered:*

- *Treatment of capital gains upon the sale/transfer of the business.* Tax events need to be planned far in advance. This includes available tax elections to minimize taxes incurred when all or a portion of your interest in a business is sold.

- *Corporate and personal taxes.* Proper structuring can strike an optimal balance between corporate and personal taxes and avoids double taxation.

- *Title to any real property owned.* Certain property may be best owned by partners/shareholders individually and leased to the business in order to achieve the lowest overall tax bill.

- *Reasonable compensation limits.* The IRS and state taxing authorities can set limits on the level of salaries to owner employees. Payments in excess of these limits become dividends that are taxable to the owner and not allowed to be deducted by the corporation.

- *Retirement plans.* A strong retirement plan can be a key tool for attracting high quality employees as well as providing for the owners' retirement. A wide variety of plans exist ranging from simple IRAs to complicated 401K plans. Each has advantages and limitations.

- *Unrelated business income.* If you are planning to start a not-for-profit corporation, which is not subject to normal income taxes, you will need to follow specific guidelines restricting the types of revenue you can generate. Sales of products unrelated to your not-for-profit business purpose may subject the organization to taxation.

EXIT PLANNING JUST MAKES GOOD SENSE!

By now you can see that thinking in terms of your future exit strategy will help you with your financing decisions and with your legal and tax considerations as you write your business plan. Obviously, the less complex your business is, the fewer decisions you will have to make.

It does not matter whether you are writing a business plan for a new business or an existing one that is moving in a new direction. Business planning is an ongoing process. As you continue to operate your goals may change radically. The current and future goals and their impact on your exit strategy need to be continually reflected in your business plan.

With your vision established and sound financial, legal, and tax strategies decided upon, you can confidently build your business plan and. . .

Start the race with the finish line in sight!

DEVELOPING FINANCIAL ASSUMPTIONS

WHAT ARE FINANCIAL ASSUMPTIONS?

Financial assumptions are the rationale upon which you base the numbers that you enter in your financial statements. A simplified example would be explaining that a marketing expense projection of $28,000 is based on sending out four mailings during the year (January, April, August, and October) at a cost of $10,000 for the initial mailing and $6,000 for each subsequent mailing.

ADDING FINANCIAL ASSUMPTION EXPLANATIONS TO YOUR BUSINESS PLAN

When you are writing the text portion of your business plan, each part of the plan should be developed not only as a conceptual idea, but in terms of how it will generate revenues and/or incur expenses. For example, when you decide which legal structure suits your purpose, go one step further and find out what costs you will incur during the process. When you make decisions on who your management will be and what their jobs will entail, plan also what their compensation and your costs will be in terms of salary, taxes, and benefits. When you consider a marketing campaign, determine its costs, probable response, and projected revenues.

In essence, every financial statement could have a sheet appended to it that explains how you arrived at your numbers. There are several scenarios you can choose to follow.

1. You can develop a full sheet of assumptions for your pro forma cash flow statement and append it to the back of the cash flow statement. On the other statements you can clarify only items that need explanation.

2. On all financial statements you can add explanations at the bottom to clarify any items that would be confusing to the reader. In this instance, you would make no reference at the bottom to numbers that you feel need no clarification.

3. You can include a page labeled Financial Assumptions either before or after your financial documents (or at some other location that is documented in your table of contents). On this page(s), you can list your financial assumptions. It is best in this instance to divide them into categories: revenues, inventory expenses, fixed and variable expenses, loans received, loan repayments, fixed asset purchases, etc. Also have a start-up cost category if you are a new business.

My choice is number 1. After a certain amount of time, even the most astute business planner tends to get confused about where some of the numbers came from. This method puts the clarification in close proximity to the number it describes.

Having the pro forma cash flow statement fully explained has an additional advantage if you are approaching a lender or investor. The pro forma cash flow statement is of the highest priority in determining the validity of your request for funding. If you take the time to develop a full assumptions sheet for your cash flow statement, it saves the lender or investor valuable time in trying to determine the premises upon which your numbers are based.

WHAT IS THE PROCESS FOR DEVELOPING YOUR ASSUMPTIONS?

There is a logical process for creating financial assumptions. The steps are as follows:

1. As you develop each piece of your business plan, remember to develop it in terms of revenues you expect to generate and expenses you expect to incur (as in the examples above).

2. Keep a piece of paper at your side. As you determine the revenue and expense dollars related to the task you are working on, jot down the assumptions that you have developed. Be sure to include explanations of when revenues will be realized and when expenses will be incurred.

3. When you are ready to develop your financial plan, gather your assumptions together in one place and use them as the basis for the dollar amounts you input. Finally, append your assumptions to your financial statements where they are needed for clarification.

Oh, No! Another Job to Do!

Every time I revise this book or its companion software and think of something more to add to the business planning process, I also think the reader will cringe because there is one more job to do. Let me assure you that the benefit of going through the financial assumption process will be extremely valuable to you.

One of the most frequent errors made by people writing a business plan is that what they say in the text portion of the plan does not correlate with the numbers they use in their financial documents. In fact, some people try to develop their financial plans first and then develop their organizational and marketing plans. *This is a fatal error.* You must develop the qualitative information and then quantify it in your financial plan. If the numbers do not work out, then you go back to the drawing board and make new decisions that will give you better financial results.

By utilizing the financial assumption process, you will be developing your plan the right way—write the text, thinking in terms of revenues and expenses; list the assumptions on a sheet of paper; transfer the numbers into your financial documents; append any assumptions that are needed for clarification of numbers to your financial documents.

The financial assumption process will do two things for you. It will save you time because you will have all of your numbers at your finger tips when you are ready to develop your financial plan. The most important benefit, however, will be that your business plan will have absolute continuity between what you say in words in the text portion of your plan and what you say in numbers in the financial plan. In other words, *the qualitative part of your plan will say the same thing as the quantitative part of your plan and the plan will be both credible and defensible.*

Qualitative = Quantitative = Credibility + Defensibility

• • • • •

On page 32 of the Dayne Landscaping, Inc. sample business plan (Appendix II), you will find an example of one way of documenting a list of financial assumptions. The writer in this example chose to include it as one of the Financial Documents. You can also see an example of a clarification of a single line item in the pro forma cash flow statement at the bottom of page 24 of the same plan.

STEPS TO E-TAILING

ARE YOU PLANNING TO BE AN E-TAILER?

If you are planning to sell via the Internet, the following are steps to follow as you plan, design, and set up your Web site. As you write your business plan, incorporate the steps into the appropriate sections of your plan—organization, marketing, and financial.

Step 1: *Set Your Goals.*
- ❑ Be consistent with your business plan.
- ❑ Address potential problems from the start.
- ❑ Reinforce your marketing strategy.

Step 2: *Access the Internet.*
- ❑ Determine which connection components should be upgraded.
- ❑ Implement changes (ISP, transmission speed, etc.) as needed.
- ❑ Will your current methods work to support your e-commerce goals?

Step 3: *Promote Your Web Site.*
- ❑ Establish your presence on the Internet (domain name registration, keywords).
- ❑ Link to and from other sites that serve your target market.

Step 4: *Design Your Web Site.*
- ❑ Project a professional image.
- ❑ Consider EDI compliance.
- ❑ Consider intranets and extranets.

Step 5: *Create an Electronic Catalog.*
- ❑ Determine if Cyber Malls are for you.
- ❑ Achieve the best balance of graphics and text.

Step 6: *Identify Your Distribution Channel.*
- ❑ Determine your supply chain.
- ❑ Create appropriate links.

Step 7: *Develop a Method of Order Processing.*
- ❑ Have electronic funds transfer capability.
- ❑ Offer real-time payment solutions (credit cards, e-cash, smart cards).

Step 8: *Select Security Systems.*
- ❑ Safeguard your customers' privacy.
- ❑ Protect your confidential company records/data.

Step 9: *Develop Inventory Tracking Procedures.*
- ❑ Cut your costs by tracking and controlling.
- ❑ Link to suppliers and/or customers as needed.

Step 10: *Refine Your Customer Interface.*
- ❑ Encourage feedback from your customers.
- ❑ Track customer purchase patterns.
- ❑ Communicate with your customers.

THE COVER SHEET AND TABLE OF CONTENTS

The cover sheet of your business plan is like the cover of a book. It provides the first impression of your business plan to the reader. It should be neat and attractive and should contain information that will grab the reader's attention.

The table of contents is also an important element of every good business plan. It enables the reader to quickly find information on the various aspects of your business.

The next three pages cover the following:

➡ **What to Include on a Cover Sheet**

➡ **Sample Cover Sheet**

➡ **Table of Contents Help**

THE COVER SHEET

The first page of your business plan will be the cover sheet. It serves as the title page and should contain the following information:

- Company name
- Company address
- Company phone number (including area code)
- Web address, if you have a Web site
- Logo, if you have one
- Names, titles, addresses, and phone numbers of the owners or corporate officers
- Month and year in which plan is issued
- Number of the copy
- Name of the preparer

The company name, address, phone number, and Web site address should appear in the top one-third of the page. If you have a logo it will be an added enhancement to the page, especially if it is printed in color.

Information regarding the owners or corporate officers of the business will appear in the center of the page.

The bottom third of the page will contain the remaining information. The month and year in which the plan was written lets the lender know if it is up-to-date. For instance, if your plan is five months old, a lender or investor might request an update on certain financial information. Many lenders and investors prefer that the plan be written by one or more of the business owners or officers. This signifies a hands-on approach to the running of the company. Numbering your copies helps you keep track of them.

Keep a log with the following information: number of copy, name of person reviewing the copy, reviewer's phone number, and date submitted. This way you can keep up with the reviewing process and make follow-up calls to the lender if necessary.

A **Sample Cover Sheet** follows. As you can see, this one page contains a lot of information. It provides the name, location, and phone number of your business. By listing the sole proprietor, partners, or corporate officers, a lender or investor will know the legal structure of the business and how to contact key people directly for additional information. Keep in mind that lenders and investors must review many business plans in a limited amount of time. It is to your advantage to help them by making your plan thorough and concise.

SAMPLE COVER SHEET

AEROTECH, INC.
372 East Main Street
Burke, NY 10071
207-526-4319
www.aerotech.com

John Guzman, President
742 South Street
Jamestown, NY 10081
207-814-0221

Roberta Thompson, Vice-President
86 West Avenue
Burke, NY 10071
207-764-1213

Thomas Choi, Secretary
423 Parker Place
Jessup, NY 10602
207-842-1648

Althea Johnson, Treasurer
321 Nason Street
Adams, NY 10604
207-816-0201

Plan prepared August, 2001
by the Corporate Officers

Copy 2 of 6

THE TABLE OF CONTENTS

The table of contents is an important part of your finished business plan. It needs to be well-organized so the reader can quickly find information on any aspect of your business. For example, if your executive summary gives an overview of the managers of your company, the reader should be able to look in the table of contents and find the page number in your organizational plan where you address the management. By the same token, the page in which the résumés can be found in the Supporting Documents section should also be listed. In the same way, marketing results can be traced through the marketing plan and backed up with copies of demographic studies, etc. in the supporting documents.

Obviously, the table of contents cannot be finished until your plan is complete. You can use the headings in your business plan to develop the table of contents. Once you have finished your plan you can insert the page numbers. If, at some time, you alternately choose to print and bind only portions of your plan, the table of contents can be scaled down to match that version.

The length of the table of contents will be dependent on the complexity of your plan. Most small start-up businesses will need only one page. Existing companies will have historical information and financial statements as well as projections. Larger, more complex companies will most likely have more detailed headings, especially if they are going after venture capital.

In all cases, your business plan will have the following major divisions in the table of contents. The subheadings will depend on what you decide to include in your plan.

- Executive Summary
- Part I: Organizational Plan
- Part II: Marketing Plan
- Part III: Financial Documents
- Supporting Documents

The tables of contents in the example business plans at the back of the book should help you see how your own can be organized.

Chapters 3 through 7 of this book will cover the above subjects and will guide you through the content and development of each one. At that point, it will become obvious to you what you will decide to address in your own plan and how the headings for those topics will fit within the table of contents.

EXECUTIVE SUMMARY

The executive summary is the thesis statement of your business plan. It summarizes who you are, what your company does, where your company is going, why it is going where it is going, and how it will get there. If you are seeking funding, it specifies the purpose of the funding you seek and justifies the financial feasibility of your plan for the lender or investor.

Although the executive summary appears near the front of the plan, it is most effectively written after the rest of your business plan is complete. At that time, your concepts will be well-developed and all the information and financial data needed will be available.

Use the *key word* approach mentioned earlier in the book. In a concise, one-page statement you will sum up the essence of your business plan by including answers to the following questions:

- **Who?**
- **What?**
- **Where?**
- **When?**
- **Why?**
- **How?**

EXECUTIVE SUMMARY

As mentioned the executive summary summarizes the content and purpose of your finished business plan. It is a concise statement about your business. The executive summary may be approached from different perspectives.

If your business plan is for internal use only and you are not seeking funds. This statement would summarize your business. It would be a brief overview of the company's goals and statement of how it will focus to meet its projections.

If you are seeking funding. The executive summary specifies the purpose of the funding you seek and justifies the financial feasibility of your plan for the lender or investor. A lender or investor reading only the executive summary should quickly see the name, age, legal structure, location, nature, and uniqueness of your business. The executive summary will also provide a quick overview of your business's past performance and of its future goals and how you plan to reach them. Information on the management team is imperative if you are seeking venture capital. Finally, the executive summary would include the amount and purpose of the loan or investment request, timing needs, justification for financing, and a repayment statement (lender) or statement of potential return on investment (venture capitalist).

- *For a lender.* Address the question of loan repayment. The lender needs to see your company's ability to meet interest expense as well as principal repayments. The lender will want to know when the loan is needed and what you will use as collateral.

- *For angels.* The angel investor, jokingly referred to as the "Bank of Mom and Dad," is generally a wealthy individual who becomes personally involved with a start-up company—loaning expertise, experience, and money. It is best to have a solid business plan to justify the funding. However, depending on the level of familiarity, you may be able to get by with a less than perfect plan.

- *For a venture capitalist.* The days of the easy flow of venture capital are long gone. Since the April 2000 public market correction, companies can't depend on prospective future funding. They need to show evidence of progress and strong relationships. You will need to address how you will meet his or her goals for growth and profitability. Remember that an investor will be an equity partner in your company. After funding, the venture capitalist will very likely sit on your board of directors and serve as an advisor to your management. Increasingly, investors have been looking for an annual return of 45 to 60 percent over three to five years.

Your executive summary should generate excitement and give the reader an awareness of the uniqueness of your business and the qualifications of your management team. Do not exaggerate your potential. Rather, stick to projections that you can back up with facts. One of the greatest errors of business plan writers is the overstatement of projected market share and potential revenues.

Use the key word approach mentioned earlier in this book. Be concise and clear. The executive summary is generally contained on one page if it is for internal use. If you are trying to approach a lender or investor, it should not exceed two or three pages.

As you write your business plan and refine your ideas, you will probably discover new ideas and information that you will want to incorporate into your business plan to make your business more effective and profitable. For this reason, the executive summary is most effectively written after your plan has been completed. At that time, all the information and financial data will be available and you can draw it from the written text and financial spreadsheets.

The following is an example of how the key words may be used to help you form your executive summary:

Who?

Who are the officers of the company?
(Guzman, Thompson, Choi, Johnson)
Who are the managers of the company?
(Guzman—CEO, Thompson—Marketing, Choi—Administration, Johnson—Finance, Smith—Production)

What?

What is the business name?
(*AeroTech, Inc.*)
What is its legal structure?
(S corporation)
What product or service is involved?
(Manufacturer of specialized parts for the aerospace industry.)
What will the loan do for the company?
(Modernize equipment, which will result in a 35 percent increase in production and will decrease the unit cost by 25 percent.)
What will be used for collateral?
(Property at 372 E. Main Street, Burke, NY, with an assessed valuation of $800,000 in 2001.)

Where?

Where is the business located?
(372 E. Main Street, Burke, NY 10071)

Why?

Why is the loan needed?
(To increase growth capital.)

How?

How much money is needed?
  ($250,000)
How will the loan be used?
  (For the purchase of new and more modern equipment and to train personnel in the
    use of the new equipment.)
How will the loan be repaid?
  (The end result will be a net profit increase sufficient to repay the loan and interest within
    three years.)

When?

When was the business established?
  (1993)
When is the loan needed?
  (Funding is needed so equipment can be delivered and in place by May 23, 2002. There
    is a two-month period between order placement and delivery date.)
When can repayment begin?
  (Within 30 days of receipt of funds.)

IN SUMMARY

The executive summary is just that—a summary of your business plan. If you are writing your plan to serve as a guide for your business, and not planning to seek a lender or investor, writing an executive summary will help you to formulate a good summary picture of where you are planning to go in your business. If you are seeking a lender or investor, the executive summary will be the first introduction to your business and should answer key questions regarding your business and its potential for growth and profitability.

Remember that the rest of the plan must back up what you say in the executive summary. For example, if you are purchasing a piece of equipment in order to increase production or expand services, you must not only show figures on its cost, but must also demonstrate a ready market for the additional products or services in the marketing and financial sections. In supporting documents, you can back up the amount requested with information, such as purchase orders, estimates from suppliers, rate sheets, and marketing results.

When you have finished with the formulation of your business plan and answered the key word questions, you will be ready to write your executive summary.

> **Note**
>
> To help you, there are examples on the next two pages—one for a company whose business plan is for internal purposes only and one for a company that is seeking loan funds.

SAMPLE EXECUTIVE SUMMARY

If you are not planning to seek a lender or investor, the following is an example executive summary for a company whose goal does not involve seeking financing from a lender or investor. It is different from the second example in that it does not involve justification of financing or a schedule for receipt of funds, repayment of a loan, or plans for return on investment to a venture capitalist (equity partner).

BestCARE Company
Executive Summary

BestCARE Company is a partnership established in 1995, whose purpose is to provide quality full-time care to the elderly through licensed residential board and care homes.

The company is administratively located at 1234 Hillside Drive in the city of Laguna Hills, California, the home of Jennifer Lopez, R.N., one of two partners. In addition to attending to the administration and accounting duties, Ms. Lopez also oversees medical services for the elderly residents. Her partner, Henry Johnson, oversees maintenance of the homes and does all of the shopping for food, furniture, patient supplies, etc.

BestCARE Company owns and operates three five-bedroom homes within Orange County, California. Each home provides 24-hour per day, full-care services for up to six residents. Two fully-trained caregivers have been hired for each home and live on the premises. Contract-service caregivers work on the live-ins' days off.

The three current homes have now been running profitably for the last three years. Current research shows that there are twice as many families seeking board and care homes as the preferred lifestyle for their elderly parents than was the case in 1995. This has created a high demand where the supply is short.

BestCARE Company is now planning to expand by purchasing two more homes over the next five years. The two new homes will be mortgage-free. They will be purchased with cash from previous profits from the company that have been retained and invested by the partners.

This business plan will serve as a five-year plan that will guide the company through the administrative, marketing, and financial issues that are inherent in reaching a growth goal that will double the size of the company.

SAMPLE EXECUTIVE SUMMARY

If you are seeking a lender or investor, the following is an example executive summary for a company whose goal is to seek financing from a lender or investor. Unlike the first example on the previous page, the executive summary will have to address the financing needs of the company in terms of how much money is needed, when it is needed, how the company plans to use the funds, how the use of those funds will achieve a desired outcome, and how and when repayment will take place to the lender. In the case of venture capital, you will address the investor's return on investment.

AeroTech, Inc.
Executive Summary

Formed in 1993, *AeroTech, Inc.* is an S corporation operating from a 10,000 square-foot manufacturing and warehousing space in Aerospace Tech Park, a light industrial park, located at 372 E. Main Street, Burke, New York. In the past two years, the Economic Development Corporation (EDD) of Burke has been successful in encouraging large aerospace and technology corporations to relocate to the Tech Park. *AeroTech, Inc.* has developed an excellent working relationship with the relocated companies. The company currently serves 20 percent of the total market with gross revenues of $3,650,000.

AeroTech, Inc. custom designs and manufactures specialized parts for the aerospace industry. The company is seeking growth capital in the amount of $250,000 for the purpose of purchasing automated equipment and for training existing personnel in the use of that equipment. Modernization of equipment will result in a 35 percent increase in production and will decrease the unit costs by 25 percent.

AeroTech has a strong management team as well as a board of directors comprised of several industry and community leaders. John Guzman, President and Chief Executive Officer was previously CEO for Omni Aerospace and was the force behind its well-documented growth between 1985 and 1992. Roberta Thompson Vice-President is the Marketing Director. She previously served as marketing head of the products division of *AeroTech, Inc.* Thomas Choi, Corporation Secretary, heads up Administration, capitalizing on his 12 years as an Administrative Executive with USAmerica Air. Althea Johnson, CFO, was a senior partner with JFG Accounting and successfully achieved turnarounds for several multi-million dollar corporations. Donald Smith, Production, came to AeroTech following 20 years as R&D and production engineer with Bordman Electronics. (See résumés in Supporting Documents.)

Burke EDD projections through the year 2005 indicate a 30 percent increase in tenancy in the Tech Park by aerospace companies. Federal government statistics project a 25 percent increase in the United States in aerospace development through the year 2020. Information from engineering and aerospace trade associations indicates that automation is needed to allow the company to remain competitive. By building on past working relationships with current companies and by actively marketing to new residents of the Tech Park, AeroTech, Inc. will be able to capture an additional 15 percent of the market; the Corporation's share will be 35 percent of the total market.

Funding is needed in time for the equipment to be delivered and in place by May 23, 2002. There is a two-month period between order placement and delivery date. Training of employees on the new equipment is projected to cover a two-week period following equipment placement.

The company is expected to break-even 24 months after completion of the employee training period. Repayment of the loan and interest can begin promptly within 30 days of receipt of funds. The loan can be secured by company-owned real estate that has a 2001 assessed valuation of $800,000.

PART I
THE ORGANIZATIONAL PLAN

The first major section of your business plan covers the organizational details of your business. Include information about your industry in general, and your business in particular.

Using the key words, be concise, but address all of the following elements. You may include other organizational areas that you feel are key to your particular industry.

- **Summary Description of the Business**
- **Products or Services**
- **Intellectual Property**
- **Location**
- **Legal Structure**
- **Management and Personnel**
- **Accounting and Legal**
- **Insurance**
- **Security**

WHAT IS AN ORGANIZATIONAL PLAN?

The organizational plan is the section of your business plan that covers the description of your products and services and the administrative setup of your business—the details of how your business is put together in order to function in an efficient and cost-effective manner.

Keep in mind, as you write about each of the following areas, that you will need to approach them in terms of revenues and expenses that will be related to each of your decisions. That way, when you are working on the financial plan, you will have the dollar figures to carry over into your financial statements.

Examples

- If you plan to have employees, project how many hours they will work and at what rate. Also project increased revenue you might expect because you have those employees.
- If you have decided to incorporate, address associated costs (attorney, incorporation fee, etc.).
- If you are leasing a building, find out about associated costs, such as utilities, insurance, improvements, etc. If the building is larger than a previous facility, what effect will the added space have on the revenues you will generate or the costs you incur?
- If you develop a Web site, how much will you spend on the initial development? How often and at what cost will it be updated? Will you have an in-house Web specialist? What are your Web hosting costs?

SUMMARY DESCRIPTION OF THE BUSINESS

Begin the organizational plan with a summary description of your business. Give a broad overview of the nature of your business. Using the key word approach, begin by telling when and why the company was formed. Describe the nature and uniqueness of the products and/or services provided and briefly review the general history and future goals of the company. After the company has been introduced in a paragraph or two, the summary description can be completed by addressing each of the following topics:

- State your company's **mission**, projecting a sense of what your goals are regarding its future place within your industry.
- Describe your company's **business model** and why it is unique to your industry.
- Give an overview of the company's *strategy*—its short-term and long-term objectives and how you plan to realize those objectives.
- If you have **strategic relationships**, tell who they are with and how they will benefit your company.
- Finally, consider the **risks** that your company will face, both internally and externally.

The following is a *simplified* Summary Description of Business Statement for *AeroTech, Inc.* To see a fully developed example, take some time to study that section in the *Wmhinc.com* example business plan in Appendix III.

AeroTech, Inc. was established in 1993 to meet the demand in specialized parts for the aerospace industry. This industry experienced moderate growth with an increase in contracts beginning in 1997. Industry projections indicate a growing demand for the type of products the company manufactures. *AeroTech, Inc.* maintains a competitive edge with prompt order fulfillment, excellent customer relationships, and custom design capabilities. The company is adequately housed in a 10,000-square-foot facility and desires to meet the growing demand for its products through the purchase of new and more modern equipment, which will provide the opportunity for broader scope bidding, increased custom design capabilities, lower per unit costs, and faster turnaround time. In the next three to five years, *AeroTech, Inc.* plans to increase its current 20 percent market share to 35 percent.

After completing the Summary Description of the Business statement, write about each of the following topics. You may add other information that you feel is appropriate to the organizational development of your business.

PRODUCTS OR SERVICES

In this section of your marketing plan you will describe your products and services. What are you selling? In the Marketing Plan (Chapter 5) you will analyze whether or not there is a real need for *all* your products and services or if your repertoire should be limited to those items that are truly in demand. Should you start with a limited number of offerings, and expand your catalog as you strengthen your relationships with manufacturers, suppliers, distributors, and vendors?

If You Are the Manufacturer and/or Distributor of a Product

Give a detailed description of the development of your products from raw materials to the finished item. The development of a flow chart or time line can help you to identify the various stages of research and development and production.

A time line can also be used to demonstrate when raw materials must be ordered, how much time is needed in the production process, and how much time is involved in inventory storage and shipping and handling. Discuss the raw materials that are used and how much they will cost. Who are your suppliers, where are they located, and why did you choose them? Include cost breakdowns and rate sheets in the Supporting Documents section to back up your statements. Although you may order from one main supplier, include information on alternate suppliers. Address how you could handle a sudden increase in orders or a loss of a major supplier. How will the work get done, by whom, and at what cost? Project peak production times and determine when money will be needed for key purchases. Also address quality control and after-sale service activities.

Describe your production equipment and other product assets in terms of what you already own, what it is valued at, what you plan to purchase, and how much it will cost. Again think in terms of dollars. Purchase prices and depreciation on assets owned by your company will end up as balance sheet items in the Financial Documents section of your plan. Also, when you are preparing cash-flow projections, this section will provide the source for your financial assumptions regarding production equipment.

If you are anticipating importing raw materials or finished products for distribution in this country and/or abroad, expand your business plan to include global information. Be sure that you can identify the steps involved in bringing goods into this country or in shipping them overseas along with the time and costs involved. You may be working with foreign manufacturers and agents. You will deal with freight forwarders and custom brokers. The cost of their services and the time and method of payment will also affect your cash flow.

If You Are a Retailer

Describe the products you sell and provide information about your primary and secondary sources of supply. Describe your product selection process and explain why specific suppliers or vendors were chosen. Include product descriptions and rate sheets in the Supporting Documents section.

You may again want to develop some type of flow chart to demonstrate the distribution process. How do the products you sell in your shop get from the manufacturer through your industry's normal distribution channels, into your store, onto your shelves, and into your customers' hands? Again, discuss quality control and after-sale service.

What is your system for managing and tracking inventory? What volume of goods do you stock in inventory, how do you determine the value of your inventory, who will be responsible for checking the inventory?

"Bricks" and/or "clicks" retailers. Who are you? Do you have a straight brick and mortar business or are you strictly an online retailer (e-tailer)—or are you a combination of both? In many ways the retailing process is much the same whether you do your selling online or from a physical location. You still need to deal with wholesalers, product mix, promotion, etc. However, the way you deal with inventory may be significantly different. Although brick and mortar businesses often sell their goods via the Internet, they traditionally stock their full line of products and offer immediate fulfillment of orders. Retailers who sell solely via the Internet, however, frequently stock only high volume items and consignment goods. It is not uncommon for e-tailers to stock no inventory and depend on the wholesaler for fulfillment of their orders.

> **E-Tailers**
>
> If you are planning an e-tail Web site, you will find it very useful to use the "Steps to E-Tailing" on page 14.

If You Provide a Service

Tell what your service is, why you are able to provide it, how it is provided, who will be doing the work, and where the service will be performed. Tell why your business is unique and what you have that is special to offer to your customers. If you have both a product and a service that work together to benefit your customer (such as warranty service for the products you sell), be sure to mention this in your plan.

Consider equipment and supplies that you will need to perform your service and estimate the costs involved. Also project any other costs of related overhead. Will you be providing service at the customer's location or will you work from an office or shop? How much time is involved in the service you will be doing, and how many of those hours are billable to the client? Will you have vehicle expenses? List equipment and supplies that you will need to perform your service and estimate the costs involved. Also project any other costs of related overhead. Will you be providing service at the customer's location or will you work at your place of business? Remember that time involved and billable·hours are a key to success in a service business.

In All Cases

You will need to know if you will be selling the same products and/or services online as you do offline or if you will limit your Web site sales to specific items. You will also need to consider future services or products that you plan to add to your business. Try to anticipate potential problem areas and work out a plan of action.

INTELLECTUAL PROPERTY

If you own intellectual property or proprietary rights, you can address it at this point. Your designs, products, inventions, and ideas can be protected under United States and international intellectual property laws, which cover trademarks, patents, and copyrights. Intellectual property is a highly specialized area of the law and it is best to speak with an expert who can go over the unique details of your own design. You will need to back up your statements by including copies of registrations, photos, diagrams of products in development, or any other pertinent information in Supporting Documents.

- *Patents.* A patent secures an inventor's exclusive right to make, use, or sell an invention for a term of years. Your design for a new product may not be an invention in a technical sense, but the idea is certainly your intellectual property.

- *Trademarks.* These, by definition, point distinctly to the origin or ownership of merchandise to which a trademark is applied. A trademark is legally reserved to the exclusive use of the owner as maker or seller. A distinctive logo, insignia, or domain name can also be protected by a trademark. The symbol ' is used when a trademark application is in progress; the symbol " is used when the trademark is officially registered.

- *Copyright.* This type of protection exists for original works of authorship fixed in any tangible medium of expression, such as literary, musical and dramatic works, pictorial, graphic and sculptural works, sound recordings, and architectural works. Copyrights are indicated by the symbol " before the name and year of the copyright holder. Copyright protection does not apply to things, such as ideas, procedures, processes, or concepts. Web site material is usually copyrighted; so are lengthy corporate writings.

LOCATION

If location *is not* a marketing decision, you will include it in this section. Two examples of businesses of this type might be a Web seller or a manufacturer that ships by common carrier such as United Parcel Service. Their locations would not be directly tied to their target markets. However, if location is a marketing consideration, you may prefer to address it in your marketing plan. For example, if you are opening a retail shop and need to be directly accessible to your customers, your choice of location will be determined by your target market and might, therefore, be more aptly addressed in your marketing plan.

You might begin writing about your location as follows:

> *AeroTech, Inc.* is housed in 10,000-square-feet of warehouse space located at 372 E. Main Street, Burke, New York. This space was chosen because of accessibility to shipping facilities, good security provisions, low square footage costs, and proximity to sources of supply.

Now expand on each reason and back up your statements with a physical description of the site and a copy of the lease agreement. Your lease or rental agreement will contain the financial information needed for monthly cost projections for the cash flow statement. The value of property owned will be transferred to a balance sheet in the Financial Documents section. If you are a new business, you should plan for associated costs such as utilities, improvements, office furniture, and equipment.

Give background information on your site choice. List other possible locations and tell why you chose your location. You may want to include copies of pictures, layouts, or drawings of the location in the Supporting Documents section.

A **Location Analysis Worksheet** is included at the end of this section. This worksheet is intended as a guideline for writing a location (site) analysis.

LEGAL STRUCTURE

Describe the legal structure you have chosen and explain why it is the most advantageous for your business. Name the owners or corporate officers, highlight their strengths and weaknesses, and include résumés of each one in the supporting documents section of your business plan. If you anticipate changing your legal structure in the future, make projections regarding why you would change, when the change would take place, who would be involved, and how the change will benefit the company (e.g., if your exit strategy is to form an IPO).

Sole proprietor. If you are a sole proprietor, give a brief overview of your experience and abilities. As a sole proprietor, you assume 100 percent of the risk. Evaluate your strengths and weaknesses, and state your plans for getting help in needed areas. Do you have current relationships with associates who will serve as advisors in various capacities?

Partnership. If you have formed a partnership, explain why the partners were chosen, what they bring to the company, and how their abilities complement each other. Show their experience and qualifications by including copies of their résumés. Include a copy of your partnership agreement in the supporting documents section. Your agreement should include provisions for partners to exit and for the dissolution of the company. It must spell out the distribution of the profits and the financial responsibility for any losses. Explain the reasoning behind the terms of your agreement.

Corporation. If you have formed an LLC or a corporation, outline the owner/corporate structure (limited liability company, S corporation, nonprofit corporation, professional corporation, etc.) and give highlighted information on the owners or corporate officers. Who are they, what are their skills, why were they chosen, and what will they bring to the organization? Include a copy of the charter and articles in the supporting documents. If you have a Board of Directors or Advisory Board, tell who they are and what they bring to the table that will further your company's goals.

MANAGEMENT AND PERSONNEL

Your management and personnel needs will be determined by the capabilities of the business owners, the amount of time they will be able to commit to the business, and the demands of the marketplace. Small businesses usually start-up with the owners doing most of the work. As the business becomes larger and sales increase, your management and personnel needs will also change. Project your company's goals for growth and plan for the changes that will be necessitated in management and personnel.

Management

The most critical issue to be addressed in your business may well be that of management. Many potentially profitable operations have failed due to inability to effectively manage the company's overall operation. One of the first questions that a potential lender or investor will ask is, "Why should your management team be entrusted with our money?" A few years ago investment capital was flowing heavily into high tech start-ups based on great ideas, but little experience. Most of them failed. There is still available capital, but the rules have changed. The new investment business model is the company with the proper mix of entrepreneurial vision and an experienced management team.

As the decision maker in your business, two of the questions you will need to ask yourself are, "What are the key areas of management in my business?" and "What outside help will I require?" Managerial hiring policies, job descriptions, and employee contracts are all part of making the right choices. Decide how your managers will be compensated: salaries, benefits, bonuses, vacation time, or stock purchase plans.

An organizational chart (see Figure 4.1) can visually show areas of responsibility and the personnel in charge of each section along with the number of employees they will manage. For example, you may need key people in charge of administration, operations, marketing, and finance. Each of these individuals may have middle managers that they will supervise. In turn, the vice president of marketing might be directly responsible for middle managers whose responsibilities are divided into Web site marketing, media advertising, and public relations. If you are involved in global trade, you may need a manager for international marketing.

FIGURE 4.1: PARTIAL ORGANIZATIONAL CHART FOR AEROTECH, INC.

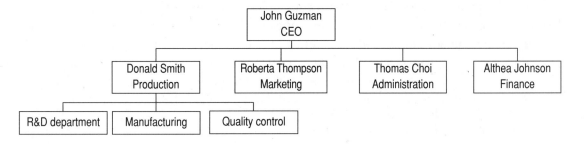

Personnel

How many employees will be needed so the company will operate efficiently? What jobs will you need them for? At what stage in the business will they be hired? What qualifications/experience will they need to have? What hours will they work? What salaries and benefits will they be paid?

Some businesses fail because they hire too many people too soon, anticipating more than their market share of business. Other businesses fail because they become too successful too soon and they are not organizationally ready. Your business plan is the key to responding promptly to the unexpected in order to keep your business progressing smoothly.

If you are seeking a lender or an investor, you will frequently hear them refer to what is known as the "Best- and Worst-Case Scenarios." They want to know that you will be able to identify potential problems and work out solutions before these difficulties occur. It is to your advantage to prepare for the unexpected so your business can continue to run smoothly. In the "best-case," do you have enough people to handle an unexpected influx in sales? In the "worst-case," if sales projections are not achieved, are there other ways in which you can generate revenue? Will you be required to reduce staff or will they be able to fill other positions? For example, if sales drop off at your sporting goods store, could personnel increase revenues by teaching in-store classes or by holding sports clinics?

I like to use this section to list the current employees on the company payroll and follow with a hiring plan for the future. For each, list the type of employee, desired qualifications, salary, and benefits, and when you expect the hiring to take place. This will provide the financial assumptions to plan your cash flow.

ACCOUNTING AND LEGAL

Accounting

Describe your accounting department. Tell what accounting system will be used and why it was chosen. What portion of your accounting/recordkeeping will be done internally? Who will be responsible for the reliability and efficiency and those records? Will you be using an outside accountant to maximize your profits? If so, who within your company will be skilled at working with the accountant—and who will be responsible for reading and analyzing the financial statements provided by the accountant?

It is important to show not only that your accounting will be taken care of, but that you will have some means of using your financial statements to implement changes to make your company more profitable. After reading this section, a lender or investor should have confidence in your company's ability to keep and interpret a complete set of financial records. Information regarding your accounting and the auditing of your books is often requested on the Business Financial Statement provided by potential lenders and investors. If you plan to hire someone to do internal accounting, the salaries should be covered under management or personnel. If you will be retaining outside accounting professionals, be sure to incorporate their retainers into your financial plan.

Legal

Murphy's Law will prevail in this area for sure. Just when you think you don't need legal help, you do. Before your company suddenly finds itself in a position that requires the immediate services of a good attorney (contracts, proprietary issues, disputes, etc.), you should practice due diligence and align yourself with a legal firm that specializes in working with your type of business. Larger firms often have an in-house legal department. Again—budget for in-house staff in your personnel plan. If you plan to keep an attorney on retainer, be sure to include the amount in your financial assumptions.

INSURANCE

Insurance is an important consideration for every business. The goal is to protect your company against common claims and against serious risks for your particular industry. Talk with a reputable insurance agent. Consider the types of coverage appropriate to your business and plan to adopt aggressive policies to reduce the likelihood of insurance claims.

Product liability is a major consideration, especially in certain industries. Service businesses are concerned with personal liability, insuring customers' goods while on the premises, or during the transporting of those goods. If a vehicle is used for business purposes, your insurance must reflect that use. If you own your business location, you will need property insurance. If you lease, you may need insurance relating to content or inventory. Some types of businesses require bonding. Partners may want life insurance naming each other as the beneficiary. Decisions will need to be made about major medical insurance that you intend to provide for management and/or employees.

Exporters may reduce risks by purchasing export credit insurance from the Export-Import Bank of the U.S. agent, the Foreign Credit Insurance Association. Policies for exporters include insurance for financing or operating leases, medium-term insurance, the new-to-export policy insurance for the service industry, and the umbrella policy.

Keep your insurance information current. An **Insurance Update Form** has been included at the end of this section. Use it to maintain information on alternate insurance companies. If your premiums are suddenly raised or your coverage is canceled, you will be able to refer to the form in order to quickly find another carrier. A filled-in example of the form can be found in the *Wmhinc.com* business plan on page 258. The Business Financial Statement from the lender or investor asks for information that can be taken from this section.

SECURITY

As many as a third of small business failures are the result of dishonesty. Security involves not only theft of office supplies, equipment, and inventories by employees and/or customers, but also the theft of information. Address the issue of security as it relates to your business.

Again there will be some important decisions to be made. Product businesses will probably have inventory controls to establish. Service businesses may need to protect client information as well as their own business information. In this age of advanced technology, major concerns have surfaced regarding Internet, Intranet, and Extranet security. Among the important questions to be answered are those relating to the transfer of information via the Internet. Businesses that accept credit cards online need to protect their customer's vital information through the establishment of a secure Web site. They also need to protect their own proprietary information from intruders into their systems.

Anticipate problem areas in your business and identify security measures you will put into practice. Tell why you chose them, and what you project they will accomplish. Discuss this area with your insurance agent. You may be able to lower certain insurance costs while protecting your business.

SUMMARY

You have now covered all of the areas that should be addressed in the Organizational Plan. Use the key words, be thorough, anticipate any problem areas, and be prepared with solutions. Analyze industry trends and be ready to project your business into the future. When the Organizational Plan section has been completed, you are ready to go to the next chapter and begin formulating your Marketing Plan.

Location Analysis Worksheet

Address: _____

Name, address, phone number of realtor/contact person: _____

Square footage/cost: _____

History of location: _____

Location in relation to your target market: _____

Traffic patterns for customers: _____

Traffic patterns for suppliers: _____

Availability of parking (include diagram): _____

Crime rate for the area: _____

Quality of public services (e.g., police, fire protection): _____

Notes on walking tour of the area: _____

_____

Neighboring shops and local business climate: _____

Zoning regulations: _____

Adequacy of utilities (information from utility company representatives): _____

Availability of raw materials/supplies: _____

Availability of labor force: _____

Labor rate of pay for the area: _____

Housing availability for employees: _____

Tax rates (state, county, income, payroll, special assessments): _____

Evaluation of site in relation to competition: _____

_____

_____

Insurance Update Form

Company Name: **Updated as of**

Company	Contact Person	Coverage	Cost Per Year
			$
			$
			$
			$
			$
			$
			$
1. TOTAL ANNUAL INSURANCE COST			**$**
2. AVERAGE MONTHLY INSURANCE COST			**$**

Notes:

1.
2.

PART II
THE MARKETING PLAN

The marketing section of your business plan defines all of the components of your marketing strategy. When you write your Marketing Plan, you will address the details of your market analysis, sales, advertising, and public relations campaigns. The plan should also integrate traditional (offline) programs with new media (online) strategies.

This chapter describes a very comprehensive list of marketing plan components. These components represent a full spectrum of marketing possibilities.

If your business is larger, and more complex, and you are financially able. If you meet all the criteria, you will address most of these components in order to develop an aggressive marketing plan.

If your business is very small. You will not need to include all of the components if your business is small. You will have to decide which ones fit within the scope of your business. However, your marketing plan should still contain the following major sections:

> ➡ **Market Analysis (Target Market, Competition, Industry Trends)**

> ➡ **Sales Strategy (Online and Offline)**

> ➡ **Advertising (Traditional and Web)**

> ➡ **Public Relations**

> ➡ **Customer Service**

Note

You can use the headings and subheadings in the Marketing Plan Outline at the end of the chapter as a guide to follow in laying out your own marketing plan, leaving out only those that do not apply to you.

OVERVIEW AND GOALS OF A MARKETING STRATEGY
(MARKETING PLAN: SECTION I)

Your marketing strategy is the comprehensive approach your business will take to achieve your business objectives.

DEFINITION OF A MARKETING STRATEGY

Your marketing strategy integrates the activities involved in marketing, sales, advertising, public relations, and networking. Each of these components of your overall marketing strategy serves a unique purpose, offers specific benefits, and complements every other component. All components must work together to enhance your company image, reinforce your brand strength, and ensure that your company is distinct from your competitors. A list of the major components of a successful multimedia (online and offline) marketing strategy is shown in Figure 5.1, pages 62–64.

The traditional (offline) and new media (online) components of your marketing strategy should all fit together precisely. These components include promotion of your range of services and products; determination of your prices or rate structure; creation of an advertising plan, public relations endeavors, and promotional campaigns; and a long list of multimedia considerations. It is important to think through your strategy and gather information about your market and your competition *before* you set your fee structure or book ad space. Trial-and-error marketing plans are too expensive.

Marketing is one area in which assistance is offered through a wide variety of local and national sources. At its best, marketing is a specialized field where you can learn a lot quickly by listening to experts. Your local Small Business Development Center (SBDC) offers workshops on marketing, publications, and reference materials at little or no cost to you. They will have consultants on staff or readily available to help you out. Self-help business books are also available in abundance on every aspect of your marketing plan. The purpose of this chapter is to outline marketing fundamentals as they relate to formation of the marketing section of your business plan.

GOALS OF YOUR MARKETING STRATEGY

What do you hope to accomplish through your marketing strategy? Your market research, advertising campaigns, sales incentives, public relations efforts, and networking plans should all move your business in the direction of achieving your marketing goals. Many companies hope to expand their customer base, increase sales, achieve profitability, promote new products and services, and reach other similar idealistic objectives. Not every business owner, however, can articulate precisely what these goals mean for their own company.

The best marketing plans are results-oriented; they define specific, realistic, and measurable goals within time parameters. All sales, advertising, and public relations efforts are then designed to work together to achieve these goals. If the goals are not accomplished within a planned schedule, individual components of the marketing plan should be reassessed and redesigned.

Goals of your marketing strategy, for example, could include creating a brand, building a strong customer base, and increasing product/service sales. Each goal should be explained in specific terms, that is, what do these goals mean to your company? As an illustration, examine these three examples of goals:

- *Create a strong brand.* What is the current level of brand awareness for your company/product/service? Are you starting from scratch or building on a familiar name? What are the characteristics of this brand that you want to reinforce in the minds of consumers? What level of brand awareness do you hope to achieve?

- *Build a strong customer base.* Who are your best customers? What customers are most likely to spend money and return? What is the profile (demographics, psychographics) of your ideal customer? How can you reach this market, online and offline? What particular characteristics of your company/product/service are most likely to inspire loyalty in your ideal customers?

- *Increase product/service sales.* If this is an existing business, what is your current level of sales? If this is a start-up, or new division of an existing business, how can you predict the future demand for your product/service? What new level of sales growth can your business handle? What quantities of your product can you produce/distribute? What level of service can you support through existing or additional staff?

Your marketing activities will comprise a significant portion of your overall business expenses, so investors and bankers will need to understand the importance of the results you are seeking. Make it clear in the statement of your marketing goals that the expenditures you are about to delineate are crucial to the development and growth of your company. By clearly identifying the goals of your marketing plan, you will make a convincing case to support your financial projections.

Basic Marketing Questions

Four fundamental questions should be answered in order to identify your marketing goals: Who, what, where, when, and how? Specifically:

- **Who** are your customers? Who are your competitors?

- **What** are you selling? What quantities and prices of your products will you sell?

- **Where** is your target market located? Where can you reach your target market?

- **When** are your customers most likely to buy? When are your busy seasons?

- **How** will you reach your customers (stores, offices, Web site, catalogs)?

Marketing Musts

Four activities will help you organize your marketing efforts in the most effective direction to achieve your goals. Worksheets are available at the end of this section for each of the following marketing musts.

- *Sell selectively.* This will help you define your market niche. What will *you* offer that is distinctly different (better, less expensive, faster, higher quality, etc.) from *your competitors*? Why should anyone buy from you? What market share can you seek?

- *Know your niche.* What type of individuals and/or businesses do you plan to serve? Start by answering in general terms (professionals, service companies, manufacturing, retail, etc.), then try to be very specific. Spell out the demographics first—age, sex, income, etc. Then you can move on to psychographics, or lifestyle considerations. When you clearly define the population you hope to sell to, you'll have a better view of what services they require. Where do they spend their free time? What activities are they involved in? How do they spend their disposable income? This information leads you to details about what they read (therefore, where you'll want publicity and advertising coverage), where they hang out (for promotions and appearances), what they watch and listen to (if television and radio spots are on your mind). Then *go out and ask them what they want—don't try to guess*. Find out what they really *need*. If your market is local (and where *is* local, anyway?), your local newspapers offer affordable ad packages; chambers of commerce and professional organizations have newsletters that offer insert opportunities. But if you don't know *exactly where your market is*, you can't determine what your market reads.

- *Create your pitch.* Define precisely what "your product/service attributes" mean so that your product or service comes *alive* for your prospective clients. Make it *so* important that they will no longer want to live or work without it. Appeal to their individual needs.

- *Price for profits.* The goal of your business is to make a profit. Many start-up businesses fail to make a profit as early as projected because they didn't price properly. Know what your competition charges, and determine if you should be less than, equal to, or higher priced. Be sure for product pricing that you have covered your materials, labor, and overhead costs. Don't forget shipping, handling, or storage in the total price. Service, like consulting, can be difficult to pinpoint. Some products and services will fall into an hourly rate structure; others are better suited to a service fee. If you provide a service, you may even be on-call for a monthly service fee. Remember that small businesses often do not have big budgets, so if this is your market, your pricing decisions will have to take into account what your market will bear. Learn what your competition charges.

MARKET ANALYSIS
(MARKETING PLAN: SECTION II)

The market analysis section of your marketing plan contains information about your target market, competitors, and marketing trends. Market research methods and results are also delineated in this section. Details about each of these components follow.

IDENTIFY TARGET MARKETS

Who are you selling to? Who are your ideal customers? Your target market should be defined in terms of demographics, psychographics, and special characteristics of niche markets, if applicable. For research information about your target market, visit <www.marketingplan.com/aybp.html>. This Web site provides a full listing of market research resources with direct links to resources.

- *Demographics.* This refers to the statistical data of a population, including average age, income, and education. Government census data is a common source of demographic information.

- *Psychographics.* Psychographics uses demographics to determine the attitudes and tastes of a particular segment of a population. Psychographics examines lifestyles: where people spend their vacations, where they shop, how they spend their disposable income, what sports they participate in or watch, which clubs/organizations they join, and more.

- *Niche markets.* These are a small segment of the population that shares common characteristics, interests, spending habits, etc. Successful niche marketing focuses on a small segment of a total market. It is the best strategy for a small business to achieve a market leadership position. It is expensive, and bland, to try to be all things to all people. Examples of niche markets include "SOHO's" (small office/home office), Generation X or Y, cultural niches, hip hop, to name a few. (The Web site <www.nichemarkets.com> offers a longer list.) Niche markets are better informed than the mass market experts in a particular area of special interest. They will demand communication that is content-rich and substantial to match their level of intelligence and depth of understanding.

BONUS

On pages 58–61, you will find a discussion on "The Product-Market Analysis." If you take the time to read and study it, you will learn the "Four Rules of Target Marketing"—or how to narrow your target market by making two important decisions: which customer needs you will satisfy and who the specific customers are to whom you wish to sell your product or services.

RESEARCH YOUR COMPETITION

Who is competing with you? After you have identified your target market, it is important to discern what other companies are after the same market. What are their strengths and weaknesses relative to your business? If you are not certain who your competitors are, use several search engines to see what company names are presented when you seek your own products and services online. Remember that because it is so easy to check out any company online and obtain far more detail than you could have acquired by a telephone call or brochure, many individuals and businesses will follow this procedure. If you don't do it, you'll be working in the dark.

Check trade associations, manufacturing company listings, and other directories available in your library. Also check the reference section if you want to do an offline search. An easier place to start, however, is to hunt for information about your competitors at <www.marketingplan.com/aybp.html>. Click on the link to "Using the Internet for Competitive Intelligence" and you can go directly to an article archived on the CIO.com Web site.

In researching your competitors, check out the general health of the business, their approach to marketing, and their financial information. In addition, specifically investigate the following indepth:

- *Check out their Web site.* Examine their design, format, and content. Is the site professional and complete? What features and benefits do they promote? How do they position their product/services to their target market? What Web sites do they link to? What is the nature of the content they provide? Do they offer any community-building, message boards, or chat rooms? Do they feature special events?

- *Investigate the prices of their products and services.* How do they compare to yours? Do they offer the same products/services? Do they offer discounts? Any other special offers?

- *Determine who their advertisers are.* Who advertises on their Web site now? What rates do they charge for advertising? What are the terms of their affiliate programs, if any?

ASSESS MARKET TRENDS

Your marketing plan should reflect your observations and insight about trends in your industry and your target market. Information about the general direction of the marketplace can help you target *what people want.* Futurist Faith Popcorn identified 16 market trends in her book, *Clicking* (HarperCollins, 1996) that are still accurate today. She coined the phrase, "cocooning" to describe the phenomenon of staying-at-home to relax and unwind. Dramatic increases in the sales of home theatre equipment, rentals of VHS/DVD movies, and take-out food are a testimonial to the longevity of this trend. Another of her trends called "small indulgences," which describes our desire to reward ourselves for our hard work with affordable luxuries, is evident as Starbucks coffee and Godiva chocolate shops become neighborhood staples and shopping mall anchors. What market trends will have an impact on your business, influencing the demand for your products and services? Are you on-trend?

- **Industry trends.** These influence almost every business within its segment. These are major trends such as the increase in service businesses in the United States, the decline of manufacturing, the precarious position of Internet pure-plays, to name a few.

- **Target market trends.** Like the events categorized by Faith Popcorn and other marketing gurus, these have an impact on the direction of a smaller segment of the population or business community. Trends can be influenced by demographics, such as the aging of our population and huge number of baby-boomers reaching age 50 every minute, or by cultural and social influences outside the realm of demographics. Examples of market trends that evolve from demographic shifts include the increase in the number of assisted-living facilities, and the growth of innovative products and services designed for a more "youthful" retired population.

The shifting demographics of online shoppers will have an important influence on companies that plan to reach their target market via Internet sales. The fastest-growing online demographic group today is 45- to 64-year-old Internet users. This means baby boomers are reaching critical mass online as well as offline. The number of online female shoppers is increasing more rapidly than male shoppers in every age bracket. Your marketing plan should demonstrate that you have analyzed market trends and have considered these trends in the creation of your marketing strategy.

CONDUCT MARKET RESEARCH

Market research can prevent your company from making erroneous decisions that result in expensive design mistakes in new products, marketing campaigns, and more. Market research has traditionally been conducted through techniques such as questionnaires, polls, surveys, and focus groups. Today your business can take advantage of both online and offline market research techniques.

Methods of Research

- **Questionnaires.** These can be administered by paper or online surveys. In either case, questionnaires are more likely to be answered if there is an incentive for the consumer to respond (a reward, that is). Questionnaires should be administered to a representative sample of the target market. Online questionnaires that are nonintrusive, optional, and offer a "thanks for your time" reward can provide the most timely and valuable information. The reward could be a discount on the respondent's next purchase, for example, or a coupon for a popular business product or service.

- **Focus groups.** Offering more insight regarding customer preferences and thought processes than questionnaires, focus groups are small groups of consumers brought together under the direction of a moderator while researchers record their observations (usually behind one-way mirrors or on videotape), responses, reactions, and comments. Consumer feedback about new product developments, pricing structures, and branding issues can be analyzed quickly using the focus group technique. Participants are usually paid for their time. Focus groups can also be conducted online using an Internet chat room. The greatest advantage of online focus groups is the speed with which they can be arranged and the reduced travel costs. Observers can watch from their computers, interject questions to probe an issue in more depth, and no one is inconvenienced.

- *Surveys.* Telephone surveys are the terror of many quiet dinners, and have become increasingly unpopular (and unreliable). Online surveys, on the other hand, meet with surprising success if presented positively. Web sites can include several questions (unintrusive, simple, quick to answer) in their format to elicit comments and suggestions from Web site visitors, particularly shoppers. Because surveys are shorter than questionnaires, a reward isn't necessary. With guarantees of privacy and a promise not to resell or relay the respondents' information to other sources, it is often possible to acquire constructive information quickly.

Database Analysis

What kinds of information will you want to collect and store to help you make better executive decisions about your business? If you store information in a data warehouse for later analysis, your data warehouse systems can help you identify trends within your company in sales, marketing, production, and finance. The sales and marketing data will be particularly useful for managing your marketing plan.

CONTENTS OF YOUR MARKETING STRATEGY
(MARKETING PLAN: SECTION III)

In this section of your marketing plan, the contents shift from descriptive to extremely detailed. You will describe your sales strategy, for example, and also elaborate on the materials you will produce and the campaigns you will organize. When you define your advertising strategy, you will need to identify how you will spend your money on each medium and in what markets. Web advertising campaigns will be described in terms of specific portals, size of banner ads, frequency of e-mail marketing, and more.

General Description

This section of your marketing plan introduces the sections which follow and provides a brief synopsis. This section should include: (1) the allocation of your efforts (i.e., the percentage of your total budget dedicated to online marketing versus offline marketing), and (2) the components that are expected to generate the greatest percentage of new business.

METHOD OF SALES AND DISTRIBUTION

How will your company reach your customers? Are your sales primarily handled by bricks (physical stores), clicks (Web site), catalogs (direct mail), or hybrid (multiple channels)? Do you have plans to expand your methods of sales/distribution as sales increase?

- *Stores or physical offices.* These should be described by size, location, and physical characteristics in reasonable detail. Kiosks and other additional methods of sales should also be included.

- *Catalogs.* Described in terms of size, frequency of mailings, and approximate number of items offered.

- *Web site.* This should include design information, description of contents and major features, hosting arrangements, technological considerations, credit card processing, security arrangements, and other details about the creation and maintenance of a Web site. If your business will operate primarily as an online store or distributor, some of this information will already be covered in other sections of your business plan. If your company will be listed in online malls (zShops at Amazon.com, iMall, shopping@Yahoo!, to name a few) include details about your arrangement and fees in this section of your marketing plan.

PACKAGING

If you provide a product, your *packaging* will be a crucial early consideration. If you are not a trained or talented designer, seek assistance for this. Packaging has a huge impact on the consumer's decision to buy.

If you provide a service, the "package" is you. Your company *image* should be defined before you begin any other marketing efforts. The image of a professional such as a lawyer or accountant, for example, involves building a private practice that will be distinctly different from an advertising agency seeking clients in the fashion industry. Your message should come across loud and clear. Are you conservative? Trendy? Cost-conscious? Flashy? Keep your message consistent and simple for your market. All your online and offline marketing efforts, your sales pitch, public relations activities, advertising, and promotional campaigns should be supportive of one another and of your image.

PRICING POLICY

How much flexibility is there in your pricing strategy? What is your price floor (the lowest price you can charge and still cover your costs) and what is your price ceiling (the highest price the market will bear)? Your marketing plan must address your pricing policy and how prices can be adjusted if necessary to increase demand or cover unanticipated revenue shortfalls.

Price strategy. You may find the range between your price floor and price ceiling offers considerable leeway. Somewhere in this range is the right price point for your product or service. How do you find out what that point is? Your pricing strategy can be tested through focus groups and surveys. What price is the average customer willing to pay? Another way to determine pricing that has become a new trend with entrepreneurs is to test-market through online sales on the auction Web site eBay <www.ebay.com>. This Web site can provide insight to what the market will bear and how hot the product really is perceived to be. eBay has become such a popular resource for small business owners that the site now offers special services for small companies to sell their products directly through eBay.

Competitive position. Should your prices be greater than, less than, or equal to your competitors? Do you need to adjust your prices when your competitors make a change? If you are claiming to offer the highest quality and most personalized service, you may be able to justify charging more than your competitors. If you are appealing to a more "elite" clientele than your competitors, you will also be able to establish your pricing independently. If you hope to beat your competitors on price by going lower, you'll have to be sensitive to your price floor—what you can truly afford to discount and still be a profitable business. If you want to remain equal to your competitors you'll have to be extremely sensitive to any "value-added" offerings and special promotions they are offering that can work as sales incentives, drawing customers away from your business and toward theirs. Your quick and well-formulated response to your competitors' special offers will be critical.

BRANDING

What do current and prospective customers think of your brand? Branding defines and focuses a company's image. Strong brands today are reinforced through a mix of advertising online and offline, sales and customer service efforts, sales incentives that combine online and offline offerings, and public relations strategies that incorporate all sales channels. Consumer reaction defines the brand in the long run. Branding emphasizes the need to build an emotional connection between your products and your purchasers.

DATABASE MARKETING

Database analysis enables a company to personalize their marketing campaign. With personalization, information is presented to customers based on the study of their previous buying patterns. Personalized, or one-to-one marketing attempts to anticipate what customers are seeking, predicting future behavior from past choices.

If your business integrates customer information from databases that track their shopping behavior from their catalog purchases to their shopping mall trips to their e-commerce buys, you can maximize personalization. Personalization can be used most effectively in Web sales. For example, you can send personalized e-mail notices about upcoming sales, special promotions, or new product releases that may be of special interest based on the individual's past purchases.

SALES STRATEGIES

This section outlines your use of online and offline sales materials to reach your target market. Traditional sales involve the creation of printed materials to accompany your sales efforts. Online sales involve refinement of your Web strategy in order to present your products and services in the best possible manner.

Direct Sales

If you are a start-up company, you may find yourself working as both CEO and chief salesperson (not to mention, head of office maintenance). Your marketing plan should identify how you plan to contact prospects, what materials you will send out or deliver, and what follow-up will occur. Your direct sales approach should combine both offline (personal) contact with prospective customers, and online sales through your Web site.

Offline sales. These require materials that can be sent to prospective customers and brought with a salesperson (or you) to presentations. Do you have to design new sales materials? What is required? Will you have to create a new logo and graphics for your material? Consider the traditional list of printed materials: brochures, pamphlets, flyers, stationery, business cards, catalog, promotional flyers, etc. Identify the specific materials that you will need to design and print for use in your sales campaign.

Online sales. These require a Web site that doubles as a marketing tool. In addition to the technological considerations of Web site design, special attention must be directed to engaging the site visitor and providing incentives to buy. Web sites that contain creative features that attract new visitors and encourage them to return to the site are called "sticky," which refers to the ability of a site to bring visitors back for additional shopping. For details about successful online selling techniques, check *E-Tailing* (Dearborn, 1999), which prescribes specific Web site marketing strategies. Your online "pitch" must be just as engaging and irresistible as your in-person sales appeal.

In addition to creating a Web site design that makes your company and your products/services stand out, another important early step of your online sales strategy is to *register with the search engines*. Search engines direct traffic to your Web site, and you are unlikely to be discovered by your target market without their help, unless you are already a major brand name. When you register with the major search engines, you have a greater opportunity for your Web site to keep on working for you 24/365.

Direct Mail

The cost of direct mail campaigns has been estimated to be about $1 to $2 per item. As postage and paper costs escalate, direct mail becomes a less attractive sales option. If your business decides to conduct a direct mail campaign, you may find it preferable to create your own mailing list rather than purchase a list, unless you deal with a reputable list supplier that guarantees their list is current and highly accurate. But even with the best mailing list, be prepared for a low rate of return. Direct mail coupled with incentive offerings can be slightly more effective.

E-Mail Marketing

Compared to direct mail, e-mail marketing is a bargain at $.01 to $.25 per item. E-mail market-ing is expected to outpace direct mail by the year 2004, according to experts. E-mail correspon-dence is more likely to be read than direct mail. It offers opportunities to send personalized offers, based on your understanding of your customers' preferences. However, your company must avoid spamming, or sending unwanted e-mail (like junk mail) to large lists of recipi-ents. To avoid any perception of spamming, your e-mail marketing strategy should allow for "opt-in" and "opt-out"—the method by which your customers and Web site visitors elect to receive future e-mail correspondence from you or decline if they are not interested.

Affiliate Marketing

Affiliate marketing engages the services of a virtually limitless sales force through some type of commission structure for sales, leads, or Web site visits. Affiliates are only paid for the actual sales, and their commission is a small percentage of the total sale. One of the most pop-ular affiliate programs is run by Amazon.com <www.amazon.com>. Affiliates of Amazon, who link their Web site visitors to Amazon's Web site, earn a 5 percent commission on com-pleted sales. If they elect to sell Amazon products on their own Web site they can earn a larger commission of 15 percent. Affiliate programs can offer a creative strategy for service-based businesses to sell related products on their Web site without having to develop the products themselves.

Reciprocal Marketing

Arrangements in which one company offers customers a discount for another company's goods, either in their store or on their Web site, are examples of reciprocal marketing. Creative opportunities within local communities or online communities can make this a beneficial and inexpensive alternative to promote your company. Chambers of commerce often extend these offers within their own circle of member businesses. Online opportunities can cross these geo-graphic boundaries to offer virtually limitless possibilities among complementary companies.

Viral Marketing

Viral marketing occurs when a company offers something that people find so intriguing they spread the word on their own. In order to be effective, your company offering must be simple, entertaining, or engaging in some way. It also must include your company's insignia or the whole point is missed. Viral marketing by word-of-mouth has been highly effective, but viral marketing by the Web has even greater impact. Word can spread more quickly, and to greater numbers of people, by e-mail and forwarded Web links than by telephone calls. And when people see an e-mail from someone they know, they are more likely to read it.

SALES INCENTIVES/PROMOTIONS

Sales incentives can be offered at physical stores and offices, through direct mail, and by your Web site. A combination of promotional offers that reach customers through multiple channels are most likely to give you the best return on your investment. The most important consideration is that your sales incentives should have a direct tie-in to your company so that customers remember your business as well as your promotional offer.

Promotions like *free samples* (give-aways), *incentive items* (pens, pads, gadgets, etc.) are important components of any trade show exhibit—they're expected. *Sweepstakes* have the potential to attract attention both online and offline. *Cash-back coupons* and *discount coupons* also work well in both channels. The combination of discount coupons and an e-mail marketing campaign can be particularly effective.

ADVERTISING STRATEGIES

Advertising is the most potentially expensive investment of your marketing strategy. Because of the high costs involved, the efforts should be researched thoroughly before you begin. This is not an area for amateurs. If you hire no other consultants, and you know you need to advertise your business, hire someone with advertising expertise. The standards today are very high, even in the smallest local papers. Online advertising is a relatively new field and uses different guidelines than print. Graphics, photos, layouts, text, and design have to be completely professional for a positive impact in both the online and offline advertising options.

If you can pinpoint your target market in the finest detail, you can specify precisely where your ad campaign should be located. Size, timing, duration, and frequency all come into play. Don't try this by trial and error. Get guidance from an expert.

Traditional Advertising

How will you invest your advertising dollars in traditional media? Traditional media includes television, radio, print, and extreme advertising. Your investment in market research truly pays off when you begin to determine how to allocate your advertising budget. Only the venues that have an impact on your target market are worth your investment. What television shows do they watch? What radio programs do they listen to? What do they read for business and for entertainment? Where are they traveling and by what method of transportation? With accurate market research to guide you, you can avoid costly advertising mistakes.

- *Television (network and cable).* Network television advertising remains the most costly advertising investment. Within this top tier, the highest price for commercial time is still the Super Bowl. Network prime time follows in rank-order, followed by nonprimetime network buys. In spite of the recent growth of national cable television, network television advertising still has the power to create brands in a way that few other advertising alternatives can. Major corporations seek prime advertising spots, and are willing to pay exorbitant rates to reach huge audiences and create a major impact.

  Cable advertising, which is predicted to assume an increasing share of the total television advertising dollars, works at several levels. National cable advertising can be as costly as network television programming, but local cable television offers rates that may be affordable for even very small businesses.

The additional expenses incurred with advertising—such as creating your commercials and identifying your media plan—must be factored into the total cost of your television advertising. A poorly crafted commercial placed in the wrong time slot may be worse than no commercial, and certainly will be worse for your budget.

- *Radio.* Radio advertising offers small businesses an opportunity to reach a national or local audience with a rate schedule far below television advertising. Radio advertisements can reach your target market during business hours as well as personal time, during commute time, and midday programming. Since many businesspeople spend inordinate amounts of time driving from meeting to meeting, and others keep a radio on in the background while they work, radio advertising has become increasingly desirable.

- *Print.* Your marketing research should provide you with information about the newspapers, magazines, periodicals, and professional or trade journals that are of interest to your target market. Print ads are most effective when they have a single focal point, a distinctive picture, and an explicit headline message of nine words or less.

- *Extreme advertising.* Extreme advertising includes billboards, bus wraps, blimp, and any other form of oversize outdoor ads. Extreme advertising is most effective when the message is straightforward and simple, without complex graphics and extended narratives.

Web Advertising/New Media

Your online advertising dollars should be invested with the same care and precision as your investment in traditional media. Web advertising options include banner ads, PDA advertising, advertising on portals and vortals, and interactive television. Market research again serves as the foundation from which to build your campaign, directing your strategy to include the online options that are most visible to your target market. What Web sites do they visit? Where do they shop online? What portals do they use?

- *Banner ads.* Banner ads have been widely criticized, but they are still a popular form of online advertising. New standards for online ads, which include a more advertiser-friendly format that closely resembles a traditional print ad and a new form of sidebar, have breathed new life into banner ads. Even critics agree that banner ads offer a method of headlining a brand name over and over again, building brand awareness, even if the "click through" rate is lower than 5 percent. Rich media (or multimedia) banner ads are believed to be three to five times more effective than standard ads, because they can be designed to be more creative and interactive. However, many experts fear that the consumer target market may not have the equipment or modem speed to take advantage of a multimedia presentation. You need to understand your target market and their capabilities before you invest in this option.

- *PDA advertising.* Personal Digital Assistant (PDA) advertising meets the unique space and size requirements of specific wireless devices. PDA advertising is most effective when it is specifically designed for these devices rather than personal computers. Web marketing campaigns need to be restructured to meet restrictions of smaller screen space, lack of color and font choices, graphic restrictions, and slow content delivery due to narrow bandwidth—restrictions that will eventually be eliminated. The best use of this form of advertising is to reach consumers on-the-go for things like travel arrangements, comparison pricing, auction bidding, hotel and entertainment plans, and stock activities.

- *Portals/vortals. Portals* guarantee a tremendous number of viewers at an extremely high cost. Advertising on a portal is beyond the scope of most small businesses, but placement in a marketplace on a portal may be a way to build online traffic. Amazon.com's zShops, Shopping@Yahoo.com, iMall, and other similar locations offer the opportunity for broader exposure without the high price tag of a portal ad. Advertising on portals requires an understanding of consumer behavior in your target market to achieve the best results.

  Vortals, or vertical portals like iVillage.com, Oxygen.com, and Women.com, offer access to niche markets on a larger scale. Vortal advertisements are about twice as expensive as portal advertising, but can reach a more responsive audience if properly identified.

- *Interactive television.* Interactive advertising, or advertising on "smart television," has evolved from the need to engage consumers in new and different ways to make an impact. Interactive television units are expected to increase worldwide in the next five years to over 81 million units, accompanied by an increase in interactive advertising. Interactive advertising is most effective when it is completely innovative, entertaining, and provides interesting content in a creative way.

Long-Term Sponsorships

Sponsorships can be designed to meet the marketing goals of any company. Long-term sponsorships offer the benefit of helping to strengthen brand awareness in niche markets. In both the online and offline areas, long-term sponsorships help to build strong relationships with a business or organization and it's direct market, offering opportunities to co-brand multiple events, functions, advertisements, and more, providing high visibility for the advertiser. Co-branding can be set up as an exclusive arrangement or as a joint sponsorship among several complementary companies.

PUBLIC RELATIONS

The primary difference between advertising and public relations is that you always pay for advertising space, while press coverage from your public relations efforts is "free" (aside from the fact that you may have paid to orchestrate the event that subsequently became newsworthy). Activities that demonstrate your strengths and the terrific qualities of your business in a newsworthy way can be of more value in the long run than the most expensive advertising campaign. Public relations campaigns strive to build credibility in the marketplace through routes that are more discreet than direct advertising.

Building an Online Presence

Your Web site offers a vehicle for public relations that companies without an online presence can't imitate. Community groups or clubs, chat groups, and message boards offer incentives for people to return to your Web site more frequently. *Community groups* can be established on your Web site to allow individuals with common interests access to shared information. What community group and club activities can be included on your Web site? *Chat groups* facilitate dynamic interaction among visitors to your Web site. Chat groups can be set up by topic according to a regular schedule for maximum effectiveness. *Message boards* encourage a running dialogue of questions and answers, and allow visitors to your Web site to exchange information or request information from a subject expert on your site.

Events (Online and Offline)

Can you create an event that will attract people to your Web site or to your physical store or office location? Grand openings, anniversary celebrations, celebrity visits, and other creative events serve a dual purpose. If they are done well, they will reinforce your relationship with existing customers and attract new business. If they are significant and newsworthy events, you may be fortunate enough to receive press coverage.

Publicizing Your Efforts

Seek opportunities for press coverage of your work and your accomplishments whenever you can. The impact of public relations is cumulative. You won't see immediate results in most cases, so consistency is critical.

Press Releases

A simple *press release*, preferably one page, accompanied by a photo, can gain more visibility for you than an advertisement if the newspapers pick it up. Press releases should be interesting, newsworthy, concise, and sent to the right person. Watch the newspapers carefully to determine who the correct contact for your press release is. The business editor generally receives huge numbers of releases. If a specific reporter tends to cover stories about your industry or interests, try addressing the release to that individual instead. The media brings you into broader public view than your advertising can. It is your way to reach larger numbers in less time. Use it wisely.

Send your press releases to:

- *Weekly newspapers.* Reporters are always looking for great new stories.

- *Daily newspapers.* Dailies usually want only a local twist, so stay close to home, unless it's a national story.

- *Wire services.* These seek up-to-the-second news items, so move quickly if you have a hot item to report.

- *Magazines.* Offer you a chance to look like an expert, but you will need longer lead time. Plan ahead.

- *Radio.* Radio attracts the attention of the mobile and the sedentary. A guest spot can boost you into a whole new spectrum.

- *Television.* This is the most important medium to be prepared for. Take the time to learn how to present yourself on television to make effective use of the incredible power of this medium. With television, you need to be concise and controlled, speaking in sound bites to be sure your point gets across the way you want it to and so it isn't edited out.

Press kits. Press kits can also be helpful. You can prepare your own press kit or hire a marketing consultant to help you out. Your press kit should build your credibility as an expert in your field or profession. It should include:

- a biography (short and directed to events that are significant today).

- a photo (headshot, 8 x 10 or 5 x 7 black and white).

- your brochure.

- copies of articles that have quoted or featured you.

The press kit doesn't accompany every press release. It is used to introduce you as a resource, an "expert" available when members of the media need a resource for quotes, opinions, inside information, validation, and more.

NETWORKING

Networking can mean the difference between isolation and involvement for any business owner. For home-based businesses networking takes on a particularly significant role. It replaces the water-cooler and coffee-pot contact that occurs daily in every corporate office. Networking is by definition a supportive system of sharing information and services among individuals and groups having a common interest. Networking will keep you in contact with the outside world, help you avoid isolation and stagnation, and build your business contacts for current and future plans.

Networking is a two-way street, an *exchange* of information. Real networking requires that you do *more* than reach out to give and receive business cards. *Give* a little information, and *get* a sincere grasp of what one another's skills are. Then you've really reached out.

You will need to become involved in several levels of networks to provide contacts for you within:

- the business community at large.

- your peer group of professionals.

- your local community.

- the community at-large.

Involvement in some organization at each of these levels of networks will provide public relations opportunities that will not develop from within your own home. The following are a few ideas to get you started in each of these four areas.

The Business Community

Small business organizations offer the potential for small business owners to pull together for a bigger impact. The impact can be political, as it is in organizations whose mission is to lobby, or economic, as in those organizations that emphasize member benefits and discounts. In larger numbers there is certainly more influence. As a member of these groups, you may qualify for corporate rates on products and services, special discounts, and/or group rate health insurance. Examples include: the National Association for the Self-Employed (NASE), National Small Business United (NSBU), and a host of local home-based business support groups.

It is a comfort to know that other business owners share your concerns and interests. The organizations mentioned are very large national groups. Subsets of the business community may find what they need in other organizations, and often will join more than one as time and finances permit. The National Association of Women Business Owners (NAWBO), for example, is designed for women business owners of any size firm. NAWBO has statewide chapters that independently run monthly meetings and events, as well as a strong nationwide offering of conferences and workshops. New corporate discount packages are made available fairly often as this group draws the attention of major corporate sponsors.

Industry organizations often combine large corporations and small businesses, offering business owners an opportunity to meet with a diverse group of individuals. Statewide chamber of commerce and regional industry associations may be worth exploring.

Your Peer Group of Professionals

Professional associations are your link with other business leaders or owners, prospective customers/clients, sales leads, and sources for general business information. Membership fees vary, and benefits of membership include a wide range of products/services, such as membership directories, newsletters and other publications, discounts, group rates for programs, educational opportunities, and more. Membership in these groups serves a different purpose for you. These groups are your resource for new information in your profession. Mentors also support resources when your business grows and you need to hire help, virtually or actually. You may find it difficult to sell here, if you're among a group all selling the same thing. But you will absolutely need these contacts. And if you achieve a leadership position, you can also achieve public recognition. Not bad for public relation purposes.

Trade associations are available for almost every profession. You'll learn the secret handshake for your peer group, just as in professional associations. Membership rates and offerings vary. Monthly and annual meetings can help to keep you current in your own field, and help you find the best suppliers, vendors, etc. for your work. But the same word of caution applies here as above—you may not be closing sales deals within a group of your peers, but you need these contacts to thrive. As a leader, your opportunity for public recognition in your field will help you grow your business.

The Community

Civic organizations provide an opportunity for you to become active in local community service groups. Your local chamber of commerce is a good start. Local chambers will promote their own members' products and services over anyone else in the community. They will often publish their own directory and run their own schedule of business functions. If the mission of the group doesn't track with your objectives, keep the time you spend to a minimum but don't be a stranger. Let your specialty be well known, and define your area of expertise so that referrals will be passed your way. Lead a workshop. Be a speaker at a meeting.

Volunteer activities at local hospitals, schools, libraries, and colleges are almost endless. Fundraising activities are usually a top priority. Volunteer to help with a task that offers you an opportunity to demonstrate your skill and talent. In this way, you'll not only help the organization, but also promote your talent through demonstration of your abilities.

The World At-Large

Don't lose your national and international focus, no matter how regional your business is today. Watch for events and opportunities that can bring you in contact with a wide range of people around the country, even if your business is geared to your own community. You can do a better job of serving any market you select if you are in touch with the outside world.

As soon as you realize your business has potential beyond the borders of the United States, start making connections in the global community. Use the contacts of corporations that have already opened doors to gain introductions and entry into this rapidly growing area of opportunity. Seek the international organizations that will give you both support and recognition.

Commitment

Your degree of involvement in any organization should reflect the importance of this organization or association to your business success—unless, of course, you are joining for purely social reasons. The best use of your time, however, will be to find and focus on a few organizations that offer both business and personal satisfaction. Why waste your time? In a position of leadership of any type of organization you will give the most time and you will gain the best contacts. You will get to know the most people. You will have the most opportunity for media exposure.

If you know that one particular organization is a great source of direct leads for your business, work your way into an active role in the leadership of the group. Start by participating on a committee to get a sense of the group and the internal dynamics. Determine how you can volunteer your time in a way that also provides you with an opportunity to showcase your skills. Your talents will be most visible to the group if you share them and help the association accomplish its goals. If you are only a name on a mailing list, you are less likely to be approached personally.

CUSTOMER SERVICE
(MARKETING PLAN: SECTION IV)

Consumer expectations of high quality service must be met if you want to keep your customers. Consumers expect to be able to contact a customer representative with questions, concerns, problems, complaints, and returns. Business customers expect the same. Your business will need to identify your plans to meet these needs.

Description of Customer Service Activities

Will you offer 24/7 access to customer service representatives? Can your customers reach you by phone, fax, or e-mail at any time? As your business grows, you will probably need to consider the addition of the services of a call center, which offers uninterrupted service for your customers. How will you deal with customer contact in the meantime?

Expected Outcome of Achieving Excellence

It's an old marketing maxim that it is far less expensive to retain existing customers than to add new ones, so your business gains an immediate benefit from building a loyal customer base. For an excellent resource with insight and techniques about building a solid customer base, check *Loyalty Marketing in the Internet Age* (Dearborn, 2000).

IMPLEMENTATION OF MARKETING STRATEGY
(MARKETING PLAN: SECTION V)

As the scope of your marketing plan expands to include complex multimedia campaigns, the resources and skills of professionals may be needed to design the best approach.

IN-HOUSE RESPONSIBILITIES

Whether or not you outsource any or all of your marketing work, you and your team remain responsible for keeping your marketing plan on track. Your marketing plan should support your overall business objectives and work within the framework of your total Business Plan. You are ultimately responsible for ensuring that occurs.

OUTSOURCED FUNCTIONS

Advertising, public relations, and marketing firms. These firms specialize in each component of your marketing plan identified in the previous pages. You may decide to hire an outside firm for only a portion of your marketing activities, such as advertising. Advertising companies can generally offer as much or little support as you choose, from media planning to creating commercials. As a small business, you may be able to find a small advertising business that will offer a fee schedule that fits your budget. It's worth checking out.

Advertising networks. Networks operate in a manner similar to traditional advertising companies, but they specialize in online advertising. Advertising networks like DoubleClick and 24/7 Media serve as brokers of Internet time and space. These companies collect online advertising inventory and sell spots to advertisers, saving clients the effort of examining advertising sites and negotiating deals. Ad networks can also focus on a specific target market segment and identify pertinent Web sites. Their fee is paid as a percentage of ad sales or cost-per-thousand rate.

ASSESSMENT OF MARKETING EFFECTIVENESS
(MARKETING PLAN: SECTION VI)

Once your marketing plan is implemented, you will need to assess your results. You will need to continuously monitor the effectiveness of each online and offline campaign.

- Are your Web site promotions reaching your target market?

- What online advertising methods are the most effective in driving traffic to your Web site?

- What is the cross-over from online promotions to offline sales, and from offline promotions to online sales?

- Should certain radio, print, or television advertisements be strengthened?

- Should any be abbreviated or eliminated?

Assessment of the effectiveness of your marketing plan provides the management information you need to direct your future efforts and to make the wisest investment of your marketing dollars.

· · · · ·

This completes the presentation of the components of a winning marketing plan.

To help you. The remaining pages in this chapter are as follows:

- *Product-market analysis.* Bonus discussion referred to under the Target Market section on pages 58–61.

- *Marketing worksheets.* These will make it easier to develop your own marketing plan, Figures 5.1 to 5.5 on pages 62–68.

- *The Marketing Plan Outline.* This provides you with an overview of the components and to help you with the formatting of your own marketing plan on pages 69–70.

THE PRODUCT-MARKET ANALYSIS

developed and contributed by
Donald R. McCrea
Director of Executive Education, University of California, Irvine

Before you write your marketing plan. The most important thing you need to do is to analyze your market and make a product-market decision. There are two parts to this decision:

1. The choice of which customer needs you will satisfy as reflected in the specific product or service you will sell to your customers.

2. The choice of the specific customers to whom you wish to sell your product or service (your target market segment).

Once you have made these decisions, you will be ready to write your marketing plan, as described in the next part of these instructions. If you take the time to do this analysis and carefully choose which customers you will market your product or service to, you will find that almost every prospect you talk to will have a need for what you're selling.

Choosing a group of customers to sell to (i.e., selecting a target market segment) means selecting potential customers according to some criteria you have determined are related to the likelihood these customers will want to buy your product or service. These criteria might include demographic factors, such as age, income, or where they live; or lifestyle factors, such as interest in sports, antique collecting, reading mystery novels, or seeing foreign movies. Your job as a business person is to determine what factors relate to your customers likelihood of buying your product or service.

FOLLOW THE FOUR RULES FOR MARKETING AND SALES SUCCESS

The following four rules for marketing and sales success are designed to help you analyze your market and choose the customers who are more likely to want to buy your product or service. Focusing your marketing and selling efforts on these customers will make finding and keeping new customers easier for you than if you are less selective about which customers you target.

Note
These rules apply equally whether you are selling to consumers or to other businesses. The rules also apply to you whether you are a start-up or an existing business.

RULE #1

FIND POTENTIAL CUSTOMERS WHO WANT YOUR PRODUCT OR SERVICE

If your potential customers are consumers, will they recognize that they have a need or want? If your customers are businesses, will they recognize that they have a business problem to solve or an opportunity to exploit?

If the group of customers you have chosen to sell to clearly recognize their need, want, problem, or opportunity, then they are more likely to want to buy your product or service. Note, though, that it's not enough for you to recognize that your prospects have a need or problem: you will have to determine if they will recognize this, as well.

If your prospects do not recognize their need or problem, then the first action plan of your marketing and selling activities will be to create or heighten your prospects' awareness of their need or problem. This will require specific effort on your part, and is typically done through an integrated marketing communications program.

It's far simpler and less costly, however, if (during your analysis) you can identify that there is a selected group of potential customers who already recognize their need or problem. This group then validates your plan by becoming your target market segment, and your marketing and selling tasks become easier with this group.

The question you must answer. What are the characteristics of your potential customers that are related to their need or desire for your product or service? For example, if you are selling an electric toothbrush, people who visit a dentist regularly are more likely to be interested in your toothbrush than those who don't visit the dentist very often. Customer characteristics that relate to the likelihood of visiting a dentist might include income and education. You might therefore choose to sell your electric toothbrush only to individuals making more than $50,000 a year and with at least a college degree.

RULE #2

IDENTIFY CUSTOMERS WHO ARE READY TO BUY

Will the want/need/problem/opportunity cause your prospects enough pain or the prospect of enough pleasure that they will be willing to take action?

If your prospects are ready to act to fill their need or solve their business problem, then they will be more likely to buy your product or service. On the other hand, if your potential customer's need or problem is not strong enough to motivate them to take action, then you will be required to expend more sales and marketing effort to convince them that they will benefit from filling the need or solving the problem. Keep in mind that your prospects probably have several needs or problems, so you must show them that the one you can fill or solve is of high enough priority that they should fill it before the others.

This again would require specific effort on your part, and will become another requirement for your integrated marketing communications program. You will be able to save yourself much of this effort, however, if you plan to refine your target market segment to include only those prospects who already recognize their need or problem and are willing to act on it.

To continue your analysis, you must ask yourself this next question. Are there additional customer characteristics that will tell me that these customers will be ready to buy? To expand on the example above: Of those who visit the dentist regularly, those with a higher likelihood of gum disease may be more ready to buy your electric toothbrush than those with healthy teeth and gums. One customer characteristic that is related to a higher incidence of gum disease is age. You might therefore choose to sell your electric toothbrush to those individuals who are over 45 years of age.

When you combine this characteristic with the income and education characteristics selected previously, your analysis has determined that your target market segment would now become those individuals earning $50,000 or more per year, with four or more years of college education, and who are over 45 years of age.

To complete your analysis, there are two more rules to apply once you have identified your target market segment. Both rules will help your business achieve success.

RULE #3
LET THE CUSTOMERS KNOW THAT YOU CAN FILL THEIR NEED

Will your prospects recognize that you can fulfill their need or want, or solve their business problem? If you are an existing business, do your prospects already recognize your ability to fill their need or want, or solve their business problem?

If you are an existing business, and your customers have recognized this, then your marketing communications program has already done its job or you have already built good relations with these prospects so you can move on to Rule #4.

If your prospects do not yet recognize your ability to meet their need or solve their problem, then you must figure out how to demonstrate to them your ability to do so. This activity will become a part of your marketing communications program, and form the core of your initial selling activities. Your prospects must recognize that you have a solution to their need or problem before they will commit to spending time or resources with you.

If you have chosen a target market segment satisfying Rules #1 and #2, then the bulk of your marketing and sales activities and expenditures will be dedicated to satisfying Rule #3 and Rule #4. Rule #3 will be satisfied by your advertising and promotional activities.

Once you have figured out how to educate your prospects on your ability to satisfy their need or solve their problem, you can move on to Rule #4.

RULE #4
FIND CUSTOMERS WHO WILL PAY

Will your prospects pay you *to meet their need or solve their business problem?*

There are two parts to this rule:

1. Will your prospect *pay*?

    and

2. Will your prospect *pay you*?

Even though your prospects recognize their need or problem, are motivated to take action, and recognize that you have a solution, they may not be ready or able to pay, or to pay you.

You must ensure your prospect will have funds budgeted or available to fill this need or solve this problem. You also must ensure you are dealing with the decision makers. In the case of a family, the husband and wife may make joint decisions, especially on large purchases. In the case of a business, several individuals may comprise the "buying center," including a purchasing agent, an executive, a financial officer, and possibly others.

Once you have determined your prospects' ability and willingness to pay, you must ensure they are willing to pay you (i.e., they recognize you can fill their need or solve their problem in a way that no other competitor or substitute product can do). They must clearly see greater value in what you have to offer them, and trust you to stand behind your product or service's ability to meet their need or solve their problem. If your prospects can't distinguish you from your competitors, don't trust you, or can't distinguish your product or service from other products or services offered to them, then a portion of your marketing and sales activities will have to be spent on educating them about your uniqueness and trustworthiness. Of course, uniqueness and trustworthiness must have value to your prospects before they will be willing to pay for them.

CONCLUSION

If you are a new business, analyzing your market, remember that every firm must satisfy these four rules for marketing and sales success. If you an existing business and having difficulty finding customers to purchase your product or service or are spending a lot of time "convincing" your prospects to buy, consider targeting your market segment to satisfy Rules #1 and #2. Then you'll find that almost every prospect you talk to has a need for what you're selling. You'll be able to concentrate your marketing and sales efforts on satisfying Rules #3 and #4, to ensure they easily see how you can fulfill their needs better than any of your competitors.

If the results of your product-market analysis show that there are valid customers for your product or service, you are now ready to write your marketing plan. The benefit to you of following the four rules will be shorter sales cycles, a higher percentage of prospects converted to customers, and more productive use of your marketing and sales dollars.

FIGURE 5.1: COMPONENTS OF A SUCCESSFUL MULTIMEDIA MARKETING STRATEGY

Marketing—Traditional (offline) +	New Media (online)
Identify target market(s) • demographics • psychographics • niche market specifics	Identify online target market(s) • online demographics • online psychographics • online niche market specifics
Research/assess competition	Research /assess competitors' Web sites
Assess industry trends	Assess online industry trends
Conduct market research • questionnaires • focus groups • surveys	Conduct market research • e-mail questionnaires • online focus groups (structured chats) • online (Web site) surveys
Create packaging/image	Mirror branding/image online
Determine pricing strategy	
Create branding/image strategy • logo • slogan • pitch	Design online customer database assessment Merge online/offline database analysis
Develop customer database assessment	
Identify co-marketing opportunities.	Identify online co-marketing opportunities
Design reciprocal marketing strategies.	Identify links to/from other Web sites
Evaluate effectiveness of all components of the marketing plan.	Evaluate effectiveness of online marketing

Sales—Traditional (offline) +	New Media (online)
Refine the sales "pitch"	Determine the online sales pitch
Design and print all sales materials • brochures • pamphlets, folders • stationery, business cards, etc. • catalog • promotional flyers, other	Design/implement the Web site • introduce the company • define products/services • identify additional content needs
Create direct mail campaign	Register with search engines
Instigate viral marketing	Create an e-mail marketing campaign
	Create affiliate programs
	Create viral marketing opportunities online

FIGURE 5.1: COMPONENTS OF A SUCCESSFUL MULTIMEDIA MARKETING STRATEGY, CONTINUED

Sales Incentive/Promotions (offline)   +   New Media (online)

Create in-store campaigns and mailers:	Create campaigns on the Web site and via e-mail for:
• cash back coupons • discounts/coupons • special introductory offers • free samples	• cash back coupons • discounts/coupons • special offers (i.e., free shipping)
Design sweepstakes and contests	Design online sweepstakes or points programs (e.g., points for frequent Web shoppers)
Identify give-aways	
Identify trade show opportunities • determine involvement (exhibit v. attend)	Identify give-aways (e.g., as a thank you for completing a Web site survey)

Advertising—Traditional (offline)   +   New Media (online)

Determine if an advertising agency should be hired	Determine if an advertising network should be hired
Determine placement, frequency, and prices for each of the following options • television (network, cable) • radio (national, local) • print (newspapers, magazines, trade journals, bulletins, yellow pages, newsletters, etc.) • extreme advertising (billboards, buses, blimps, etc.) • other (event signage, T-shirts, point-of-purchase signs, etc.)	Determine placement, frequency, and prices for each of the following options • banner ads (vertical, rectangle, click thru) • portal advertising • vortal (vertical portal) advertising • online newsletters, newspapers • interactive television • direct TV • links to/from • advertorials on other Web sites
Identify opportunities for sponsorship (of events, programs, materials, etc.)	Identify opportunities for online sponsorships (of Web events, of portions of a Web site, of online newsletters)

FIGURE 5.1: COMPONENTS OF A SUCCESSFUL MULTIMEDIA MARKETING STRATEGY, CONTINUED

Public Relations—Traditional (offline) +	New Media (online)
Determine if a public relations agency should be hired.	Determine if the public relations function should be outsourced.
Conduct scheduled events for public/niche: • workshops • open house • seminars • celebrations	Arrange for online events: • special guest expert chats • regularly scheduled chat groups • community-building activities • message boards • Web site simulcast of offline events
Arrange for: • participation in other events (special lectures, speeches, workshops) • guest appearances (radio, television, guest columnist) • interviews (print)	Arrange for guest appearances on other Web sites: • chat groups • message board (ask the expert) • interviews (in online newsletters, magazines)
Identify community and charitable events for personal and financial contributions.	

Networking—Traditional (offline) +	New Media (online)
Identify groups, associations, organizations, and conferences: • your local community • trade associations • business organizations • professional groups	Identify online networking opportunities to participate in: • chat rooms • message boards • professional association Web sites
Determine level of involvement in each: • join • seek a leadership position • attend meetings/events only	Establish regular e-mail contact with: • current clients • prospective clients • business and professional associates

FIGURE 5.2: SELL SELECTIVELY WORKSHEET

Marketing Musts

Sell Selectively

Describe your products and/or services. _____

_____

_____

_____

_____

_____

What trends today have an impact on your products and services? _____

_____

_____

_____

_____

_____

How can you apply information about these trends to your own marketing strategy? _____

_____

_____

_____

_____

_____

FIGURE 5.3: KNOW YOUR NICHE WORKSHEET

Marketing Musts

Know Your Niche

Describe your customers in detail. In addition to demographic data, consider psychographic issues: _____

- Hobbies _____

- Disposable income _____

- Leisure activities _____

- Memberships _____

- Vacations _____

- Family status _____

- Other lifestyle information _____

What additional information should you obtain about your customers? _____

_____

_____

_____

_____

_____

How does this information have an impact on your marketing strategy? _____

- Marketing_____

- Sales _____

- Advertising _____

- Public relations_____

- Networking _____

FIGURE 5.4: CREATE YOUR PITCH WORKSHEET

Marketing Musts

Create Your Pitch

Define precisely the attributes of your products and services. _____

_____

- Product/service A: _____

  _____

  _____

- Product/service B: _____

  _____

  _____

- Product/service C: _____

  _____

  _____

How can you make your products and services come alive for your prospective customers/clients? _____

_____

_____

_____

For one of your products or services, write a brief pitch that grabs attention. Focus on the *needs* of your customers and the product/service *benefits*.

_____

_____

_____

_____

FIGURE 5.5: PRICE FOR PROFITS WORKSHEET

Marketing Musts

Set Prices for Profits

How does your present pricing structure compare to your competitors? (equal to, more than, or less than)

_____

_____

_____

_____

Have you covered all of your expenses to produce this product or provide this service, considering:

- Materials _____

- Labor _____

- Overhead expenses_____

- Shipping costs _____

- Handling costs _____

- Storage _____

For services you provide, what are the advantages and disadvantages of the following pricing structures:

- Hourly billing rates _____

- Project by project estimates_____

- Monthly retainer structure _____

What is your price floor? Ceiling? _____

_____

_____

_____

_____

MARKETING PLAN OUTLINE

I. Overview and Goals of Marketing Strategy

   A. Overview of Marketing Strategy

   B. Goals of Marketing Strategy

      1. Creating a strong brand

      2. Building a strong customer base

      3. Increasing product/service sales

II. Market Analysis

   A. Target Market(s)

      1. Demographics

      2. Psychographics

      3. Niche market specifics

   B. Competition

      1. Description of major competitors

      2. Assessment of their strengths/weaknesses

   C. Market Trends

      1. Industry trends

      2. Target market trends

   D. Market Research

      1. Methods of research

      2. Database analysis

      3. Summary of results

III. Marketing Strategy

   A. General Description

      1. Allocation of marketing efforts (percentage of budget dedicated to online versus offline)

      2. Expected return on investment from most significant components

   B. Method of Sales and Distribution

      1. Stores, offices, kiosks

      2. Catalogs, direct mail

      3. Web site

   C. Packaging

      1. Quality considerations

      2. Packaging

   D. Pricing

      1. Price strategy

      2. Competitive position

   E. Branding

   F. Database Marketing (personalization)

MARKETING PLAN OUTLINE, CONTINUED

G. Sales Strategies
1. Direct sales
2. Direct mail
3. E-mail marketing
4. Affiliate marketing
5. Reciprocal marketing
6. Viral marketing

H. Sales Incentives/Promotions
1. Free samples
2. Cash back coupons
3. Sweepstakes
4. Online promotions
5. Add-ons
6. Rebates
7. Other

I. Advertising Strategies
1. Traditional advertising (television, radio, print, extreme)
2. Web advertising/new media (banner ads, PDA advertising, portals/vortals, interactive television)
3. Long-term sponsorships

J. Public Relations
1. Building an online presence (communities, chats, message boards)
2. Events (online and offline)
3. Press releases (print, radio, television, online)
4. Interviews (online newsletters and Web sites, print, radio, television, chat rooms, online events)

K. Networking (memberships and leadership positions)

IV. **Customer Service**
A. Description of Customer Service Activities
B. Expected Outcomes of Achieving Excellence

V. **Implementation of Marketing Strategy**
A. In-House Responsibilities
B. Outsourced Functions
1. Advertising, public relations, marketing firms
2. Advertising networks
3. Other

VI. **Assessment of Marketing Effectiveness** *
*Note: The assessment is for existing businesses and is added after periodic evaluations.

CHAPTER 6

PART III
FINANCIAL
DOCUMENTS

Y ou learned earlier that the body of a Business Plan is divided into three main sections. Having completed the Organizational and Marketing Plans, you are now ready to develop the third area of your plan.

Financial Documents are those records used to show past, current, and projected finances. This section contains the major documents you will want to consider and include in your Business Plan. They will consist of both pro forma (projected) and actual financial statements. Your work will be easier if these are done in the following order.

- **Summary of Financial Needs**

- **Dispersal of Loan Funds Statement**

- **Cash Flow Statement (Budget)**

- **Three-Year Income Projection**

- **Break-Even Analysis**

- **Balance Sheet**

- **Profit & Loss Statement**

- **Loan Application/Financial History**

- **Financial Statement Analysis**

BEFORE YOU BEGIN

You are now beginning the Financial Document section of your business plan. I would strongly suggest that you prepare these documents in the order presented because it will simplify the process. In the same way that a house builder must lay the foundation, build the walls, and finally put on the roof, you will find that your financial statements will build on each other. Each one will use information from the previous ones. If you try to jump ahead, you will make your task more difficult.

Before you begin work on your financial statements go back to Chapter 1 and reread the section on "Developing Financial Assumptions." Remember that the numbers in your financial plan are derived through the development of organizational and marketing concepts in terms of revenues that will be generated and expenses that will be incurred.

PURPOSE OF FINANCIAL DOCUMENTS

In the first two sections, you have written about the physical setup of your operation and your plans for finding and reaching your customers. The Financial Documents section is the quantitative interpretation of everything you have stated in the text portion of your plan. Well-executed financial statements will provide you with the means to look realistically at your business in terms of profitability. The Financial Documents section is often the first examined by a potential lender or investor.

The financial documents included in your plan are not just for the purpose of satisfying a potential lender or investor. The primary reason for writing a business plan is so that it will serve as a guide during the lifetime of your business. It is extremely important that you keep it updated frequently. This means examining your financial statements on a periodic basis, measuring your actual performance against your projections, and revising your new projections accordingly.

TYPES OF FINANCIAL DOCUMENTS

There are four types of financial documents covered in this chapter under Sections I, II, III, and IV. Before you start to develop your financial plan, it is best to gain a basic understanding of what they are and why they are important to your business.

- *Statements of sources and uses of funds from a lender or investor.* The first two documents covered are the "Summary of Financial Needs" and the "Loan Fund Dispersal Statement." These two documents, explained in Section I of the chapter, are the only ones that are written in paragraph form rather than as spreadsheets in rows and columns. They are included only if your business is seeking funds from a lender or investor (or other source).

- *Pro forma statements.* The word "pro forma" in accounting means "projected." These are the statements (cash flow, income projections, etc.) that are used for you to predict the future profitability of your business and will be covered in Section III of this chapter.

You are not a magician and will not be able to be 100 percent right. However, your projections should be based on realistic research and reasonable assumptions. *It is dangerous to overstate your revenues and understate your expenses.*

- **Actual performance statements.** These are the historical financial statements reflecting the past performance of your business. If you are planning a new business, you have no history. Therefore, you will not have these statements to include. However, once you have been in business for even one accounting period, you will have a Profit & Loss Statement and a Balance Sheet for those periods. The actual performance statements will be explained and illustrated in Section III of this chapter.

- **Financial statement analysis.** Once you have completed the financial documents described above, it is also important to use them as tools to look at your business and enable you to make future decisions that will make your business more profitable. Financial statement analysis utilizes the income statement and the balance sheet and is the study of relationships and comparisons of single components in a single or in comparative financial statements. In Section IV of this chapter, you will learn how to use your income statement and balance sheet to prepare a financial statement analysis of your business.

HOW TO PROCEED

The financial documents will be presented in the order discussed in the paragraphs above. It will be necessary for you to determine your individual situation and decide which documents to include in your own business plan. Below are five descriptions. Decide which one fits your business and proceed accordingly:

1. **If yours is a new business—and—you are going to seek a lender or investor.** Include the Application of Loan Funds and the Loan Fund Dispersal Statement. You will also include all of the pro forma statements. Since you have no financial history, you cannot include actual performance statements. Financial statement analysis will be based on projections only and will utilize your three-year profit & loss (income) projection.

2. **If yours is a new business—and—you are not going to seek a lender or investor.** You will not include the Application of Loan Funds and the Loan Fund Dispersal Statement. You will include all pro forma statements. Again, financial statement analysis will be based only on projections and will utilize your three-year profit & loss (income) projection.

3. **If yours is an existing business—and—you are going to seek a lender or investor.** You will need to include all financial documents discussed in this chapter.

4. **If yours is an existing business—and—you are not seeking a lender or investor.** You will include all financial documents discussed in this chapter with the exception of the Application of Loan Funds and the Loan Fund Dispersal Statement.

5. **If this business plan is being written for a division within a larger business.** Consider your division as being a business within a business and include financial documents as indicated in whichever of the above scenarios fits your situation.

Now You Are Ready to Prepare Your Financial Documents

The four types of financial documents will be presented in the following order:

➡ **Section I: Statements of financial needs and uses of lender/investor funds**

➡ **Section II: Pro forma statements**

➡ **Section III: Actual financial statements**

➡ **Section IV: Financial Statement Analysis**

Work in order. You should work on financial documents in the order that they are presented in the book. It will make your job easier. Most of your financial documents will use information from the ones you will have already completed.

Add explanations when needed. When you prepare your financial statements, it is a good idea to append a written explanation of any items that are unusual or that would not be immediately clear to your lender or investor. Some examples are as follows:

- If you are a manufacturing business and have shut down operations for a period to put in new equipment, appending an explanation would clear up any queries about the reason for decreased revenues or inventory levels during that time.

- If you have a heavy increase in advertising expenses, but the increased revenues will not materialize until a future financial statement period, you can attach a note of explanation about your projected benefits for future periods.

Example Financial Spreadsheets
in this chapter have no correlation with each other

Do not try to follow the numbers from one spreadsheet to the next. The three business plans in Appendix I, II, and III have 100 percent correlation between spreadsheets. You will be able to see from them how the numbers build on each other throughout the financial plan.

Section I

STATEMENTS OF FINANCIAL NEEDS AND USES OF FUNDS FROM A LENDER OR INVESTOR

The financial text document and example on the next two pages describes your needs for capital to be infused into your company through borrowed or invested funds. It also outlines your intended use of those funds. *Include this statement only if you are seeking funds from a lender or investor.* This statement has two parts:

➡ **Summary of Financial Needs**

➡ **Loan Fund Dispersal Statement**

SUMMARY OF FINANCIAL NEEDS

If you are applying for a loan, your lenders and investors will analyze the requirements of your business. They will distinguish among the three types of capital as follows:

Working capital. Fluctuating needs to be repaid through cash (liquidity) during the business's next full operating cycle, generally one year.

Growth capital. Needs to be repaid with profits over a period of a few years. If you seek growth capital, you will be expected to show how the capital will be used to increase your business profits enough to be able to repay the loan (plus interest) within several years (usually not more than seven).

Equity capital. This is for permanent needs. If you seek equity capital, it must be raised from investors who will take the risk for dividend returns or capital gains, or a specific share of the business.

Keeping the above in mind, you must now prepare a Summary of Financial Needs. This document is an *outline* giving the following information:

- *Why* you are applying for a loan or investment funds.

- *How much* you need to accomplish your goals.

LOAN FUND DISPERSAL STATEMENT

Uses of financing. The potential lender will require a statement of how the money you intend to borrow will be used. It will be necessary for you to tell:

- *How* you intend to utilize the loan funds.

- *Back up your statement* with supporting data. The backup statement will show the lender that you have done your homework properly.

The following are two examples that will help to clarify your understanding of the above.

Example 1   **How money will be used.** Funds for advertising.

Backup statement. Refer to the advertising section of your plan. That section must contain a breakdown of how you intend to do your advertising. Include rate sheets in the Supporting Documents.

Example 2   **How money will be used.** Funds for expansion. Include a concise statement explaining how you intend to expand.

Backup statement. Include the following information:
- Projected costs of carrying out plans.
- Projections as to how that expansion will ultimately result in increased profits for your business and thereby enable you to repay your loan.
- References to other sections of your business plan that relate to projected expansion.

SAMPLE PAGE
SUMMARY OF FINANCIAL NEEDS AND LOAN FUND DISPERSAL STATEMENT

Summary of Financial Needs

1. Genesis Multimedia is seeking a loan to increase growth capital in the following areas of production:

   A. Equipment (new and more modern)

   B. Training of personnel in operation of above

2. Funds needed to accomplish the above goal will be $100,000.

Loan Fund Dispersal Statement

1. **Dispersal of Loan Funds**

   Genesis Multimedia will utilize anticipated loan funds in the amount of $100,000 to modernize its production equipment. This will necessitate the purchase of two new pieces of equipment and the training of present personnel in the operation of that equipment.

2. **Backup Statement**

   A. The equipment needed is as follows:

      1. High-speed F-34 Atlas Press (purchase price: $123,000)

      2. S71 Jaworski Ebber (purchase price: $110,000)

   B. The training is available from the manufacturer as a three-week intensive program (cost: 10 employees @ $1,200 = $12,000).

   C. The remaining $5,000 of loan funds will be used to make the first monthly installment on loan repayment (a period of low production training off the premises).

   D. The equipment will result in a 35 percent increase in production and will decrease unit cost by 25 percent. The end result will be a net profit increase sufficient to repay the loan and interest within three years with a profit margin of 15 percent.[*]

   [*]**Note**: Refer to page 17 for production plan of Genesis Multimedia. See pages 27 and 28 of the marketing section for market research and projected trends in the industry. (See footnote at bottom of page.)

Page numbers at the bottom of the sample page above are hypothetical and do not refer to page numbers in *Anatomy of a Business Plan*. The production plan referred to in the example would include a description of the equipment, how the work will be done, by whom, and at what cost. Market research would show projected demand for the product, and thus would show how increased production would result in increased sales and ultimately in the company's capability to repay the loan in a timely fashion.

Be sure that your supporting data can be easily found by the loan officer who is examining your application. If your information is not well-organized and easily retrievable, you risk having your loan turned down simply because information cannot be located. The necessity of having a well-written Table of Contents will be discussed in Chapter 9, "Packaging Your Plan and Keeping It Up-to-Date."

SECTION II
PRO FORMA STATEMENTS

The financial statements that follow are pro forma statements. They show your projections for the future profitability of your business.

All business plans must contain the following pro forma statements:

➡ **Cash Flow Statement**

➡ **Three-Year Income Projection**

➡ **Break-Even Analysis**

Blank forms are included of all three pro forma statements in Appendix IV of *Anatomy of a Business Plan*. They are ready for you to customize and input your numbers.

Projected balance sheet. A potential lender or investor may also require that you include a pro forma (or projected) balance sheet for a specific target date in the life of your business (e.g., "end of year one"). You will find instructions for the development of a balance sheet under Actual Financial Statements in the next part of this chapter. There are also examples in the sample business plans in the Appendix.

Also included in this section are:

- *Cash to be Paid Out and Sources of Cash worksheets.* These worksheets will help you to develop your cash flow statement and may be included in your business plan.

- *Quarterly Budget Analysis spreadsheet.* This is your tool for comparing your company's projections with its actual performance. Your cash flow statement will be effective only if it is revised quarterly reflecting the results of a budget analysis.

If you are a new business. You have no actual performance to measure against projections. Therefore, you will not have a quarterly budget analysis until you have been in business for three months.

If you have been in business for one or more quarters. Do a quarterly budget analysis, revise your cash flow statement accordingly, and insert the revised cash flow statement in your business plan.

PRO FORMA CASH FLOW STATEMENT (BUDGET)

It is a fact that a third or more of today's businesses fail due to a lack of cash flow. The cash flow statement is usually the first thing a lender or investor examines in your business plan. What is cash flow?

What Is a Cash Flow Statement?

The Pro Forma Cash Flow Statement is the financial document that *projects* what your business plan means in terms of dollars. A cash flow statement is the same as a budget. It is a pro forma (or projected) statement used for internal planning and estimates how much money will flow into and out of a business during a designated period of time, usually the coming tax year. Your profit at the end of the year will depend on the proper balance between cash inflow and outflow.

The **Cash Flow Statement** identifies when cash is expected to be received and when it must be spent to pay bills and debts. It also allows the manager to identify where the necessary cash will come from.

This statement deals only with **actual cash transactions** and not with depreciation and amortization of goodwill or other noncash expense items. Expenses are paid from cash on hand, sale of assets, revenues from sales and services, interest earned on investments, money borrowed from a lender, and influx of capital in exchange for equity in the company. If your business will require $100,000 to pay its expenses and $50,000 to support the owners, you will need at least an equal amount of money flowing into the business just to maintain the status quo. Anything less will eventually lead to an inability to pay your creditors or yourself.

The availability or nonavailability of cash *when* it is needed for expenditures gets to the very heart of the matter. By careful planning, you must try to project not only *how much* cash will have to flow into and out of your business, but also *when* it will need to flow in and out. A business may be able to plan for gross receipts that will cover its needs. However, if those sales do not take place in time to pay the expenses, your venture will soon be history unless you plan ahead for other sources of cash to tide the business over until the revenues are realized.

Time period. The cash flow statement should be prepared on a monthly basis for the next tax year (or more) of your business. To be effective, it must be analyzed and revised quarterly to reflect actual performance in the preceding three months of operations.

Steps for Planning Your Cash Flow Statement

Prepare individual budgets. Begin by compiling individual projections and budgets. They might be as follows:

- Revenue projections (product and service)
- Inventory purchases
- Variable (selling) expense budget (with marketing budget)
- Fixed (administrative) expense budget

Prepare planning worksheets. Because the cash flow statement deals with cash inflow and cash outflow, the first step in planning can be best accomplished by preparing two worksheets.

1. *Cash to be Paid Out.* This worksheet documents the cash flowing out of your business. It identifies categories of expenses and obligations and the projected amount of cash needed in each category. Use the information from your individual budgets (inventory purchases, direct expenses, administrative expenses, owner draws, etc.).

   These expenditures are not always easy to estimate. If yours is a new business, it will be necessary for you to do lots of market research. If you are an existing business, you will combine information from past financial statements with trends in your particular industry.

2. *Sources of Cash.* Use this worksheet to document the cash flowing into your business. It will help you to estimate how much cash will be available from what sources. To complete this worksheet, you will have to look at cash on hand, projected revenues, assets that can be liquidated, possible lenders or investors, and owner equity to be contributed. This worksheet will force you to take a look at any existing possibilities for increasing available cash.

Check out the examples. On the next four pages, you will see examples of the two worksheets along with accompanying information explaining each of the categories used. The worksheets are filled in for the fictitious company, Genesis Multimedia, to help you understand the process.

Please note that the Cash to be Paid Out worksheet shows a need for $131,000. It was necessary in projecting Sources of Cash to account for $131,000 without the projected sales because payment is not expected to be received until November and December (too late for cash needs January through October). Next year, those revenues will be reflected in cash on hand or other salable assets.

When you do your own worksheets:

- Try to be as realistic as possible. *Do not understate revenues and/or overstate expenses*, a deadly error frequently made during the planning process.

- Be sure to figure all of your estimates on both worksheets for the same time period (i.e., annually, quarterly, and monthly).

Note. Blank forms of the two worksheets are provided in Appendix IV.

CASH TO BE PAID OUT WORKSHEET
Explanation of Categories

1. *Start-Up Costs*
   These are the costs incurred by you to get your business underway. They are generally one-time expenses and are capitalized for tax purposes.

2. *Inventory Purchases*
   Cash to be spent during the period on items intended for resale. If you purchase manufactured products, this includes the cash outlay for those purchases. If you are the manufacturer, include labor and materials on units to be produced.

3. *Variable expenses (selling or direct expenses)*
   These are the costs of all expenses that will relate directly to your product or service (other than manufacturing costs or purchase price of inventory).

4. *Fixed expenses (administrative or indirect expenses)*
   Include all expected costs of office overhead. If certain bills must be paid ahead, include total cash outlay even if covered period extends into the next year.

5. *Assets (Long-term purchases)*
   These are the capital assets that will be depreciated over a period of years (land, buildings, vehicles, equipment). Determine how you intend to pay for them and include all cash to be paid out in the current period. *Note*: Land is the only asset that does not depreciate and will be listed at cost.

6. *Liabilities*
   What are the payments you expect to have to make to retire any debts or loans? Do you have any accounts payable as you begin the new year? You will need to determine the amount of cash outlay that needs to be paid in the current year. If you have a car loan for $20,000 and you pay $500 per month for 12 months, you will have a cash outlay of $6,000 for the coming year.

7. *Owner Equity*
   This item is frequently overlooked in planning cash flow. If you, as the business owner, will need a draw of $2,000 per month to live on, you must plan for $24,000 cash flowing out of your business. Failure to plan for it will result in a cash flow shortage and may cause your business to fail.

> **Variable and Fixed Expense Categories Must Be Determined By You**
>
> Every business has expenses that are specific to its industry. You will have to customize your variable and fixed expense categories to match your business. Some have been suggested in the examples to get you started. Type in your own headings in the working spreadsheets. As you begin to operate your business, you will be better able to determine what your true expenditures are. **However, for your business plan, you will need to set your expense headings beginning with this worksheet and use the same ones throughout your spreadsheets.** You can change later if you find that your current categories do not meet your needs.

Note. Be sure to use the same time period throughout your worksheet.

Cash To Be Paid Out Worksheet

Business Name: Genesis Multimedia

Time Period Covered: Jan 1–Dec 31, 2002

1. START-UP COSTS		1,450
Business license	30	
Corporation filing	500	
Legal fees	920	
Other start-up costs:		
a.		
b.		
c.		
d.		
2. INVENTORY PURCHASES		
Cash out for goods intended for resale		32,000
3. VARIABLE EXPENSES (SELLING)		
Advertising/marketing	8,000	
Freight	2,500	
Fulfillment of orders	800	
Packaging costs	0	
Sales salaries/commissions	14,000	
Travel	1,550	
Miscellaneous	300	
TOTAL SELLING EXPENSES		27,150
4. FIXED EXPENSES (ADMINISTRATION)		
Financial administration	1,800	
Insurance	900	
Licenses and permits	100	
Office salaries	16,300	
Rent expense	8,600	
Utilities	2,400	
Miscellaneous	400	
TOTAL ADMINISTRATIVE EXPENSE		30,500
5. ASSETS (LONG-TERM PURCHASES)		6,000
Cash to be paid out in current period		
6. LIABILITIES		
Cash outlay for retiring debts, loans,		9,900
and/or accounts payable		
7. OWNER EQUITY		
Cash to be withdrawn by owner		24,000
TOTAL CASH TO BE PAID OUT		**$131,000**

SOURCES OF CASH WORKSHEET
Explanation of Categories

1. *Cash on Hand*

   Money that you have on hand in your bank accounts and other resources. Be sure to include petty cash and income that you have not yet deposited.

2. *Sales (revenues)*

   This includes projected revenues from the sale of your product and/or service. If payment is not expected during the time period covered by this worksheet, do not include that portion of your sales. Think about the projected timing of sales. If receipts will be delayed beyond the time when a large amount of cash is needed, make a notation to that effect and take it into consideration when determining the need for temporary financing. Include deposits you require on expected sales or services. To figure collections on accounts receivable, you will have to project the percentage of invoices that will be lost to bad debts and subtract it from your accounts receivable total.

3. *Miscellaneous Income*

   Do you, or will you have, any moneys out on loan or deposited in accounts that will yield interest income during the period in question?

4. *Sale of Long-Term Assets*

   If you are expecting to sell any of your fixed assets such as land, buildings, vehicles, machinery, equipment, etc., be sure to include only the cash you will receive during the current period.

Important. At this point in your worksheet, add up all sources of cash. If you don't have an amount equal to your projected needs, you will have to plan sources of cash covered under numbers 5 and 6.

5. *Liabilities*

   This figure represents the amount you will be able to borrow from lending institutions such as banks, finance companies, the SBA, etc. Be reasonable about what you think you can borrow. If you have no collateral, have no business plan, or if you have a poor financial history, you will find it difficult, if not impossible, to find a lender. This source of cash requires *preplanning*.

6. *Equity*

   Sources of equity come from owner investments, contributed capital, sale of stock, or venture capital. Do you anticipate the availability of personal funds? Does your business have the potential for growth that might interest a venture capitalist? Be sure to be realistic in this area. You cannot sell stock (or equity) to a nonexistent investor.

Sources of Cash Worksheet

Business Name: Genesis Multimedia

Time Period Covered: From January 1, 2000 to December 31, 2002

---

1. CASH ON HAND — $20,000

2. SALES (REVENUES)

Product sales income* — 90,000
Most of this sales revenue will not be received until Nov. or Dec.

Services income — 22,000

Deposits on sales or services — 0

Collections on accounts receivable — 3,000

3. MISCELLANEOUS INCOME

Interest income — 1,000

Payments to be received on loans — 0

4. SALE OF LONG-TERM ASSETS — 0

5. LIABILITIES — 40,000

Loan funds (to be received during current period; from banks, through the SBA, or from other lending institutions)

6. EQUITY

Owner investments (sole proprietors/partners) — 10,000

Contributed capital (corporation) —

Sale of stock (corporation) —

Venture capital — 35,000

TOTAL CASH AVAILABLE

A. Without product sales = **$131,000**

B. With product sales = **$221,000**

Using the worksheets. Now that you have completed the two worksheets, you are ready to use that information. You have estimated **how much** cash will be needed for the year and you now know what sources are available. In the next phase of cash flow planning you will break the time period of one year into monthly segments and predict **when** the cash will be needed to make the financial year flow smoothly.

Project sales on a monthly basis based on payment of invoices, demand for your particular product or service, and ability to fill that demand. Figure the cost of goods and fixed and variable expenses in monthly increments. Most will vary. When do you plan to purchase the most inventory? What months will require the most advertising? Are you expecting a rent or insurance increase? When will commissions be due on expected sales? Determine your depreciable assets needs. How much will the payments be and when will they begin? Fill in as much of the cash flow statement as you can using those projections and any others that you can comfortably determine.

To clarify the process of filling in a cash flow statement, we will walk you through January and February again using Genesis Multimedia as the example.

January Projections

1. Genesis Multimedia projects a beginning cash balance of $20,000.
2. Cash Receipts: Product manufacturing will not be completed until February, so there will be no sales. However, service income of $4,000 is projected.
3. Interest on the $20,000 will amount to about $100 at current rate.
4. There are no long-term assets to sell. Enter a zero.
5. Adding 1, 2, 3, and 4 the Total Cash Available will be $24,100.
6. Cash Payments: Product will be available from the manufacturer in February, and payment will not be due until pickup. However, there will be prototype costs of $5,000.
7. Variable (Selling) Expenses: Estimated at $1,140.
8. Fixed (Administrative) Expenses: Estimated at $1,215.
9. Interest Expense: No outstanding debts or loans. Enter zero.
10. Taxes: No profit for previous quarter. No estimated taxes would be due.
11. Payments on Long-Term Assets: Genesis plans to purchase office equipment to be paid in full at the time of purchase. Enter $1,139.
12. Loan Repayments: No loans have been received. Enter zero.
13. Owner Draws: Owner will need $2,000 for living expenses.
14. Total Cash Paid Out: Add 6 through 13. Total $10,494.
15. Cash Balance: Subtract Cash Paid Out from Total Cash Available $13,606.
16. Loans to be Received: Being aware of the $30,000 to be paid to the manufacturer in February, a loan of $40,000 is anticipated to increase Cash Available. (This requires advance planning.)
17. Equity Deposit: Owner plans to add $5,000 from personal CD.
18. Ending Cash Balance: Adding 15, 16, and 17 the sum is $58,606.

February Projections

1. February Beginning Cash Balance: January Ending Cash Balance ($58,606).
2. Cash Receipts: Still no sales, but service income is $2,000.
3. Interest Income: Projected at about $120.
4. Sale of Long-Term Assets: None. Enter zero.
5. Total Cash Available: Add 1, 2, 3, and 4. The result is $60,726.
6. Cash Payments: $30,000 due to manufacturer, $400 due on packaging design.
7. Continue as in January. Don't forget to include payments on your loan.

Partial Cash Flow Statement

Genesis Multimedia

	Jan	Feb
BEGINNING CASH BALANCE	20,000	58,606
CASH RECEIPTS		
A. Sales/revenues	4,000	2,000
B. Receivables	0	0
C. Interest income	100	120
D. Sale of long-term assets	0	0
TOTAL CASH AVAILABLE	24,100	60,726
CASH PAYMENTS		
A. Cost of goods to be sold		
1. Purchases	0	30,000
2. Material	0	0
3. Labor	5,000	400
Total Cost of Goods	5,000	30,400
B. Variable Expenses (Selling)		
1. Advertising	300	
2. Freight	120	
3. Fulfillment of orders	0	
4. Packaging costs	270	
5. Sales/salaries	0	
6. Travel	285	
7. Miscellaneous selling expense	165	
Total Variable Expenses	1,140	
C. Fixed Expenses (Administrative)		CONTINUE as in JANUARY
1. Financial administration	80	
2. Insurance	125	
3. License/permits	200	
4. Office salaries	500	
5. Rent expenses	110	
6. Utilities	200	
7. Miscellaneous administrative expense	0	
Total Fixed Expenses	1,215	
D. Interest expense	0	
E. Federal income tax	0	
F. Other uses	0	
G. Long-term asset payments	1,139	
H. Loan payments	0	
I. Owner draws	2,000	
TOTAL CASH PAID OUT	10,494	
CASH BALANCE/DEFICIENCY	13,606	
Loans to be received	40,000	
Equity deposits	5,000	
ENDING CASH BALANCE	58,606	

INSTRUCTIONS FOR COMPLETING
YOUR PRO FORMA CASH FLOW STATEMENT

This page contains instructions for completing the cash flow statement on the next page. A blank form for your own projections can be found in Appendix IV.

- **Vertical columns** are for the 12 months plus 6-month and 12-month period columns.

- **Horizontal positions** on the statement contain all sources of cash and cash to be paid out (chart of accounts). Figures are retrieved from worksheets and individual budgets.

Assumptions are projected for each month, reflecting the flow of cash in and out of your business for a one-year period. Begin with the first month of your business cycle and proceed as follows:

1. Project the Beginning Cash Balance. Enter under "January."

2. Project the Cash Receipts for January. Apportion your total year's revenues throughout the 12 months. Try to weight revenues as closely as you can to a realistic selling cycle for your industry.

3. Add Beginning Cash Balance and Cash Receipts to determine Total Cash Available.

4. Project cash payments to be made for cost of goods to be sold (inventory that you will purchase or manufacture). Apportion your total inventory budget throughout the year, being sure you are providing for levels of inventory that will fulfill your needs for sales projected.

5. Customize your Variable and Fixed Expense categories to match your business.

6. Project Variable, Fixed, and Interest Expenses for January. Fill out any that you can for all 12 months.

7. Project cash to be paid out on Taxes, Long-Term Assets, Loan Repayments, and Owner Draws.

8. Calculate Total Cash Paid Out (Total of Cost of Goods to Be Sold, Variable, Fixed, Interest, Taxes, Long-Term Asset Payments, Loan Repayments, and Owner Draws).

9. Subtract Total Cash Paid Out from Total Cash Available. The result is entered under "Cash Balance/Deficiency." Be sure to bracket this figure if the result is a negative to avoid errors.

10. Look at Ending Cash Balance in each of the months and project Loans to be Received and Equity Deposits to be made. Add to Cash Balance/Deficiency to arrive at Ending Cash Balance for each month.

11. Ending Cash Balance for January is carried forward and becomes February's Beginning Cash Balance (as throughout the spreadsheet. Each month's ending balance is the next month's beginning balance).

12. Go to February and input any numbers that are still needed to complete that month. The process is repeated until December is completed.

To Complete 6-Month and 12-Month Period Columns

1. The Beginning Cash Balance for January is entered in the first space of the 6-month and 12-month period column.

2. The monthly figures for each category (except Beginning Cash Balance, Total Cash Available, Cash Balance/Deficiency, and Ending Cash Balance) are added horizontally and the result entered in the corresponding Total category.

3. The 6- and 12-month period columns are then computed in the same manner as each of the individual months. If you have been accurate, your computations for the December Ending Cash Balance will be exactly the same as the Total Ending Cash Balance.

Note. If your business is new, you will have to base your projections solely on market research and industry trends. If you have an established business, you will also use your financial statements from previous years.

Pro Forma Cash Flow Statement
Genesis Multimedia

Year: 2003

	Jan	Feb	Mar	Apr	May	Jun	6-MONTH PERIOD	Jul	Aug	Sep	Oct	Nov	Dec	12-MONTH PERIOD
BEGINNING CASH BALANCE	10,360	72,840	54,488	60,346	65,125	79,253	10,360	81,341	71,401	68,974	55,974	54,718	59,032	10,360
CASH RECEIPTS														
A. Sales/revenues	14,000	9,500	9,500	15,000	18,000	12,000	78,000	9,000	8,000	9,500	16,000	28,000	43,000	191,500
B. Receivables	400	400	300	500	450	425	2,475	500	750	650	600	1,250	8,000	14,225
C. Interest income	234	240	260	158	172	195	1,259	213	303	300	417	406	413	3,311
D. Sale of long-term assets	2,000	0	4,000	0	0	0	6,000	0	0	0	0	0	0	6,000
TOTAL CASH AVAILABLE	26,994	82,980	68,548	76,004	83,747	91,873	98,094	91,054	80,454	79,424	72,991	84,374	110,445	225,396
CASH PAYMENTS														
A. Cost of goods to be sold														
1. Purchases	800	16,500	3,700	200	200	300	21,700	9,000	430	540	6,700	14,000	12,000	64,370
2. Material	2,000	1,430	200	300	250	200	4,380	359	750	5,000	400	300	350	11,539
3. Labor	4,000	2,800	400	600	500	450	8,750	600	1,500	8,000	750	500	540	20,640
Total cost of goods	6,800	20,730	4,300	1,100	950	950	34,830	9,959	2,680	13,540	7,850	14,800	12,890	96,549
B. Variable expenses														
1. Advertising	900	300	900	250	300	700	3,350	350	300	640	1,300	1,200	1,400	8,540
2. Freight	75	75	75	75	180	70	550	75	75	90	180	300	560	1,830
3. Fulfillment of orders	300	300	300	400	350	300	1,950	300	280	325	450	600	975	4,880
4. Packaging costs	2,100	0	0	0	600	0	2,700	0	200	230	0	0	0	3,130
5. Sales/salaries	1,400	900	1,300	1,400	1,100	900	7,000	1,400	1,400	1,400	1,400	1,400	1,400	15,400
6. Travel	0	500	700	0	0	400	1,600	0	540	25	80	0	0	2,245
7. Misc. variable expense	100	100	100	100	100	100	600	100	100	100	100	100	100	1,200
Total variable expenses	4,875	2,175	3,375	2,225	2,630	2,470	17,750	2,225	2,895	2,810	3,510	3,600	4,435	37,225
C. Fixed expenses														
1. Financial administration	75	75	75	475	75	75	850	75	75	75	75	75	75	1,300
2. Insurance	1,564	0	0	0	0	0	1,564	1,563	0	0	0	0	0	3,127
3. License/permits	240	0	0	0	0	0	240	0	0	0	0	0	125	365
4. Office salaries	1,400	1,400	1,400	1,400	1,400	1,400	8,400	1,400	1,400	1,400	1,400	1,400	1,400	16,800
5. Rent expenses	700	700	700	700	700	700	4,200	700	700	700	700	700	700	8,400
6. Utilities	200	200	140	120	80	80	820	75	75	75	90	120	155	1,410
7. Misc. fixed expense	100	100	100	100	100	100	600	100	100	100	100	100	100	1,200
Total fixed expenses	4,279	2,475	2,415	2,795	2,355	2,355	16,674	3,913	2,350	2,350	2,365	2,395	2,555	32,602
D. Interest expense	0	0	0	234	233	232	699	231	230	225	223	222	220	2,050
E. Federal income tax	1,200	1	1	1,200	1	1,200	3,603	0	0	1,200	0	0	0	4,803
F. Other uses	0	0	0	0	0	0	0	0	0	0	0	0	0	0
G. Long-term asset payments	0	0	0	214	214	214	642	214	214	214	214	214	214	1,926
H. Loan payments	0	1,111	1,111	1,111	1,111	1,111	5,555	1,111	1,111	1,111	1,111	1,111	1,111	12,221
I. Owner draws	2,000	2,000	2,000	2,000	2,000	2,000	12,000	2,000	2,000	2,000	3,000	3,000	3,000	27,000
TOTAL CASH PAID OUT	19,154	28,492	13,202	10,879	9,494	10,532	91,753	19,653	11,480	23,450	18,273	25,342	24,425	214,376
CASH BALANCE/DEFICIENCY	7,840	54,488	55,346	65,125	74,253	81,341	6,341	71,401	68,974	55,974	54,718	59,032	86,020	11,020
LOANS TO BE RECEIVED	65,000	0	0	0	0	0	65,000	0	0	0	0	0	0	65,000
EQUITY DEPOSITS	0	0	5,000	0	5,000	0	10,000	0	0	0	0	0	0	10,000
ENDING CASH BALANCE	72,840	54,488	60,346	65,125	79,253	81,341	81,341	71,401	68,974	55,974	54,718	59,032	86,020	86,020

QUARTERLY BUDGET ANALYSIS

Your Pro Forma Cash Flow Statement (yearly budget) is of no value to you as a business owner unless there is some means to evaluate the actual performance of your company and measure it against your projections.

What Is a Quarterly Budget Analysis?

A quarterly budget analysis is the financial analysis tool that is used to compare your projected cash flow statement with your business's actual performance. Its purpose is to let you know whether you are operating within your projections and help you maintain control of all phases of your business operations. When your analysis shows that you are over or under budget in any area, it will be necessary to determine the reason for the deviation and implement changes for the future that will enable you to get back on track.

Example. If you have budgeted $1,000 in advertising funds for the first quarter and you find that you have actually spent $1,600, the first thing you should do is look at the sales that have occurred as a result of increased advertising. If they are over projections by an amount equal to or more than the $600, your budget will still be in good shape. If not, you will have to find expenses in your budget that can be revised to make up the deficit. You might be able to take a smaller draw for yourself or spend less on travel. You might even be able to increase your profits by adding a new product or service.

It should be clear at this point that the correct process to keep you from running out of operating capital in the middle of the year is to make yearly projections, analyze at the end of each quarter, and then revise your budget based on that analysis and current industry trends.

How to Develop a Quarterly Budget Analysis

The Quarterly Budget Analysis needs the following seven columns:

1. **Budget Item.** The list of budget items is taken from headings on the Pro Forma Cash Flow Statement. All items in your budget should be listed.

2. **Budget this Quarter.** Fill in the amount budgeted for current quarter from your Pro Forma Cash Flow Statement.

3. **Actual this Quarter.** Fill in actual expenditures or receipts for quarter.

4. **Variation this Quarter.** Subtract the amount spent or received from the amount budgeted for the current quarter. This will be the amount spent or received over or under budget.

5. **Year-to-Date Budget.** Amount budgeted from beginning of year through and including current quarter (from cash flow statement).

6. **Actual Year-to-Date.** Actual amount spent or received from beginning of year through current quarter.

7. **Variation Year-to-Date.** Subtract the amount spent or received from the amount budgeted from the start of the year through the current quarter.

Note. You will not have any information to input into column numbers 3, 4, 5, 6, and 7 until you have been in business at least one quarter.

All items contained in the budget are listed on this form. The second column is the amount budgeted for the current quarter. By subtracting the amount actually spent, you will arrive at the variation for the quarter. The last three columns are for year-to-date-figures. If you analyze at the end of the 3rd quarter, figures will represent the first nine months of your tax year.

Making Calculations. *When you calculate variations, the amounts are preceded by either a plus (+) or a minus (–), depending on whether the category is a revenue or an expense. If the actual amount is greater than the amount budgeted, (1) Revenue categories will represent the variation as a positive (+); and (2) Expense categories will represent the variation as a negative (–).*

Quarterly Budget Analysis

Business Name: Genesis Multimedia   **For the Quarter Ending: September 30, 2002**

BUDGET ITEM	THIS QUARTER			YEAR-TO-DATE		
	Budget	Actual	Variation	Budget	Actual	Variation
SALES REVENUES	145,000	150,000	5,000	400,000	410,000	10,000
Less cost of goods	80,000	82,500	(2,500)	240,000	243,000	(3,000)
GROSS PROFITS	65,000	67,500	2,500	160,000	167,000	7,000
VARIABLE EXPENSES						
1. Advertising/marketing	3,000	3,400	(400)	6,000	6,200	(200)
2. Freight	6,500	5,750	750	16,500	16,350	150
3. Fulfillment of orders	1,400	950	450	3,800	4,100	(300)
4. Packaging	750	990	(240)	2,200	2,300	(100)
5. Salaries/commissions	6,250	6,250	0	18,750	18,750	0
6. Travel	500	160	340	1,500	1,230	270
7. Miscellaneous	0	475	(475)	0	675	(675)
FIXED EXPENSES						
1. Financial/administrative	1,500	1,500	0	4,500	4,700	(200)
2. Insurance	2,250	2,250	0	6,750	6,750	0
3. Licenses/permits	1,000	600	400	3,500	3,400	100
4. Office salaries	1,500	1,500	0	4,500	4,500	0
5. Rent	3,500	3,500	0	10,500	10,500	0
6. Utilities	750	990	(240)	2,250	2,570	(320)
7. Miscellaneous	0	60	(60)	0	80	(80)
NET INCOME FROM OPERATIONS	36,100	39,125	3,025	79,250	84,895	5,645
INTEREST INCOME	1,250	1,125	(125)	3,750	3,700	(50)
INTEREST EXPENSE	1,500	1,425	75	4,500	4,500	0
NET PROFIT (Pretax)	35,850	38,825	2,975	78,500	84,095	5,595
TAXES	8,500	9,500	(1,000)	25,500	28,500	(3,000)
NET PROFIT (After Tax)	27,350	29,325	1,975	53,000	55,595	2,595

NON-INCOME STATEMENT ITEMS

1. Long-term asset repayments	2,400	3,400	(1,000)	7,200	8,200	(1,000)
2. Loan repayments	3,400	3,400	0	8,800	8,800	0
3. Owner draws	6,000	6,900	(900)	18,000	18,900	(900)

BUDGET DEVIATIONS	This Quarter	Year-to-Date
1. Income statement items:	$1,975	$2,595
2. Non-income statement items:	($1,900)	($1,900)
3. Total deviation	$75	$695

THREE-YEAR INCOME PROJECTION

What Is a Three-Year Income Projection?

A three-year income projection is a pro forma income (or profit & loss) statement. This statement differs from a cash flow statement in that it includes only projected income and deductible expenses. This difference is illustrated as follows: Your company will make payments of $9,000 on a vehicle in 2002. Interest accounts for $3,000 of that amount. The full amount ($9,000) will be recorded on a cash flow statement; only the interest ($3,000) will be recorded on a projected income statement. Principal paid on your loan ($6,000) is not a deductible expense.

Variation in Period Covered

There is some difference of opinion as to the period of time that should be covered and whether it should be on an annual or month-by-month basis. If you are seeking funds, talk to the lender about his or her specific requirements. If not, a three-year projection with annual rather than monthly projections is suggested. With the rapidly-changing economy, it is difficult to make accurate detailed projections.

Account for Increases and Decreases

Increases in income and expenses are only realistic and should be reflected in your projections. Industry trends can also cause decreases in both income and expenses. An example of this might be in the computer industry where heavy competition and standardization of components has caused a decrease in cost and sale price of both hardware and software. The state of the economy will also be a contributing factor in the outlook for your business.

Sources of Information

Information for a three-year projection can be developed from your pro forma cash flow statement and your business and marketing analysis. The first year's figures can be transferred from the totals of income and expense items. The second and third years' figures are derived by combining these totals with projected trends in your particular industry. Also remember that certain expenses from your first year may not be repeated in future years. You may also have new expenses to take into account. For instance, you may have a new product or service, you may begin importing or exporting internationally and have customs and freight, or you may begin offering merchant credit card services and have associated fees. Again, if you are an established business, you will also be able to use past financial statements to help you determine what you project for the future of your business. Be sure to take into account anticipated fluctuations in costs, efficiency of operation, and changes in your market.

At the end of each year, you can compare your company's projections against its actual performance. You may be required by some lenders or investors to extend your projection to five years. The process will be the same.

Note. A filled-in example of a Three-Year Income Projection form is provided on the next page. A blank form for your use is located in Appendix IV.

Three-Year Income Projection

Business Name: Updated: September 26, 2001

Genesis Multimedia	YEAR 1 2002	YEAR 2 2003	YEAR 3 2004	TOTAL 3 YEARS
INCOME				
1. Sales revenues	500,000	540,000	595,000	1,635,000
2. Cost of goods sold (c – d)	312,000	330,000	365,000	1,007,000
a. Beginning inventory	147,000	155,000	175,000	147,000
b. Purchases	320,000	350,000	375,000	1,045,000
c. C.O.G. available Sale (a + b)	467,000	505,000	550,000	1,192,000
d. Less ending inventory (12/31)	155,000	175,000	185,000	185,000
3. GROSS PROFIT ON SALES (1 – 2)	188,000	210,000	230,000	628,000
EXPENSES				
1. Variable (selling) (a thru h)	67,390	84,300	89,400	241,090
a. Advertising/marketing	22,000	24,500	26,400	72,900
b. Freight	9,000	12,000	13,000	34,000
c. Fulfillment of orders	2,000	3,500	4,000	9,500
d. Packaging costs	3,000	4,000	3,500	10,500
e. Salaries/wages/commissions	25,000	34,000	36,000	95,000
f. Travel	1,000	1,300	1,500	3,800
g. Miscellaneous selling expense	390	0	0	390
h. Depreciation (prod/serv assets)	5,000	5,000	5,000	15,000
2. Fixed (administrative) (a thru h)	51,610	53,500	55,800	160,910
a. Financial administration	1,000	1,200	1,200	3,400
b. Insurance	3,800	4,000	4,200	12,000
c. Licenses and permits	2,710	1,400	1,500	5,610
d. Office salaries	14,000	17,500	20,000	51,500
e. Rent expense	22,500	22,500	22,500	67,500
f. Utilities	3,000	3,500	3,600	10,100
g. Miscellaneous fixed expense	0	0	0	0
h. Depreciation (office equipment)	4,600	3,400	2,800	10,800
TOTAL OPERATING EXPENSES (1 + 2)	119,000	137,800	145,200	402,000
NET INCOME OPERATIONS (GP – Exp)	69,000	72,200	84,800	226,000
OTHER INCOME (Interest income)	5,000	5,000	5,000	15,000
OTHER EXPENSE (Interest expense)	7,000	5,000	4,000	16,000
NET PROFIT (LOSS) BEFORE TAXES	67,000	72,200	85,800	225,000
TAXES 1. Federal, self-employment	21,700	24,200	28,500	74,400
2. State	4,300	4,800	5,700	14,800
3. Local	0	0	0	0
NET PROFIT (LOSS) AFTER TAXES	41,000	43,200	51,600	135,800

BREAK-EVEN ANALYSIS

What Is a Break-Even Point?

This is the point at which a company's costs exactly match the sales volume and at which the business has neither made a profit nor incurred a loss. The break-even point can be determined by mathematical calculation or by development of a graph. It can be expressed in:

1. *Total dollars of revenue* (exactly offset by total costs).

2. *Total units of production* (cost of which exactly equals the income derived by their sale).

To apply a break-even analysis to an operation, you will need three projections:

1. *Fixed costs.* Administrative Overhead plus Interest. Many of these costs remain constant even during slow periods. *Interest expense* must be added to fixed costs for a break-even analysis.

2. *Variable costs.* Cost of Goods plus Selling Expenses. Usually varies with volume of business. The greater the sales volume, the higher the costs.

3. *Total sales volume.* Projected sales for same period.

Source of Information

All of your figures can be derived from your three-year projection. Since breakeven is not reached until your total revenues match your total expenses, the calculation of your break-even point will require that you add enough years' revenues and expenses together until you see that the total revenues are greater than the total expenses. Retrieve the figures and plug them into the following mathematical formula. (By now you should be able to see that each financial document in your business plan builds on the ones done previously.)

Mathematically

A firm's sales at a break-even point can be computed by using this formula:

B-E Point (Sales) = Fixed Costs + [(Variable Costs/Est. Revenues) x Sales]

Terms used: a. Sales = volume of sales at Break-Even Point

                b. Fixed Costs = administrative expense, depreciation, interest

                c. Variable Costs = cost of goods and selling expenses

                d. Estimated Revenues = income (from sales of goods/services)

Example: a. S (Sales at B-E Point) = the unknown

                b. FC (Fixed Costs) = $25,000

                c. VC (Variable Costs) = $45,000

                d. R (Estimated Revenues) = $90,000

Using the formula, the computation would appear as follows:

$$S \text{ (at B-E Point)} = \$25,000 + [(\$45,000/\$90,000) \times S]$$

$$S = \$25,000 + (1/2 \times S)$$

$$S - 1/2\,S = \$25,000$$

S = $50,000 (B-E Point in terms of $ of revenue exactly offset by total costs)

Graphically

Break-even point in graph form for the same business would be plotted as illustrated below. There is a blank form for your use in Appendix IV.

Break-Even Analysis Graph

Business Name: Genesis Multimedia   Date of Analysis: Sept 31, 2002

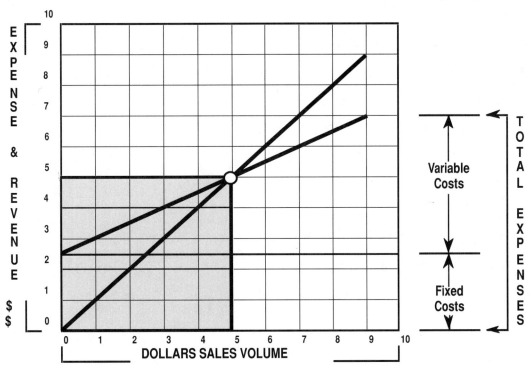

NOTE: Figures shown in 10's of thousands of dollars (Ex: 2 = $ 20,000)

To Complete the Graph. Determine the following projections.

1. *Fixed Costs for Period.* Those costs that usually remain constant and must be met regardless of your sales volume (administrative, rent, insurance, depreciation, salaries, etc.). Also add interest expenses (e.g., $25,000).

2. *Variable Costs.* Cost associated with the production and selling of your products or services. If you have a product, you will include cost of goods (inventory purchases, labor, materials) with your variable costs (freight, packaging, sales commissions, advertising, etc.) If you wish, these costs may be expressed by multiplying the unit cost by the units to be sold for a product (e.g., $1.50 per unit x 30,000 units = $45,000). For a service having no cost of goods, use total of projected selling expenses (variable).

3. *Total Sales Volume.* This figure represents your total projected revenues. You may also calculate revenues by multiplying projected units of product to be sold by sale price per unit (e.g., 30,000 units @ $3.00 = $90,000). For a service, you can multiply your projected billable hours by your hourly rate (e.g., 900 hours x $100 = $90,000).

To Draw Graph Lines

1. **Draw Horizontal Line** at point representing Fixed Costs (25).

2. **Draw Variable Cost Line** from left end of Fixed Cost Line sloping upward to point where Total Costs (Fixed + Variable) on vertical scale (7) meet Total Revenues on the horizontal scale (9).

3. **Draw Total Revenues Line** from zero through point describing total Revenues on both scales (where 9 meets 9).

Break-Even Point. That point on the graph where the Variable Cost Line intersects the Total Revenue Line. This business estimates that it will break even at the time sales volume reaches $50,000. The triangular area below and to the left of that point represents company losses. The triangular area above and to the right of the point represents expected company profits.

Section III
ACTUAL PERFORMANCE (HISTORICAL) FINANCIAL STATEMENTS

The financial statements covered on the following pages are actual performance (or historical) statements. They reflect the *past* activity of your business.

If You Are a New Business Owner

Being a new business owner, you have no business history. Your financial section will end with the projected statements and a Personal Financial History.

If You Are an Established Business

With an established business you will include the following actual performance financial documents:

➡ **Balance Sheet**

➡ **Profit & Loss (Income) Statement**

➡ **Business Financial History**

or

➡ **Loan Application**

BALANCE SHEET

What Is a Balance Sheet?

The balance sheet is a financial statement that shows the financial position of the business as of a fixed date. It is usually done at the close of an accounting period. The balance sheet can be compared to a photograph. It is a picture of what your business owns and owes at a particular given moment and will show you whether your financial position is strong or weak. By regularly preparing this statement, you will be able to identify and analyze trends in the financial strength of your business and thus implement timely modifications.

Assets, Liabilities, and Net Worth

All balance sheets are divided into three categories. The three are related in that, at any given time, a business's assets equal the total contributions by its creditors and owners. They are defined as follows:

- **Assets**. Anything your business owns that has monetary value.

- **Liabilities**. Debts owed by the business to any of its creditors.

- **Net Worth (Capital)**. An amount equal to the owner's equity.

The relationship between the three is simply illustrated in the following mathematical formula.

Assets − Liabilities = Net Worth

Examined as such, it becomes apparent that if a business possesses more assets than it owes to creditors, its net worth will be a positive. Conversely, if the business owes more money to creditors than it possesses in assets, the net worth will be a negative.

Categories and Format

The balance sheet must follow an accepted accounting format and contain the previously mentioned categories. By following this format, anyone reading the Balance Sheet can readily interpret it.

> **Note**
>
> A sample filled-in Balance Sheet and Explanation of Balance Sheet Categories are provided for you on the next two pages.
>
> There is also a blank form for your own use in Appendix IV.

BALANCE SHEET
Explanation of Categories

Assets. Everything owned by or owed to your business that has cash value.

1. ***Current assets.*** Assets that can be converted into cash within one year of the date on the Balance Sheet.
   - *Cash.* Money you have on hand. Include moneys not yet deposited.
   - *Petty cash.* Money deposited to petty cash and not yet expended.
   - *Accounts receivable.* Money owed to you for sale of goods and/or services.
   - *Inventory.* Raw materials, work in process, and goods manufactured or purchased for resale.
   - *Short-term investments.* Expected to be converted to cash within one year—stocks, bonds, or CDs. List at lesser of cost or market value.
   - *Prepaid expenses.* Goods or services purchased or rented prior to use (e.g., rent, insurance, prepaid inventory purchases, etc.).

2. ***Long-term investments.*** Stocks, bonds, and special savings accounts to be kept for at least one year.

3. ***Fixed assets.*** Resources a business owns and does not intend for resale.
   - *Land.* List at original purchase price.
   - *Buildings.* List at cost less depreciation.
   - *Equipment, Furniture, Autos/Vehicles.* List at cost less depreciation. "Kelley Blue Book" can be used to determine current value of vehicles.

Liabilities. What your business owes; claims by creditors on your assets.

1. ***Current liabilities.*** Those obligations payable within one operating cycle.
   - *Accounts payable.* Obligations payable within one operating cycle.
   - *Notes payable.* Short-term notes; list the balance of principal due. Separately list the current portion of long-term debts.
   - *Interest payable.* Interest accrued on loans and credit.
   - *Taxes payable.* Amounts estimated to have been incurred during the accounting period.
   - *Payroll accrual.* Current liabilities on salaries and wages.
   - *Long-term liabilities.* Outstanding balance less the current portion due (e.g., business loans, mortgages, vehicle, etc.).

Net Worth. Also called Owner Equity. The claims of the owner or owners on the assets of the business (document according to the legal structure of your business.)

1. ***Proprietorship or partnership.*** Each owner's original investment plus earnings after withdrawals.

2. ***Corporation.*** The sum of contributions by owners or stockholders plus earnings retained after paying dividends.

Balance Sheet

Business Name: **Genesis Multimedia**   Date: September 30, 2001

ASSETS

Current assets

Cash	$	8,742
Petty cash	$	167
Accounts receivable	$	5,400
Inventory	$	101,800
Short-term investments	$	0
Prepaid expenses	$	1,967

Long-term investments $ 0

Fixed assets

Land (valued at cost)		$	185,000
Buildings		$	143,000
1. Cost	171,600		
2. Less acc. depr.	28,600		
Improvements		$	0
1. Cost			
2. Less acc. depr.			
Equipment		$	5,760
1. Cost	7,200		
2. Less acc. depr.	1,440		
Furniture		$	2,150
1. Cost	2,150		
2. Less acc. depr.	0		
Autos/vehicles		$	16,432
1. Cost	19,700		
2. Less acc. depr.	3,268		

Other assets

1.	$	
2.	$	

TOTAL ASSETS $ 470,418

LIABILITIES

Current liabilities

Accounts payable	$	2,893
Notes payable	$	0
Interest payable	$	1,842
Taxes payable		
Federal income tax	$	5,200
Self-employment tax	$	1,025
State income tax	$	800
Sales tax accrual	$	2,130
Property tax	$	0
Payroll accrual	$	4,700

Long-term liabilities

Notes payable	$	196,700

TOTAL LIABILITIES $ 215,290

NET WORTH (EQUITY)

Proprietorship	$	
or		
Partnership		
John Smith, 60% equity	$	153,077
Mary Blake, 40% equity	$	102,051
or		
Corporation		
Capital stock	$	
Surplus paid in	$	
Retained earnings	$	

TOTAL NET WORTH $ 255,128

Assets – Liabilities = Net Worth
and
Liabilities + Equity = Total Assets

PROFIT & LOSS (INCOME) STATEMENT

What Is a Profit & Loss (Income) Statement?

This statement shows your business financial activity over a period of time, usually your tax year. In contrast to the balance sheet, which shows a picture of your business at a given moment, the Profit & Loss Statement (P&L) can be likened to a moving picture—showing what has happened in your business over a period of time. It is an excellent tool for assessing your business. You will be able to pick out weaknesses in your operation and plan ways to run your business more effectively, thereby increasing your profits. For example, you may find some heavy advertising that you did in March did not effectively increase your sales. In following years, you may decide to utilize your advertising funds more effectively by using them at a time when there is increased customer spending taking place. In the same way, you might examine your profit & loss statement to see what months have the heaviest sales volume and plan your inventory accordingly. Comparison of your P&Ls from several years will give you an even better picture of the trends in your business. Don't underestimate the value of this particular tool when planning your tactics.

How to Develop a Profit & Loss Statement

The profit & loss statement (income statement) is compiled from actual business transactions, in contrast to pro forma statements, which are projections for future business periods. The P&L shows where your money has come from and where it was spent over a specific period of time. It should be prepared not only at the end of the fiscal year, but at the close of each business month. It is one of the two principal financial statements prepared from the ledgers and the records of a business.

Income and expense account balances are used in the profit & loss statement. The remaining asset, liability, and capital information provides the figures for the balance sheet covered on the last three pages. At the end of each month, the accounts in the General Ledger are balanced and closed. Balances from the revenue accounts (numbered 400–499) and the expense accounts (numbered 500–599) must be transferred to your profit & loss statement.

If you use an accounting professional or have a good in-house software program, either should generate a profit & loss statement and balance sheet for you at the end of every month as well as at the end of your tax year. Many owners of smaller businesses set up their own set of manual books. If your general records are set up properly, the transfer of information should still be fairly simple as long as you understand what information is needed and which general records are to be used as sources.

Format and Sources of Information

The profit & loss (or income) statement must also follow an accepted accounting format and contain certain categories.

On the next page, you will see the correct format and a brief explanation of the items to be included or computations to be made in each category in order to arrive at "The Bottom Line" or owner's share of the profit for the period.

PROFIT & LOSS STATEMENT
Correct Format and Explanation of Categories

Income

1. ***Net sales (Gross sales less Returns and Allowances).*** What were your cash receipts for the period? If your accounting is on an accrual basis, what amount did you invoice out during the period? You may wish to have subcategories for different types of sales.

2. ***Cost of goods sold (COG).*** The cost of manufacturing or purchase of products sold for the period. The cost of goods is calculated using a, b, and c below (a + b − c = COG).
   - *Beginning inventory.* Product on hand at beginning of accounting period.
   - *Purchases.* Material, labor, or cost on inventory purchased during accounting period.
   - *Ending inventory.* Product on hand at the end of the accounting period.

3. ***Gross profit.*** Computed by subtracting Cost of Goods Sold from Net Sales (1 − 2).

Expenses

1. ***Variable expenses (selling).*** What expenses did you have that were directly related to your product or service (e.g., advertising/marketing, freight, fulfillment of orders, sales salaries/commissions, trade shows, travel, vehicles, depreciation, production equipment, etc.)? These expenses vary and are usually directly proportional to your volume of business. Divide into subcategories customized to your business.

2. ***Fixed expenses (administrative).*** What expenses did you have during the period on office overhead (accounting/legal, insurance, office supplies, office salaries, rent, utilities, depreciation of office equipment, etc.)? These expenses are often fixed and remain the same regardless of your volume of business. They should also be divided into subcategories customized to your business.

Net income from operations. Gross Profit (3) minus Total Fixed (selling) Expenses and Variable (administrative) Expenses (Expenses numbers 1 and 2).

> *Other income.* Interest received during the period
>
> *Other expense.* Interest paid out during the period

Net profit (loss) before income taxes. The Net Income from Operations plus Interest Income minus Interest Expense. The amount of profit prior to income taxes.

> *Income taxes.* List taxes paid out during the period (federal, state, local, self-employment).

Net profit (loss) after income taxes. Subtract all income taxes paid out from the net profit (or loss) before income taxes. This is what is known as "the bottom line."

Sample Forms

The next two pages contain two profit & loss statement forms. As you will see in the example 12-Month Profit & Loss Statement, the spreadsheet is divided into columns representing each of the 12 months plus 6-month and annual total columns. At the end of your tax year, you will have filled in all monthly columns. After calculating your annual totals, your P&L will be complete. At the end of the year, this form will provide an accurate moving picture of the year's financial activity. The second one is a single form to be used for either a monthly, quarterly, or annual profit & loss statement. Blank forms for your own use are provided in Appendix IV.

Profit & Loss (Income) Statement

Genesis Multimedia

For the Year: 2002

	Jan	Feb	Mar	Apr	May	Jun	6-MONTH TOTALS	Jul	Aug	Sep	Oct	Nov	Dec	12-MONTH TOTALS
INCOME														
1. Net sales (Gr - R&A)	14,400	10,140	10,060	15,658	18,622	12,620	81,500	11,500	9,850	10,150	16,600	29,250	51,000	209,850
2. Cost of goods to be sold	2,800	2,900	4,200	7,700	7,350	2,750	27,700	2,959	2,580	2,740	6,250	13,400	23,290	78,919
a. Beginning inventory	27,000	31,000	48,500	48,600	42,000	35,600	27,000	33,800	40,800	40,900	51,700	53,300	54,700	27,000
b. Purchases	6,800	20,400	4,300	1,100	950	35,600	34,500	9,959	2,680	13,540	7,850	14,800	12,890	96,219
c. C.O.G. available for sale	33,800	51,400	52,800	49,700	42,950	36,550	61,500	43,759	43,480	54,440	59,550	68,100	67,590	123,219
d. Less ending inventory	31,000	48,500	48,600	42,000	35,600	33,800	33,800	40,800	40,900	51,700	53,300	54,700	44,300	44,300
3. Gross profit	11,600	7,240	5,860	7,958	11,272	9,870	53,800	8,541	7,270	7,410	10,350	15,850	27,710	130,931
EXPENSES														
1. Variable (selling) expenses														
a. Advertising	900	300	900	250	300	300	2,950	350	300	640	1,300	1,200	1,400	8,140
b. Freight	75	75	75	75	180	70	550	75	75	90	180	300	560	1,830
c. Fulfillment of orders	300	300	300	400	350	300	1,950	300	280	325	450	600	975	4,880
d. Packaging costs	2,100	0	0	0	600	0	2,700	0	200	230	0	0	0	3,130
e. Sales salaries/commissions	1,400	900	1,300	1,400	1,100	900	7,000	1,400	1,400	1,400	1,400	1,400	1,400	15,400
f. Travel	0	500	700	0	0	400	1,600	0	540	25	80	0	0	2,245
g. Misc. variable expense	50	47	73	40	28	62	300	90	73	46	39	74	87	709
h. Depreciation	0	0	0	0	0	0	0	0	0	0	0	0	2,660	2,660
Total variable expenses	4,825	2,122	3,348	2,165	2,558	2,032	17,050	2,215	2,868	2,756	3,449	3,574	7,082	38,994
1. Fixed (admin) expenses														
a. Financial administration	75	75	75	475	75	75	850	75	75	75	75	75	75	1,300
b. Insurance	1,564	0	0	0	0	0	1,564	1,563	0	0	0	0	0	3,127
c. Licenses/permits	240	0	0	0	0	0	240	0	0	0	0	0	125	365
d. Office salaries	1,400	1,400	1,400	1,400	1,400	1,400	8,400	1,400	1,400	1,400	1,400	1,400	1,400	16,800
e. Rent expenses	700	700	700	700	700	700	4,200	700	700	700	700	700	700	8,400
f. Utilities	200	200	140	120	80	80	820	75	75	75	90	120	155	1,410
g. Misc. fixed expense	54	38	42	57	28	64	283	60	72	31	48	45	89	628
h. Depreciation	0	0	0	0	0	2,660	2,660	0	0	0	0	0	2,660	5,320
Total fixed expenses	4,233	2,413	2,357	2,752	2,283	4,979	19,017	3,873	2,322	2,281	2,313	2,340	5,204	37,350
Total operating expense	9,058	4,535	5,705	4,917	4,841	7,011	36,067	6,088	5,190	5,037	5,762	5,914	12,286	76,344
Net Income From Operations	2,542	2,705	155	3,041	6,431	2,859	17,733	2,453	2,080	2,373	4,588	9,936	15,424	54,587
Other Income (interest)	234	240	260	158	172	195	1,259	213	303	300	417	406	413	3,311
Other Expense (interest)	0	0	0	234	233	232	699	231	230	225	223	222	220	2,050
Net Profit (Loss) Before Taxes	2,776	2,945	415	2,965	6,370	2,822	18,293	2,435	2,153	2,448	4,782	10,120	15,617	55,848
Taxes: a. Federal	1,950	0	0	1,950	0	1,950	5,850	0	0	1,950	0	0	0	7,800
b. State	350	0	0	350	0	350	1,050	0	0	350	0	0	0	1,400
c. Local	0	0	0	0	0	0	0	0	0	0	0	0	0	0
NET PROFIT (LOSS) AFTER TAXES	476	2,945	415	665	6,370	522	11,393	2,435	2,153	148	4,782	10,120	15,617	46,648

Profit & Loss (Income) Statement
Genesis Multimedia

Beginning: January 1, 2002   **Ending: December 31, 2002**

INCOME		
1. Sales revenues		$ 209,850
2. Cost of goods sold (c – d)		78,919
a. Beginning inventory (1/01)	27,000	
b. Purchases	96,219	
c. C.O.G. avail. sale (a + b)	123,219	
d. Less ending inventory (12/31)	44,300	
3. Gross profit on sales (1 – 2)		$ 130,931
EXPENSES		
1. Variable (selling) (a thru h)		38,994
a. Advertising/marketing	8,140	
b. Freight	1,830	
c. Fulfillment of orders	4,880	
d. Packaging costs	3,130	
e. Salaries/wages/commissions	15,400	
f. Travel	2,245	
g. Misc. variable (selling) expense	709	
h. Depreciation (prod/serv assets)	2,660	
2. Fixed (administrative) (a thru h)		37,350
a. Financial administration	1,300	
b. Insurance	3,127	
c. Licenses and permits	365	
d. Office salaries	16,800	
e. Rent expense	8,400	
f. Utilities	1,410	
g. Misc. fixed (administrative) expense	628	
h. Depreciation (office equipment)	5,320	
Total operating expenses (1 + 2)		76,344
Net income from operations (GP – Exp)		$ 54,587
Other income (interest income)		3,311
Other expense (interest expense)		2,050
Net profit (loss) before taxes		$ 55,848
Taxes		
a. Federal	7,800	
b. State	1,400	9,200
c. Local	0	
NET PROFIT (LOSS) AFTER TAXES		$ 46,648

BUSINESS FINANCIAL HISTORY

The business financial history is the last of the financial statements required in your business plan. It is a summary of financial information about your company from its start to the present.

If Yours Is a New Business

You will have only projections for your business. If you are applying for a loan, the lender will require a Personal Financial History. This will be of benefit in that it will show the manner in which you have conducted your personal business, an indicator of the probability of your succeeding in your business.

If Yours Is an Established Business

The loan application and your Business Financial History are the same. When you indicate that you are interested in obtaining a business loan, the institution considering the loan will supply you with an application. The format may vary slightly. When you receive your loan application, be sure to review it and think about how you are going to answer each item. Answer all questions and by all means be certain your information is accurate and that it can be easily verified.

Information Needed and Sources

As you fill out your Business Financial History (loan application), it should become immediately apparent why this is the last financial document to be completed. All of the information needed will have been compiled previously in earlier parts of your plan and in the financial statements you have already completed.

To help you with your financial history, the following is a list of information most frequently required. Also listed are some of the sources you can refer to for that information.

- *Assets, liabilities, and net worth.* You should recognize these three as balance sheet terms. You have already completed the Balance Sheet for your company and need only to go back to that record and bring the dollar amounts forward.

- *Contingent liabilities.* These are debts you may come to owe in the future (e.g., default on a cosigned note or settlement of a pending lawsuit).

- *Inventory details.* Information derived from your inventory record. Also, in the organizational plan you should already have a summary of your current policies and methods of evaluation.

- *Profit & loss statement.* This is revenue and expense information. You will transfer the information from your annual profit & loss (last statement completed) or from compilation of several if required by the lender.

- ***Real estate holdings, stocks, and bonds.*** Refer back to your Organizational Plan. You may also have to go through your investment records for more comprehensive information

- ***Legal structure information (sole proprietorship, partnership or corporation).*** There are generally three separate schedules on the financial history, one for each form of legal structure. You will be required to fill out the one that is appropriate to your business. In the Organizational section, you will have covered two areas that will serve as the source of this information—Legal Structure and Management. Supporting Documents may also contain some of the information that you will need.

- ***Audit information.*** Refer back to the organizational plan under Recordkeeping. You may also be asked questions about other prospective lenders, whether you are seeking credit, who audits your books, and when they were last audited.

- ***Insurance coverage.*** You will be asked to provide detailed information on the types of insurance coverage you have for your company (i.e., liability, earthquake, workers' compensation, inventory, machinery and fixtures, buildings, extended coverage, auto, etc.). Your organizational plan and Insurance Update form should have all the information you will need to fill in this section of the financial history.

Business Financial Statement form. You will find an example of a Business Financial History that might be required by a potential lender or investor on the next two pages.

Personal Financial Statement form. If you are a new business and need your Personal Financial Statement for this section, you will find a sample form in *Anatomy of a Business Plan,* Chapter 7, "Supporting Documents."

Please Note

Section IV: Financial Statement Analysis will follow after the Business Financial History example. Analysis of your financial statements will help you to make decisions and implement changes that will make your business more profitable.

Business Financial Statement
Page 1

Business Financial Statement
INDIVIDUAL, PARTNERSHIP, OR CORPORATION

FINANCIAL STATEMENT OF _____   Received At_____Branch

Name_____   Business_____

Address_____   At Close of Business_____ 20____

To

The undersigned, for the purpose of procuring and establishing credit from time to time with you and to induce you to permit the undersigned to become indebted to you on notes, endorsements, guarantees, overdrafts or otherwise, furnishes the following (or in lieu thereof the attached, which is the most recent statement prepared by or for the undersigned) as being a full, true and correct statement of the financial condition of the undersigned on the date indicated, and agrees to notify you immediately of the extent and character of any material changes in said financial condition, and also agrees that if the undersigned or any endorser or guarantor of any of the obligations of the undersigned, at any time fails in business or becomes insolvent, or commits an act of bankruptcy, or if any deposit account of the undersigned with you, or any other property of the undersigned held by you, be attempted to be obtained or held by writ of execution, garnishment, attachment or other legal process, or if any of the representations made below prove to be untrue, or if the undersigned fails to notify you of any material change, as above agreed, or if the business, or any interest therein of the undersigned is sold, then and in such case, at your option, all of the obligations of the undersigned to you, or held by you, shall immediately become due and payable, without demand or notice. This statement shall be construed by you to be a continuing statement of the condition of the undersigned, and a new and original statement of all assets and liabilities upon each and every transaction in and by which the undersigned hereafter becomes indebted to you, until the undersigned advises in writing to the contrary.

ASSETS	DOLLARS	CENTS	LIABILITIES	DOLLARS	CENTS
Cash In_____			Notes Payable to Banks_____		
_____(Name of Bank)					
Cash on Hand			Notes Payable and Trade Acceptances for Merchandise_____		
Notes Receivable and					
Trade Acceptance (Includes $_____Past Due)			Notes Payable to Others_____		
Accounts Receivable--$_____ Less Reserves $_____			Accounts Payable (Includes $_____Past Due)___		
			Due to Partners, Employees		
Customer's . . . (Includes $_____Past Due)			Relatives, Officers, Stockholders or Allied Companies___		
Merchandise—Finished—How Valued_____			Chattel Mortgages and Contracts Payable (Describe		
			Monthly Payments) . . . . . $___		
Merchandise—Unfinished—How Valued_____			Federal and State Income Tax_____		
Merchandise—Raw Material—How Valued_____			Accrued Liabilities (Interest, Wages, Taxes, Etc.)___		
Supplies on Hand_____			Portion of Long Term Debt Due Within One Year___		
Stocks and Bonds—Listed (See Schedule B)___					
TOTAL CURRENT ASSETS			**TOTAL CURRENT LIABILITIES**		
Real Estate—Less Depreciation of: $_____Net			Liens on Real Estate (See Schedule A) $_____		
(See Schedule A)			Less Current Portion Included Avove $_____Net		
Machinery and Fixtures—					
Less Depreciation of: $_____Net					
Automobiles and Trucks—					
Less Depreciation of: $_____Net			Capital Stock—Preferred_____		
Stocks and Bonds—Unlisted (See Schedule B)___			Capital Stock—Common_____		
Due from Partners, Employees,					
Relatives, Officers, Stockholders or Allied Companies___			Surplus—Paid In_____		
Cash Value Life Insurance_____			Surplus—Earned and Undivided Profit____		
Other Assets (Describe_____			Net Worth (If Not Incorporated)____		
TOTAL			TOTAL		

PROFIT AND LOSS STATEMENT FOR THE PERIOD FROM_____ TO_____				**CONTINGENT LIABILITIES (Not Included Above)**			
Net Sales (After Returned Sales and Allowances)___				As Guarantor or Endorser_____			
Cost of Sales:				Accounts, Notes, or Trade			
Beginning Inventory				Acceptance Discounted or Pledged___			
Purchases (or cost of goods mfd.)				Surety On Bonds or Other Continent Liability___			
TOTAL				Letters of Credit_____			
Less: Closing Inventory				Judgments Unsatisfied or Suits Pending___			
				Merchandise Commitments and Unfinished Contracts___			
Gross Profit on Sales				Merchandise Held On Consignment From Others___			
Operating Expenses:				Unsatisfied Tax Liens or Notices From the Federal or			
				State Governments of Intention to Assess Such Liens			
Salaries—Officers or Partners				**RECONCILEMENT OF NET WORTH OR EARNED SURPLUS**			
Salaries and Wages—Other				Net Worth or Earned Surplus at Beginning of Period___			
Rent				Add Net Profit or Deduct Net Loss___			
Depreciation				Total___			
Bad Debts				Other Additions (Describe)_____			
Advertising				Total___			
Interest				Less: Withdrawals or Dividends___			
Taxes—Other Than Income				Other Deductions (Explain)___			
Insurance				Total Deductions___			
Other Expenses				Net Worth or Capital Funds on This Financial Statement___			
Net Profit from Operations				**DETAIL OF INVENTORY**			
Other Income							
Less Other Expenses				Is Inventory Figure Actual or Estimated?___			
Net Profit Before Income Tax				By whom Taken or Estimated_____When?___			
Federal and State Income Tax				Buy Principally From_____			
Net Profit or Loss				Average Terms of Purchase_____Sale___			
(To Net Worth or Earned Surplus)				Time of Year Inventory Maximum_____Minimum___			

Business Financial Statement
Page 2

Business Financial Statement
INDIVIDUAL, PARTNERSHIP, OR CORPORATION – Page 2

SCHEDULE A   LIST OF REAL ESTATE AND IMPROVEMENTS WITH ENCUMBRANCES THEREON

Description, Street Number, Location	Title in Names of	BOOK VALUE		MORTGAGES OR LIENS		Terms of Payment	Holder of Lien
		LAND	IMPROVEMENTS	MATURITY	AMOUNT		
		$	$		$	$	
TOTALS		$	$		$	$	

SCHEDULE B   STOCKS & BONDS: Describe Fully. Use Supplemental Sheet if Necessary. Indicate if Stocks Are Common or Preferred. Give Interest Rate and Maturity of Bonds.

NO. OF SHARES AMT. OF BONDS	NAME AND ISSUE (DESCRIBE FULLY)	BOOK VALUE		MARKET VALUE	
		LISTED	UNLISTED	PRICE	VALUE
		$	$		$
	TOTALS	$	$		$

SCHEDULE C   Complete if Statement is for an Individual or Sole Proprietorship

Age _____ Number of Years in Present Business _____ Date of Filing Fictitious Trade Style _____

What Property Listed in This Statement is in Joint Tenancy? _____ Name of Other Party _____

What Property Listed in This Statement is Community Property? _____ Name of Other Party _____

With What Other Businesses Are You Connected? _____ Have You Filed Homestead? _____

Do You Deal With or Carry Accounts With Stockbrokers? _____ Amount $ _____ Name of Firm _____

SCHEDULE D   Complete if Statement is of a Partnership

NAME OF PARTNERS (indicate special partners)	Age	Amount Contributed	Outside Net Worth	Other Business Connections
		$	$	

Date of Organization _____ Limited or General? _____ Terminates _____

If Operating Under Fictitious Trade Style, Give Date of Filing

SCHEDULE E   Complete if Statement is of a Corporation

	AUTHORIZED	Par Value	OUTSTANDING			ISSUED FOR
			SHARES	AMOUNT	CASH	
Common Stock	$	$		$	$	
Preferred Stock	$	$		$	$	
Bonds—Total Issue	$	$		$	$	
Date Incorporated			Under Laws of State of			

Officers	Age	Shares Owned		Directors and Principal Stockholders	Shares Owned	
		COMMON	PREFERRED		COMMON	PREFERRED
President				Director		
Vice President				Director		
Secretary				Director		
Treasurer						

SCHEDULE F   Complete in ALL Cases   INSURANCE

Are Your Books Audited by Outside Accountants? _____ None _____

Date of Last Audit _____ To What Date Has the U.S. Internal Revenue Department Examined Your Books? _____

Are You Borrowing From Any Other Branch of This Bank? _____ Which? _____

Are You Applying for Credit At Any Other Source? _____ Where? _____

Have You Ever Failed In Business? _____ If So, attach a Complete Explanation and State Basis of Settlement With Creditors _____

Lease Has _____ Years to Run With Monthly Rental of $ _____

Merchandise _____ $ _____

Machinery & Fixtures _____ $ _____

Buildings _____ $ _____

Earthquake _____ $ _____ Is Extended Coverage Endorsement Included? _____

Do You Carry Workmen's Compensation Insurance? _____

Automobiles and Trucks:

Public Liability $ _____ M/$ _____ M

Collision _____ $ _____

Property Damage _____ $ _____

Life Insurance _____ $ _____ Name of Beneficiary _____

STATEMENT OF BANK OFFICER:

Insofar as our records reveal, this Financial Statement is accurate and true. The foregoing Statement is (a copy of) the original signed by the maker, in the credit files as of _____ of this Bank.

_____ Assistant Cashier-Manager

The undersigned solemnly declares and certifies that the above statement (or in lieu thereof, the attached statement, as the case may be) and supporting schedules, both printed and written, give a full, true, and correct statement of the financial condition of the under-Signed as of the date indicated.

Signature _____

By _____

(Title, If Corporation)

SECTION IV
FINANCIAL STATEMENT ANALYSIS—THE FINAL TOOL

The Financial Documents I have presented will most probably be sufficient for both your own use and that of a potential lender or investor. Some of the documents may not be required. You should also note that we may have omitted forms required by some lenders or investors. The important thing for you to be aware of when compiling financial statements is that the information must be correct, it must reflect the assumptions developed in the organizational and marketing plans, and you must have supportive records that back up your numbers.

By now you will have completed all of the pro forma and historical financial statements required for your business. There is an additional financial tool, however, that will help you as well as your lenders and/or investors to look at your business, analyze it according to industry standards, and make decisions that will increase profitability. That tool is financial statement analysis. It is accomplished by applying a set of formulas to the information on your profit & loss (income statements and balance sheets.

HOW TO ANALYZE FINANCIAL STATEMENTS

In the last pages of this section, I will explain financial statement analysis and give you examples of how you can use it to look at your business. Doing a financial statement analysis of your business is like all of the other tasks you have already completed. There is a definite process and if you follow it step-by-step, you will have added a valuable component to your business plan.

Read the following pages. When you are finished reading, go to the sample business plans in Appendixes I, II, and III and see how the analyses were done for Marine Art of California, Dayne Landscaping, Inc., and Wholesale Mobile Homes.com, Inc. You will note in all cases that there is a ratio table and spreadsheets preceded by a one-page summary. Apply the formulas to your income statements and balance sheets to figure the ratios for your business. You can also complete a vertical analysis using the income statements and balance sheets. A horizontal analysis can only be completed if you have been in business for two or more years.

Analysis Summary

Once you have figured the ratios and completed your vertical (and horizontal, if you have been in business for two or more years) analyses, be sure to develop a summary sheet for your business plan. The summary sheet allows you and/or your lenders or investors to get a quick overview of your business and how it compares to industry standards. The summary should contain: (1) a list of your projected ratios, (2) a list of historical ratios if you are a current business, and (3) a list of standard ratios for your industry. After you list the ratios, you should finish your summary with your comments regarding what your ratios indicate for the future of the company.

FINANCIAL STATEMENT ANALYSIS
Putting Your Financial Statements to Work

To better utilize the financial section of your business plan as a working tool, you will use the financial statements that you have prepared to analyze your business. The following pages are devoted to giving you the basics about financial statement analysis. After you have read the material and understand how to apply the formulas to develop ratios, you can do an analysis of your own business and append it to the end of your financial section.

> **Note**
>
> If you are a new business, your analysis will be based on projections only. If you are a current business, you will use your historical profit & loss (income) statements and your balance sheets.

Your financial statements contain the information you need to help make decisions regarding your business. Many small business owners think of their financial statements as requirements for creditors, bankers, or tax preparers only, but they are much more than that. When analyzed, your financial statements can give you key information needed on the financial condition and the operations of your business.

Relationships are expressed as ratios or percentages. Financial statement analysis requires measures to be expressed as ratios or percentages. For example, consider the situation where total assets on your balance sheet are $10,000. Cash is $2,000; Accounts Receivable are $3,000; and Fixed Assets are $5,000. The relationships of each of the three to total assets would be expressed as follows:

	Ratio	Relationship	Percentages
Cash	.2	.2:1	20%
Accounts Receivable	.3	.3:1	30%
Fixed Assets	.5	.5:1	50%

Financial statement analysis involves the studying of relationships and comparisons of:

- Items in a single year's financial statement.

- Comparative financial statements for a period of time.

- Your statements with those of other businesses.

> **Note**
>
> A **Financial Statement Analysis Ratio Table form** has been provided in Appendix IV for your use. The form has all of the formulas for figuring your ratios. Input the appropriate numbers from your income statements and balance sheets and calculate according to the formulas. This will give you the information for your analysis summary page.

ANALYZING YOUR P&L (INCOME) STATEMENTS AND BALANCE SHEETS

Many analytic tools are available, but the focus will be on the following measures, using your profit & loss (income) statements and balance sheets, that are of most importance to a small business owner in the business planning process:

- **Liquidity Analysis**
- **Measures of Investment**
- **Profitability**
- **Vertical Financial Statement Analysis**
- **Measures of Debit**
- **Horizontal Financial Statement Analysis**

Liquidity Analysis

The liquidity of a business is the ability it has to meet financial obligations. The analysis focuses on the *balance sheet* relationships for the current assets and current liabilities. The three main measures of liquidity and their formulas are as follows:

1. *Net working capital.* The excess of current assets over current liabilities is net working capital. The more net working capital a business has, the less risky it is, as it has the ability to cover current liabilities as they come due.

$$\text{Formula:} \quad \frac{\textbf{Current assets – Current liabilities}}{\textbf{Net working capital}}$$

2. *Current ratio.* The current ratio is a more dependable indication of than the net working capital. The current ratio is computed with the following formula:

$$\text{Current ratio} = \frac{\textbf{Current assets}}{\textbf{Current liabilities}}$$

There is no set criteria for the *normal* current ratio, as that is dependent on the business you are in. If you have predictable cash flows, you can operate with a lower current ratio.

A higher ratio means a more liquid position. A ratio of 2.0 is considered acceptable for most businesses. This would allow a company to lose 50 percent of its current assets and still be able to cover current liabilities. For most businesses, this is an adequate margin of safety.

3. *Quick ratio.* Since inventory is the most difficult current asset to dispose of quickly, it is subtracted from the current assets in the quick ratio to give a tougher list of liquidity. A quick ratio of 1.00 or greater is usually recommended, but that is dependent upon the business you are in. The quick ratio is computed as follows:

$$\text{Quick ratio} = \frac{\textbf{Current assets inventory}}{\textbf{Current liabilities}}$$

What Are Liquidity Ratios Good For?

Liquidity ratios can be used to see if your business is in any risk of insolvency. You will also be able to assess your ability to increase or decrease current assets for your business strategy. How would these moves affect your liquidity? Your creditors will use these ratios to determine whether or not to extend credit to you. They will compare the ratios with those of previous periods and with industry standard ratios.

Profitability Analysis

A profitability analysis will measure the ability of a business to make a profit. This type of analysis will utilize your *profit & loss (income) statements*. Three of these measures and their formulas are as follows:

1. **Gross profit margin.** The gross profit margin indicates the percentage of each sales dollar remaining after a business has paid for its goods.

$$\text{Gross profit margin} = \frac{\text{Gross profit}}{\text{Sales}}$$

The higher the gross profit margin, the better. The *normal* rate is dependent on the business you are in. The Gross Profit Margin is the actual markup you have on the goods sold.

2. **Operating profit margin.** This ratio represents the pure operations profits, ignoring interest and taxes. In other words, this is the percentage of each sales dollar remaining after a business has paid for its goods and paid for its variable and fixed expenses. Naturally, a high operating profit margin is preferred.

$$\text{Operating profit margin} = \frac{\text{Income from operations}}{\text{Sales}}$$

3. **Net profit margin.** The net profit margin is clearly the measure of a business success with respect to earnings on sales.

$$\text{Net profit margin} = \frac{\text{Net profit}}{\text{Sales}}$$

A higher margin means the firm is more profitable. The net profit margin will differ according to your specific type of business. A 1 percent margin for a grocery store is not unusual due to the large quantity of items handled; while a 10 percent margin for a jewelry store would be considered low.

Your creditors will look at these ratios to see just how profitable your business is. Without profits, a business cannot attract outside financing. As a business owner, you can see just how profitable your business is. If the ratios are too low, you will want to analyze why.

- Did you mark up your goods sold enough? Check your gross profit margin.
- Are your operating expenses too high? Check your operating profit margin.
- Are your interest expenses too high? Check your net profit margin.

Debt Measures

The debt position of a business indicates the amount of other people's money being used to generate profits. Many new businesses assume too much debt too soon in an attempt to grow too quickly. The measures of debt use the *balance sheet* to tell your business how indebted it is and how able it is to service the debts. The more indebtedness you have, the greater will be your risk of failure.

1. **Debt to assets ratio.** This is a key financial ratio used by creditors. It shows what you owe in relationship to what you own. The higher this ratio, the more risk of failure.

$$\text{Debt to assets ratio} = \frac{\text{Total liabilities}}{\text{Total assets}}$$

The acceptable ratio is dependent upon the policies of your creditors and bankers. If, for instance, you had rates of 79 percent and 74 percent for two consecutive years, these would be excessively high and show a very high risk of failure. Clearly three-quarters of the company is being financed by other people's money, and it does not put the business in a good position for acquiring new debt.

2. **Debt to equity ratio.** This is a key financial ratio used by creditors. It shows what is owed in relationship to the owner's equity in the company. Again, the higher this ratio, the more risk of failure.

$$\text{Debt to equity ratio} = \frac{\text{Total liabilities}}{\text{Total equity (net worth)}}$$

If your business plan includes the addition of long-term debt at a future point, you will want to monitor your debt ratio. If you are seeking a lender, is it within the limits acceptable to your banker?

Investment Measures

As a small business owner, you have invested money to acquire assets, and you should be getting a return on these assets. Even if the owner is taking a salary from the business, he/she also should be earning an additional amount for the investment in the company.

1. **Return on investment (ROI).** The ROI uses your *balance sheet* and measures the effectiveness of you, as the business owner, to generate profits from the available assets.

$$\text{ROI} = \frac{\text{Net profit}}{\text{Total assets}}$$

The higher the ROI, the better. The business owner should set a target for the ROI. What do you want your investment to earn? Many small business owners have successfully created jobs for themselves, but still don't earn a fair return on their investment. Set your target for ROI, and work towards it.

VERTICAL FINANCIAL STATEMENT ANALYSIS

Percentage analysis is used to show the relationship of components in a single financial statement.

- ***For a balance sheet.*** Each asset on the balance sheet is stated as a percent of the total assets, and each liability and equity item is stated as a percent of the total liabilities and owner equity (or net worth).

- ***For an income statement.*** In vertical analysis of the income statement, each item is stated as a percent of the total net sales.

An evaluation of components on single financial statements from one or more years can show changes that may alert you to investigate current expenditures. For example a high percentage increase in cost of goods sold should be cause for investigation. A decrease in gross profit from one year to the next might trigger the owner to look at the mark-up.

You can also evaluate your percentages against those of competitors or against industry standards for your trade to help you make judgments that can help your business be more profitable in the future. If your competitor is making a gross profit of 47 percent and yours is only 32 percent, you will want to know the reason why. Does he or she have a better source for purchasing product? Is your competitor's manufacturing process more efficient?

HORIZONTAL FINANCIAL STATEMENT ANALYSIS

Horizontal analysis is a percentage analysis of the increases and decreases in the items on comparative financial statements. The increase or decrease of the item is listed, and the earlier statement is used as the base. The percentage of increase or decrease is listed in the last column.

- ***For a balance sheet.*** Assets, liabilities, and owner's equity of one year are measured against a second year. The increase or decrease of the item is listed followed by the percentage of increase or decrease.

- ***For an income statement.*** In horizontal analysis of the income statement, income and expense items of one year are measured against a second year. The increase or decrease of the item is listed followed by the percentage of increase or decrease.

The horizontal financial statement analysis can also alert you to potential or current problems that can decrease your profitability. As an example, if you have an increase in sales, but a decrease in gross profit, you might look at your mark-up. If you have a large increase in advertising expense, you will need to see if the expense was justified by increased sales.

Summary

Now you can see how financial statement analysis can be a tool to help you manage your business.

- If the analysis produces results that don't meet your expectation—or if the business is in danger of failure, analyze your expenses and your use of assets. Your first stop should be to cut expenses and increase productivity of assets.

- If return on investment is too low, examine how you could make your assets (equipment, machinery, fixtures, inventory, etc.) better work to your benefit.

- If your profit is low, be sure that your mark-up is adequate, analyze operating expenses to see that they are not too high, and review your interest expenses.

- If your liquidity is low, you could have a risk of becoming insolvent. Examine the level and composition of current assets and current liabilities.

- Vertical and horizontal financial statement analysis will reveal trends and compositions that signify trouble. Using management skills, you can take corrective action.

What Is Your Situation?

Your Financial Statement Analysis will need to be set up according to your individual situation. For example, a new business will have projections only and will have no historical statements to analyze. A one-year-old business would have historical statements for the first year and projections for the second year. A business that is several years old may wish to analyze more than one year of their past financial statements and show their projections for future years.

Most plans will follow one of the two following two formats:

1. *New businesses—projected analysis for year one.* You will prepare a ratio table, filling in column three only with projected ratios for your first year of business. You will not input any information in column four. You will also prepare Projected Vertical Income Statement and Balance Sheets for your first year. After you have completed these three spreadsheets, you will do a Financial Statement Analysis Summary, filling in the *Projected* and *Industry Standard* columns. This will complete your analysis.

   When you update your plan at the end of year one, come back and fill in the *historical* column for year one and the *projected* column for year two. You can also prepare a Historical Vertical Income Statement and Balance Sheet for year one and a Projected Vertical Income Statement and Balance Sheet for year two.

2. *Current businesses—historical analysis of previous year and projected analysis for the coming year.* You will prepare a ratio table, filling in column three with historical ratios for your previous business year. In column four you will input your projections for the coming year. You will prepare a Historical Vertical Income Statement and Balance Sheet for the past year and a Projected Vertical Income Statement and Balance Sheet for the coming year. When you have completed these spreadsheets, you will do a Financial Statement Analysis Summary, filling in *Historical, Projected,* and *Industry Standard* columns.

> **Note**
>
> For a more detailed discussion of Financial Statement Analysis see my basic recordkeeping and accounting small business book, *Keeping the Books.*

CHAPTER 7

SUPPORTING DOCUMENTS

Now that you have completed the main body of your business plan, it is time to consider any additional records that pertain to your business that should be included in your business plan.

Supporting Documents are the records that back up the statements and decisions made in the three main parts of your Business Plan. This chapter covers most of the documents you will want to include. They will be discussed in the following order:

- **Personal Résumés**
- **Owner's Financial Statement**
- **Credit Reports**
- **Copies of Leases**
- **Letters of Reference**
- **Contracts**
- **Legal Documents**
- **Location Studies, Demographics, etc.**

SUPPORTING DOCUMENTS

After completing the main body of your business plan, you are now ready to consider the Supporting Documents that should be included. These are the records that back up the statements and decisions made in the three main parts of your business plan. As you are compiling the first three sections, it is a good idea to keep a separate list of the supporting documents you mention or that come to mind. Many of these documents will actually be needed as you write your plan so that you will have solid financial information to use in your projections. For instance, discussion of your business location might indicate a need for demographic studies, location maps, area studies, leases, etc. The information in the lease agreement will state the financial terms. Once you have the location, you will also know the square footage of your facility and be able to project other associated costs, such as utilities and improvements.

If you are considering applying for a loan to purchase equipment, your supporting documents might be existing equipment purchase agreements or lease contracts. If you are planning a major advertising campaign, include advertising rate sheets from your targeted advertiser.

If you are doing business internationally, you may wish to include customs documents, trade agreements, or shipping agreements. If you are exporting a product or providing a service in a foreign country, it might be beneficial to include demographics on your target market, competition evaluations, and anything else that is pertinent to your business.

By listing these items as you think of them and gathering them as you are working on your business plan, you will have a fairly complete set of all of your supporting documents by the time you finish writing your organizational, marketing, and financial sections. You can sort them into a logical sequence, add them to your working copy, and be ready to add any new ones that become pertinent during the lifetime of your business.

The following pages will cover most of the documents you will normally need to include. The end of the chapter contains examples of some types of supporting documents.

> **Note**
>
> All supporting documents would not be included in every copy of your business plan. Include only that information you think will be needed by the potential lender or investor. The rest should be kept with your copy of the plan and be easily accessible.

PERSONAL RÉSUMÉS

If you are a sole proprietor, include your own résumé. If your business is a partnership, there should be a résumé for each partner. If you are a corporation, include résumés for all officers of the corporation.

It is also a good idea to include résumés for your management and any other key personnel that will be involved in making decisions and affecting the profitability of the company, showing why they were chosen, what their skills are, and how the company will benefit from their management.

A résumé need not and should not be a lengthy document. Preferably, it should be contained on one page for easy reading. Include the following categories and information:

- **Work history.** Include the name of business with dates of employment, beginning with the most recent. Include duties, responsibilities, and related accomplishments.
- **Educational background.** Schools and dates attended, degrees earned, and fields of concentration.
- **Professional affiliations and honors.** List active affiliation with organizations that will add to credibility. Tell about any distinguishing individual or business award received.
- **Special skills.** For example, relates well to others, able to organize, not afraid to take risks, etc.

If you find it difficult to write your own résumé, there are professionals who will do it for you for a nominal fee. A well-written résumé will be a useful tool and should always be kept up-to-date. Once written, it is a simple task to update your information, adding new items and eliminating those that will not benefit you in your current endeavors. An example of a résumé is located on page 117.

OWNER'S FINANCIAL STATEMENT

This is a statement of the owner's personal assets and liabilities. Information can be compiled in the same manner as a balance sheet (see Chapter 6). It is also a statement of annual income and expenditure. If you are a new business owner, your personal financial statement will be included as a part of the Financial Documents section and may be a standard form supplied by the potential lender. See the example on pages 118–119.

CREDIT REPORTS

Credit ratings are of two types: business and personal. If you are already in business, you may have a Dun & Bradstreet rating. You can also ask your suppliers or wholesalers to supply you with letters of credit. Personal credit ratings can be obtained upon request through credit bureaus, banks, and companies with whom you have dealt on a basis other than cash.

COPIES OF LEASES

Include all lease agreements currently in force between your company and a leasing agency. Some examples are the lease agreement for your business premises, equipment, automobiles, etc. These agreements will provide solid backup for the financial information that you have projected regarding the lease of property and assets. It is important to note here that all lease agreements should be carefully entered into. In many instances they will contain clauses (especially in the case of site locations) that can eat heavily into a company's profits.

LETTERS OF REFERENCE

Reference letters recommend you as being a reputable and reliable business person worthy of being considered a good risk. There are two types of reference letters:

1. **Business references.** Written by business associates, suppliers, and customers.
2. **Personal references.** Written by nonbusiness associates who can assess your business skills, not by friends or relatives.

CONTRACTS

Include all business contracts, both completed and currently in force. Some examples are:

- Current loan contracts
- Papers on prior business loans
- Purchase agreements on large equipment
- Vehicle purchase contracts
- Service contracts
- Maintenance agreements
- Miscellaneous contracts

LEGAL DOCUMENTS

Include all legal documents pertaining to your business. Examples are:

- Articles of Incorporation
- Partnership Agreements
- Limited Partnership Agreements
- DBAs
- Business licenses
- Copyrights, trademarks, and patents
- Trade agreements (example page 120)
- Licensing agreements
- Insurance policies, agreements, etc.
- Property and vehicle titles

MISCELLANEOUS DOCUMENTS

These are all the documents (other than those above) that are referred to, but not included, in the organizational and marketing sections of your business plan.

A good example is those records related to selecting your location in the organizational or marketing plan. Your location might be finalized as the result of the development of a location plan. You can refer to this section in your Table of Contents. The potential lender or investor can then turn to this portion of your plan and examine that location plan, might include:

- Demographic studies
- Map of selected location
- Area studies (crime rate, income, etc.)

TO HELP YOU

The next four pages contain samples of a résumé, a personal financial statement, and a trade offering. You will also find examples of several other types of supporting documents in the three business plans in the Appendix.

SAMPLE RÉSUMÉ

John Smith
742 South Street
Jamestown, NY 10081
207-814-0221

WORK EXPERIENCE

1995–Present   GENESIS MULTIMEDIA
Burke, New York
Corporate President: Overall management responsibility for tool and die manufacture providing specialized parts to the aerospace industry. Specific management of Research and Development Department.

1990–1995   ABC COMPONENTS
Jamestown, New York
Sole Proprietor and General Manager: Solely responsible for research and development of specialty aircraft parts. Long-term goal of expanding to incorporate and provide specialty parts to aerospace industry.

1980–1990   JACKSON AIRCRAFT CO.
Burke, New York
Quality Control Supervisor: Responsibility for the development and implementation of a quality control program for automated aircraft assembly facility. Implemented quality control program resulting in $4.3 million in increased profits to the company.

EDUCATION

University of California, Berkeley—Master of Business Administration, Marketing emphasis on Marketing, 1990.

Stanford University, Palo Alto, CA—B.S. in Civil Engineering, 1980.

PROFESSIONAL AFFILIATIONS

American Society of Professional Engineers
New York City Industrial League
Burke Chamber of Commerce

SPECIAL RECOGNITION

New York Businessman of the Year, 1998
New York Council on Small Business, 1996–present
Director, Burke Chamber of Commerce

SPECIAL SKILLS

Resourceful and well-organized; Relates well to employees; self-motivated and not afraid to take risks.

Personal Financial History
Page 1

Personal Financial Statement

(DO NOT USE FOR BUSINESS FINANCIAL STATEMENT)

As of _____ 20_____

FINANCIAL STATEMENT OF

Name_____

Address_____

Received At_____Branch

Employed by_____

Position_____Age____Spouse_____ Name of

If Employed Less Than
1 year, Previous Employer_____

The undersigned, for the purpose of procuring and establishing credit from time to time with you and to induce you to permit the undersigned to become indebted to you on notes, endorsements, guarantees, overdrafts or otherwise, furnishes the following (or in lieu thereof the attached, which is the most recent statement prepared by or for the undersigned) as being a full, true and correct statement of the financial condition of the undersigned on the date indicated, and agrees to notify you immediately of the extent and character of any material changes in said financial condition, and also agrees that if the undersigned or any endorser or guarantor of any of the obligations of the undersigned, at any time fails in business or becomes insolvent, or commits an act of bankruptcy, or dies, or if a writ of attachment, garnishment, execution or other legal process be issued against property of the undersigned or if any assessment for taxes against the undersigned, other than taxes on real property, is made by the federal or state government or any department thereof, or if any of the representations made below prove to be untrue, or if the undersigned fails to notify you of any material change as above agreed, or if such change occurs, or if the business, or any interest therein, of the undersigned is sold, then and in such case, all of the obligations of the undersigned to you or held by you shall immediately be due and payable, without demand or notice. This statement shall be construed by you to be a continuing statement of the condition of the undersigned, and a new and original statement of all assets and liabilities upon each and every transaction in and by which the undersigned hereafter becomes indebted to you, until the undersigned advises in writing to the contrary.

ASSETS	DOLLARS	CENTS	LIABILITIES	DOLLARS	CENTS
Cash In B of_____ (Branch)			Notes Payable B of_____ (Branch)		
Cash on Hand_____ (Other – give name)			Notes Payable _____ (Other)		
Accounts Receivable-Good_____			Accounts Payable_____		
Stocks and Bonds (Schedule B) _____			Taxes Payable_____		
Notes Receivable-Good_____			Contracts Payable_____ (To Whom)		
Cash Surrender Value Life Insurance_____			Contracts Payable_____ (To Whom)		
Autos_____ (Year-Make) (Year-Make)			Real Estate indebtedness (Schedule A)____		
Real Estate (Schedule A)_____			Other Liabilities (describe)		
Other Assets (describe)			1. _____		
1. _____			2. _____		
2. _____			3. _____		
3. _____			4. _____		
4. _____			TOTAL LIABILITIES		
5. _____			NET WORTH		
TOTAL ASSETS			TOTAL		

ANNUAL INCOME			a n d ANNUAL EXPENDITURES (Excluding Ordinary living expenses)		
Salary_____			Real Estate payment (s) _____		
Salary (wife or husband) _____			Rent_____		
Securities Income_____			Income Taxes _____		
Rentals _____			Insurance Premiums _____		
Other (describe)			Property Taxes _____		
1. _____			Other (describe-include installment payments other than real estate)		
2. _____					
3. _____			1. _____		
4. _____			2. _____		
5. _____			3. _____		
TOTAL INCOME			TOTAL EXPENDITURES		

LESS TOTAL EXPENDITURES

NET CASH INCOME
(exclusive of ordinary expenses) _____

Personal Financial History
Page 2

Personal Financial Statement
Page 2

What assets in this statement are in joint tenancy? _____ Name of other Party _____

Have you filed homestead? _____

Are you a guarantor on anyone's debt? _____ If so, give details _____

Are any encumbered assets or debts secured except as indicated? _____ If so, please itemize by debt and security _____

_____

Do you have any other business connections? _____ If so, give details _____

Are there any suits or judgments against you? _____

Have you gone through bankruptcy or compromised a debt? _____

Have you made a will? _____ Number of dependents _____

SCHEDULE A — REAL ESTATE

Location and type of Improvement	Title in Name of	Estimated Value	Amount Owing	To Whom Payable
		$	$	

SCHEDULE B — STOCKS AND BONDS

Number of Shares Amount of Bonds	Description	Current Market on Listed	Estimated Value on Unlisted
		$	$

If additional space is needed for Schedule A and/or Schedule B, list on separate sheet and attach.

INSURANCE

Life Insurance $_____ Name of Company _____ Beneficiary _____

Automobile Insurance:

Public Liability → yes ☐ no ☐   Property Damage → yes ☐ no ☐

Comprehensive personal Liability → yes ☐ no ☐

STATEMENT OF BANK OFFICER:
Insofar as our records reveal, this Financial Statement is accurate and true. The foregoing Statement is (a copy of) the original signed by the maker, in the credit files of this Bank.

_____Assistant Cashier-Manager

The undersigned solemnly declares and certifies that the above statement (or in lieu thereof, the attached statement, as the case may be) and supporting schedules, both printed and written, give a full, true, and correct statement of the financial condition of the undersigned as of the date indicated.

_____
Date signed   Signature

SAMPLE TRADIING OFFER

Capital, Inc.

presents

Genesis Multimedia, Inc.

248,000 Shares of Common Stock

Resale of Securities
Under
Regulations

Trading Offer

Capital, Inc.

Capital, Inc. hereby introduces Genesis Multimedia, Inc. This company has been in operation since 1988 and currently has $7,000,000 in annual sales. The company is currently trading on the OTC Bulletin Board.

Listed below is the Bid and Ask price of Genesis Multimedia, Inc., trading symbol (GMMI), CUSIP no. 274106-12-5:

	BID	ASK
Current	34.25	35.5
Discount	5%	6%

Restricted

Capital, Inc. has purchased these shares under an agreement that shares cannot come back into the United States before one year. As a consequence, the transfer agent will issue instructions that no shares being resold under this purchase can be transferred to any person in the United States before one year. Although, Genesis Multimedia, Inc. is a fully reporting company for over one year, these shares can come back into United States pursuant to an exemption from registration or a filing of a registration before 41 days. After 41 days, any sales of these securities can be sold to any U.S. person or to an account of any U.S. person who is outside the United States.

Investor's Qualifications

The shares may be freely traded outside the United States and can be sold or transferred to any non-U.S. person within 41 days and to any U.S. person after 41 days.

U.S. TAX INFORMATION
AN IMPORTANT AID
TO WRITING YOUR BUSINESS PLAN

Abasic understanding of the U.S. tax system is an absolute necessity if you are going to write a Business Plan for a business that will operate within or do business with the U.S. It has long been a premise of the majority of taxpayers that the system is unwieldy, complicated, unfair, and a plague to most Americans. If you will try to put those feelings aside temporarily, we will show you how a basic understanding of the tax system can be an invaluable aid to you during business planning.

In this chapter, I have also included the following visual aids and lists that should help you with your business planning in relation to taxes:

➡ **Calendar of Federal Taxes**

➡ **List of Free IRS Publications**

➡ **Information Resources**

If You Are Doing Business Internationally

Business planning follows the same format throughout the world. With the spread of global trade, all countries are seeking common ground upon which to do business together and a business plan serves as an important link leading to successful international venturing. If you are in the United States and participate in foreign trade, you will need to understand the legalities pertaining to the countries with which you are doing business. By the same token, those businesses outside the United States will need to familiarize themselves with the American legal and tax systems. In this chapter, we will deal only with cursory tax information pertaining to the United States. The reader of this book should in no way construe it as legal or accounting advice.

COMPARING THE U.S. TAX SYSTEM AND BUSINESS ACCOUNTING

Comparison of the U.S. Tax System and business accounting is like studying the chicken and the egg. They cannot be separated. Many new business owners attempt to set up an accounting system without examining and understanding the IRS's tax forms to be completed at the end of the year. This is a gross error for two reasons. The first is failure to account for financial information required by the IRS at tax time. More important, however, is the failure to utilize information and services that will help you to develop effective financial accounting, which will, in turn, enable you to analyze your business and implement changes to keep it on the track to greater profitability.

To Help You Understand Taxes and Set Up a File of IRS Publications

In order to help you with your tax planning (and related business planning), the remainder of this chapter will provide you with the following:

- *Calendars of federal taxes* for which a sole proprietor, partnership, S corporation, or corporation may be liable. You will find four tax calendars. Choose the one that is appropriate to your legal structure. During the tax year, all businesses must comply with reporting regulations and periodic payments of federal taxes. Your legal structure will determine required reporting dates. They are not the same for sole proprietorships and partnerships as they are for S corporations and C corporations. Be sure to look ahead as the due dates are firm and a penalty may be imposed for not reporting on time. Your business plan financial projections need to reflect these tax liabilities. Failure to do so will result in an unbalanced budget—and it is possible that a serious cash deficiency could result.

- *A list of free IRS publications* available from the IRS that will be helpful to you as business owners. You will also find telephone number, and Internet addresses for easy access of forms and publications.

  What most of us don't know is that the United States government has spent a great deal of time and money to make free publications available for the preparation of income taxes. Make a conscious decision to send for (or download) these publications at least once a year and make it a priority to study the revisions that take place in U.S. tax laws.

  IRS forms and publications are updated every November and can be downloaded or ordered shortly thereafter. They are available either in hard copy directly from the IRS or by going on the Internet and accessing them from their Web site. If you choose to download them, they can be accessed and/or printed out in Acrobat Reader, a free software application available from Adobe at <www.adobe.com>.

Remember that developing and working with your business plan is an ongoing process requiring the implementation of many changes. You may rest assured that many of those changes will be a direct result of new tax laws.

Sole Proprietor

Calendar of Federal Taxes for Which You May Be Liable

Month	Day	Description	Form
January	15	Estimated tax	Form 1040ES
	31	Social security (FICA) tax and the withholding of income tax Note: See IRS rulings for deposit—Pub. 334	Forms 941, 941E, 942, and 943.
	31	Providing information on social security (FICA) tax and the withholding of income tax	Form W-2 (to employee)
	31	Federal unemployment (FUTA) tax	Form 940-EZ or 940
	31	Federal unemployment (FUTA) tax (only if liability for unpaid taxes exceeds $100)	Form 8109 (to make deposits)
	31	Information returns to nonemployees and transactions with other persons	Form 1099 (to recipients)
February	28	Information returns to nonemployees and transactions with other persons	Form 1099 (to IRS)
	28	Providing information on social security (FICA) tax and the withholding income tax	Forms W-2 and W-3 (to Social Security Admin.)
April	15	Income tax	Schedule C (Form 1040)
	15	Self-employment tax	Schedule SE (Form 1040)
	15	Estimated tax	Form 1040ES
	30	Social security (FICA) tax and the withholding of income tax Note: See IRS rulings for deposit—Pub. 334	Forms 941, 941E, 942, and 943
	30	Federal unemployment (FUTA) tax (only if liability for unpaid taxes exceeds $100)	Form 8109 (to make deposits)
June	15	Estimated tax	Form 1040ES
July	31	Social security (FICA) tax and the withholding of income tax Note: See IRS rulings for deposit—Pub. 334	Forms 941, 941E, 942, and 943
	31	Federal unemployment (FUTA) tax (only if liability for unpaid taxes exceeds $100)	Form 8109 (to make deposits)
September	15	Estimated tax	Form 1040ES
October	31	Social security (FICA) tax and the withholding of income tax Note: See IRS rulings for deposit—Pub. 334	Forms 941, 941E, 942, and 943
	31	Federal unemployment (FUTA) tax (only if liability for unpaid taxes exceeds $100)	Form 8109 (to make deposits)

If your tax year is not January 1st through December 31st:

- Schedule C (Form 1040) is due the 15th day of the 4th month after end of the tax year. Schedule SE is due same day as Form 1040.

- Estimated tax (1040ES) is due the 15th day of 4th, 6th, and 9th months of tax year, and the 15th day of 1st month after the end of tax year.

Partnership

Calendar of Federal Taxes for Which You May Be Liable

January	15	Estimated tax (individual who is a partner)	Form 1040ES
	31	Social security (FICA) tax and the withholding of income tax Note: See IRS rulings for deposit—Pub. 334	Forms 941, 941E, 942, and 943
	31	Providing information on social security (FICA) tax and the withholding of income tax	Form W-2 (to employee)
	31	Federal unemployment (FUTA) tax	Form 940-EZ or 940
	31	Federal unemployment (FUTA) tax (only if liability for unpaid taxes exceeds $100)	Form 8109 (to make deposits)
	31	Information returns to nonemployees and transactions with other persons	Form 1099 (to recipients)
February	28	Information returns to nonemployees and transactions with other persons	Form 1099 (to IRS)
	28	Providing information on social security (FICA) tax and on withholding income tax	Forms W-2 and W-3 (to Social Security Admin.)
April	15	Income tax (individual who is a partner)	Schedule C (Form 1040)
	15	Annual return of income	Form 1065
	15	Self-employment tax (individual who is partner)	Schedule SE (Form 1040)
	15	Estimated tax (individual who is partner)	Form 1040ES
	30	Social security (FICA) tax and the withholding of income tax Note: See IRS rulings for deposit—Pub. 334	Forms 941, 941E, 942, and 943
	30	Federal unemployment (FUTA) tax (only if liability for unpaid taxes exceeds $100)	Form 8109 (to make deposits)
June	15	Estimated tax (individual who is a partner)	Form 1040ES
July	31	Social security (FICA) tax and the withholding of income tax Note: See IRS rulings for deposit—Pub. 334	Forms 941, 941E, 942, and 943
	31	Federal unemployment (FUTA) tax (only if liability for unpaid taxes exceeds $100)	Form 8109 (to make deposits)
September	15	Estimated tax (individual who is a partner)	Form 1040ES
October	31	Social security (FICA) tax and the withholding of income tax Note: See IRS rulings for deposit—Pub. 334	Forms 941, 941E, 942, and 943
	31	Federal unemployment (FUTA) tax (only if liability for unpaid taxes exceeds $100)	Form 8109 (to make deposits)

If your Tax Year is not January 1st through December 31st:

- Income tax is due the 15th day of the 4th month after end of tax year.
- Self-employment tax is due the same day as income tax (Form 1040).
- Estimated tax (1040ES) is due the 15th day of the 4th, 6th, and 9th month of the tax year and the 15th day of 1st month after end of the tax year.

S Corporation

Calendar of Federal Taxes for Which You May Be Liable

January	15	Estimated tax (individual S corp. shareholder)	Form 1040ES
	31	Social security (FICA) tax and the withholding of income tax Note: See IRS rulings for deposit—Pub. 334	Forms 941, 941E, 942, and 943
	31	Providing information on social security (FICA) tax and the withholding of income tax	Form W-2 (to employee)
	31	Federal unemployment (FUTA) tax	Form 940-EZ or 940
	31	Federal unemployment (FUTA) tax (only if liability for unpaid taxes exceeds $100)	Form 8109 (to make deposits)
	31	Information returns to nonemployees and transactions with other persons	Form 1099 (to recipients)
February	28	Information returns to nonemployees and transactions with other persons	Form 1099 (to IRS)
	28	Providing information on social security (FICA) tax and the withholding of income tax	Forms W-2 and W-3 (to Social Security Admin.)
March	15	Income tax	Form 1120S
April	15	Income tax (individual S corp. shareholder)	Form 1040
	15	Estimated tax (individual S corp. shareholder)	Form 1040ES
	30	Social security (FICA) tax and the withholding of income tax Note: See IRS rulings for deposit—Pub. 334	Forms 941, 941E, 942, and 943
	30	Federal unemployment (FUTA) tax (only if liability for unpaid taxes exceeds $100)	Form 8109 (to make deposits)
June	15	Estimated tax (individual S corp. shareholder)	Form 1040ES
July	31	Social security (FICA) tax and the withholding of income tax Note: See IRS rulings for deposit—Pub. 334	Forms 941, 941E, 942, and 943
	31	Federal unemployment (FUTA) tax (only if liability for unpaid taxes exceeds $100)	Form 8109 (to make deposits)
September	15	Estimated tax (individual S corp. shareholder)	Form 1040ES
October	31	Social security (FICA) tax and the withholding of income tax Note: See IRS rulings for deposit—Pub. 334	Forms 941, 941E, 942, and 943
	31	Federal unemployment (FUTA) tax (only if liability for unpaid taxes exceeds $100)	Form 8109 (to make deposits)

If your tax year is not January 1st through December 31st:

- S corporation income tax (1120S) and individual S corporation shareholder income tax (Form 1040) are due the 15th day of the 4th month after end of tax year.

- Estimated tax of individual shareholder (1040ES) is due 15th day of 4th, 6th, and 9th months of tax year, and 15th day of 1st month after end of tax year.

Corporation

Calendar of Federal Taxes for Which You May Be Liable

Month	Day	Description	Form
January	31	Social security (FICA) tax and the withholding of income tax Note: See IRS rulings for deposit—Pub. 334	Forms 941, 941E, 942, and 943
	31	Providing information on social security (FICA) tax and the withholding of income tax	Form W-2 (to employee)
	31	Federal unemployment (FUTA) tax	Form 940-EZ or 940
	31	Federal unemployment (FUTA) tax (only if liability for unpaid taxes exceeds $100)	Form 8109 (to make deposits)
	31	Information returns to nonemployees and transactions with other persons	Form 1099 (to recipients)
February	28	Information returns to nonemployees and transactions with other persons	Form 1099 (to IRS)
	28	Providing information on social security (FICA) tax and the withholding of income tax	Forms W-2 and W-3 (to Social Security Admin.)
March	15	Income tax	Form 1120 or 1120-A
April	15	Estimated tax	Form 1120-W
	30	Social security (FICA) tax and the withholding of income tax Note: See IRS rulings for deposit—Pub. 334	Forms 941, 941E, 942, and 943
	30	Federal unemployment (FUTA) tax (only if liability for unpaid taxes exceeds $100)	Form 8109 (to make deposits)
June	15	Estimated tax	Form 1120-W
July	31	Social security (FICA) tax and the withholding of income tax Note: See IRS rulings for deposit—Pub. 334	Forms 941, 941E, 942, and 943
	31	Federal unemployment (FUTA) tax (only if liability for unpaid taxes exceeds $100)	Form 8109 (to make deposits)
September	15	Estimated tax	Form 1120-W
October	31	Social security (FICA) tax and the withholding of income tax Note: See IRS rulings for deposit—Pub. 334	Forms 941, 941E, 942, and 943
	31	Federal unemployment (FUTA) tax (only if liability for unpaid taxes exceeds $100)	Form 8109 (to make deposits)
December	15	Estimated tax	Form 1120-W

If your tax year is not January 1st through December 31st:

- Income tax (Form 1120 or 1120-A) is due on the 15th day of the 3rd month after the end of the tax year.
- Estimated tax (1120-W) is due the 5th day of the 4th, 6th, 9th, and 12th months of the tax year.

FREE TAX PUBLICATIONS AVAILABLE FROM THE IRS

The following is a list of IRS Publications that may prove helpful to you in the course of your business. Make it a point to keep a file of tax information. Send for these publications and update your file with new publications at least once a year. The United States government has spent a great deal of time and money to make this information available to you for preparation of income tax returns.

By phone or mail. You may call IRS toll free at **1-800-TAX-FORM (1-800-829-3676)** between 8 AM and 5 PM weekdays and 9 AM to 3 PM on Saturdays. Call them if you wish to order publications or forms by mail.

By computer and modem. If you subscribe to an online service, ask if IRS information is available and, if so, how to access it. The IRS offers the ability to download electronic print files of current tax forms, instructions, and taxpayer information publications (TIPs) in three different file formats. Internal Revenue Information Services (IRIS) is housed within Fed-World, known also as the Electronic Marketplace of U.S. government information, a broadly accessible electronic bulletin board system. FedWorld offers direct dial-up access, as well as Internet connectivity, and provides "gateway" access to more than 140 different government bulletin boards.

IRIS at FedWorld. You can reach the IRIS FedWorld by three methods.

1. Modem (dial-up). The Internal Revenue Information Services bulletin board at 703-321-8020 (not toll-free).

2. Telnet. <iris.irs.ustreas.gov>.

3. File Transfer Protocol (FTP). Connect to <ftp.irs.ustreas.gov>.

4. World Wide Web <www.ustreas.gov>.

Tax Guide for Small Business

(For Individuals Who Use Schedule S or S-EZ)
Sole proprietors should begin by reading Publication 334, *Tax Guide for Small Business*. It is a general guide to all areas of small business and will give you comprehensive information.

Listing of Publications for Small Business

If you are a business owner, the following IRS publications will provide you with fairly detailed information on specific tax-related topics.

1	*Your Rights as a Taxpayer*
15	*Circular E., Employer's Tax Guide*
15A	*Employers Supplemental Tax Guide*
17	*Your Federal Income Tax*
463	*Travel, Entertainment, Gift, and Car Expenses*

PACKAGING YOUR PLAN AND KEEPING IT UP-TO-DATE

Part I: Business planning software. Because I often get questions regarding business plan software, I will dedicate some space in the first part of this chapter to discussing what you should look for before making a purchase. *Quick fixes* may be good when it comes to saving time, but they can be the kiss of death when it comes to something as serious as business planning. On the other hand, the right software package can save you many hours of time.

Part II: The packaging of your business plan. This is an important part of the planning process. Putting your plan together the right way will increase its readability and effectiveness for the business itself and for potential lenders and investors. In the first half of this chapter, we will give you some ideas on how to organize and present your business plan for maximum effectiveness.

Part III: Keeping your business plan up-to-date. Your business plan will serve you well if you revise it often and let it serve as your guide during the lifetime of your business. In order to update it, you as the owner or key decision maker of your company will have the final responsibility to analyze what is happening and implement the changes that will make your business more profitable. The second half of this chapter will address changes to be considered in the following areas.

➡ **Changes within the Company**

➡ **Changes in Customer Needs**

➡ **Changes in Technology**

PART I: BUSINESS PLAN SOFTWARE

There are several software programs on the market today. What the prospective business plan writer hopes for is a quick solution to a difficult problem—a program with questions that can be answered by filling in the blanks after which the software will automatically generate a finished business plan.

Do Not Use a Canned Program

There are some *fill in the blanks* software packages. However, it is not advisable for you to use this type of program. There are at least two good reasons:

1. Your business plan serves as the guide for your particular business. Even though you may have the same type of business as someone else, you will have different areas of focus and you will want to fill your own special niche with things that are unique to your business. These differences should be reflected in your business plan. Therefore, a canned business plan cannot possibly serve you well.

2. If you are going to potential lenders or investors, you will find that they will readily recognize the canned statements and generic financial statements that come from a specific piece of software. The resulting "cookie cutter" business plan is an immediate indicator to that person that you have not put much time and effort into the planning process and that you may not know your business well enough to succeed at it. Since the repayment of your loan depends on your business skills, this may indicate that you will be a poor risk.

Effective Software Programs

The right software package should allow for you to do your own research and generate your own organizational and marketing statements. This is the only way that you can create a plan that will make your business unique. Well thought out, individualized organizational and marketing plans will favorably impress your lender or investor by showing them that you have thoroughly researched your business and have the expertise to run it effectively. Thorough planning will also give you the confidence to better run your business.

Automated financial statements (or spreadsheets). These can be a great help to you in the financial section of your business plan. If they are preformatted and preformulated, you will save a great deal of time. You plug in the amounts to the allocated cells and the program should do all of your calculations. Since the pro forma cash flow statement has approximately 350 figures to work with, your time will be cut considerably. It will also allow you to make changes or create "what if" situations and see the results immediately.

Even here, a note of caution is called for. Many programs have all of the spreadsheets linked into one long integrated spreadsheet. This a great feature except for its downside. Linked spreadsheets are always generic and not customized for any particular business. If you attempt to customize them and do not have the expertise to make the proper changes throughout the entire spreadsheet (without error), the spreadsheet loses its integrity.

A strong financial plan is your best friend. To preserve that strength, even preformatted spreadsheets will need to be altered to reflect the categories of revenues and expenses pertinent to your particular business. Be sure the software program allows you to *completely customize* the spreadsheets to your own Chart of Accounts.

YES! THERE IS A BUSINESS PLANNING SOFTWARE THAT ACCOUNTS FOR ALL OF THE ABOVE!

In order to further implement the writing of your business plan, I have developed a software program that will guide you neatly through the entire business planning process. **AUTOMATE YOUR BUSINESS PLAN FOR WINDOWS** is for IBM and compatibles and *does not* require any additional software. The software has its own full-powered word processor and an easy-to-use spreadsheet program with preformatted and preformulated financial statements that can be completely customized to match your business.

AUTOMATE YOUR BUSINESS PLAN is *Anatomy of a Business Plan* translated into software. It follows the book step-by-step and will print out a finished business plan.

PART II: PACKAGING FOR SUCCESS

When you have finished writing your business plan, there are a few last considerations that will help in making a favorable impression with a potential lender or investor. Good packaging will also make your plan easier for you to use.

- *Binding and cover.* For your working business plan, it is best to use a three-ring binder. That way information can be easily added, updated, or replaced. Your working plan should have a copy of all of your supporting documents. For the plan that you take to a potential lender or investor, you will want to bind it in a nice cover. You can purchase one from an office supply store or take it to your printer and have it done. Use blue, brown, or black covers as bankers are usually conservative.

- *Length.* Be concise! Generally, you should have no more than 30 to 40 pages in the plan you take to a lender, including supporting documents. As you write each section, think of it as being a summary. Include as much information as you can in a brief statement. Potential lenders do not want to search through volumes of material to get to needed information. You can always have an expanded version of your business plan in your own binder, including a complete set of your supporting documents.

- *Presentation.* Do your best to make your plan look presentable. However, do not go to the unnecessary expense of paying for professional word processing services unless you cannot do it yourself. The lender or investor is not interested in seeing an expensive looking business plan. What he is looking for is what your business plan says in terms of text and numbers. Paying for frills could even be considered as frivolous by some lenders—a first impression that might indicate that you would not use their loan funds wisely.

- *Table of contents.* Be sure to include a Table of Contents in your business plan. It will follow the Statement of Purpose. Make it detailed enough so a lender or investor can locate any of the areas addressed in the plan. It must also list the supporting documents and their corresponding page numbers. It might help you to use the Table of Contents in this book as a guide to compiling your own.

- *Number of copies.* Make copies for yourself and each lender you wish to approach. Keep track of each copy. Don't try to work with too many potential lenders at one time. If your loan is refused, be sure to retrieve your business plan.

PART III: KEEPING YOUR BUSINESS PLAN UP-TO-DATE

Revising Your Business Plan

Revision is an on-going process. Changes are constantly taking place in your business. If your plan is going to be effective either to the business or to a potential lender or investor, it will be necessary for you to update it on a regular basis. Changes necessitating such revisions can be attributed to three primary sources:

1. *Changes within the company.* Any number of changes may occur in your organization. You may choose to expand from a brick and mortar company into a more modern "clicks and bricks" venture. Conversely, with the current failure rate in dot.coms, your company may find that it has to fall back and move its focus to more traditional types of offerings—or you might find your company expanding from B to C business into the B to B arena. Changes from within the company may also necessitate changes in legal structure, the addition of new partners, or changes in management.

2. *Changes originating with the customer.* Your product or service may show surges or declines due to your customers' changes in need or taste. This is evident in all the companies that fold because they continue to offer what they like instead of what the customer will buy or use. In the clothing industry, for example, retailers have to pay close attention to current styles, popular materials, and seasonal colors.

   Marketing to a new and expanding customer base will also require careful consideration of both demographic and psychographic factors that may differ from those of current customers. Remember that your customers' buying patterns are also integrally related to the current economy. If money is scarce, you will have to be more innovative in your marketing efforts. If you sell your products and services internationally, you need to understand the cultures in order to satisfy the customers.

3. *Technological changes.* You will have to change your business to stay current with a changing world. As technology changes within your industry, bringing new products and services on the market, you will have to keep up or you will be left behind. The computer industry is a perfect example of fast changes in technology. Developers are challenged daily with the problems of keeping their products or losing their niche in the marketplace. The toy industry is another. Little girls and boys are no longer satisfied with storybook dolls and tinkertoys. They want electronic miracles that are programmed to walk, talk, fly, think, and feel.

   Technological advances, especially those in the area of communication, have also revolutionized the *ways* in which we do business. The Internet has enabled small business owners to research information, communicate instantly with venders and customers, process credit cards and transfer funds electronically, and market and sell products and services to their customers via the Internet. Yesterday's typewriters, telephones, and airmail letters have been replaced with computers, cell phones, and e-mail.

Implementing Changes in Your Business Plan

You, as the owner or manager of the company, must be aware of the changes in your industry, your market, and your community. First you must determine what revisions are needed in order for you to accomplish the goals you have set for your company. To make this determination, you will have to look at your current plan and decide what you have to do to modify it in order to reflect the changes discussed above.

If you find that writing the company business plan is an overwhelming task for one person, utilize key employees to keep track of the business trends applicable to their expertise. For example, your buyer can analyze the buying patterns of your customers and report to you. Your research and development person might look at changes in technology and materials for your products. Your Webmaster can make suggestions regarding your Web site. Your marketing department can develop a plan that will take advantage of new ways that will help you to reach your potential customers. Each department can be responsible for information that pertains to its particular area and report on a periodic basis.

You may also find that it is effective to hire an outside consultant to perform a periodic analysis of your current plan in relation to your company's goals.

Be aware, however, that the final judgment as to the implementation of changes will rest with you, the owner or CEO. You will have to analyze the information and decide on any changes to be effected. If your decision is wrong, don't dwell on it. Correct your error and cut your losses as soon as possible. With experience, your percentage of correct decisions will increase and your reward will be higher profits.

Anticipating Your Problems

Try to see ahead and determine what possible problems may arise to plague you. For example, you may have to deal with costs that exceed your projections. At the same time, you may experience a sharp decline in sales. These two factors occurring simultaneously can portend disaster if you are not ready for them.

Also, a good year can give you a false sense of security. Be cautious when things are too good. The increased profits may be temporary. Also, what sells today may not sell tomorrow. As an example, recreational equipment often sells in cycles that are related to current fads. Today's $100 item will most likely be selling for $29 next year—or it may even be no longer a viable product.

You might think about developing an alternate budget based on possible problems that are likely to be encountered. This may be the time when you will decide that emphasis on a service rather than on a product would be more profitable due to changes in the economy and decreased spending. For instance, the repair of what is already owned may far outpace the buying of replacement items. Alternately, as the buying of luxury services wanes, the company might plan instead to provide those services that are considered a necessity.

Don't Fall into the Trap!

More often than not, a business owner will spend a lot of time and effort writing a business plan when the pressure is on to borrow funds or to get a business started. The intention is there to always keep that plan up-to-date. Before long, things get hectic and the business plan is put in a drawer, never again to be seen.

Just remember, *"the business that operates by the seat of its pants will probably end up with torn pants."*

Do Remember to Revise Your Plan Often

Awareness of changes within your industry and revision of your business plan reflecting those changes will benefit you greatly. Your business plan can be your best friend. If you nurture your relationship with it, you will have a running start on the path to success.

When you are finished, your business plan should be professional. At the same time, it should be obvious to the lender or investor that it was done by the people who own and run the business. Your business plan will be the best indication the lender will have to judge your potential for success.

Be Sure that Your Business Plan Is Representative of Your Best Efforts!

It is my hope that you have been able to use this book to help you develop a concise, logical, and appropriate plan for your business. When your work is done and your business plan is complete, don't forget to:

- Operate within your business plan.

- Anticipate changes.

- Revise your plan and keep it up-to-date.

Do these things and I guarantee you that you are well on your way to improving your chances of success and growth as you continue with your business venture. Thank you for including my materials as part of your plan.

MARINE ART
OF CALIFORNIA
BUSINESS PLAN

The business plan presented in Appendix I is an actual business plan developed by Mr. Robert Garcia for his business, Marine Art of California. Mr. Garcia has generously allowed us to use it in *Anatomy of a Business Plan* and **AUTOMATE YOUR BUSINESS PLAN** to serve as an illustration that will help you with the writing of your own plan.

Mr. Garcia wrote this plan when he was in the process of organizing his business for start-up and looking for investors in the form of limited partnerships. His business has changed direction and he has now been in business for a few years and updates his plan regularly to reflect what is actually happening in the operation of his venture.

The plan was written prior to start-up. For that reason, it included projections only and the financial section ended with a break-even analysis. After one year in business, Mr. Garcia's business plan would also include historical profit & loss statements, a current balance sheet, and financial statement analysis, all of which would be based on the actual transactions of his business.

Additions to the Original Plan

In order to give you a complete example of a business plan, including historical information as well as projections (especially in the financial area), I decided to create a what if scenario for the business that would reflect the financial numbers for the first year of operation. and show how projections can be measured against performance.

Because it would be inappropriate to disclose the financial information of a current business, I created a financial scenario to show what might have happened in the year 2002. The historical financial statements and financial statement analysis documents on pages 26 through 32 of this plan are for educational purposes only and *do not* reflect the actual financial history or industry ratio standards of Marine Art of California. The remainder of the plan is presented as originally written. If it, too, had been updated, it would have included any changes in position and planning that occurred during that year of business (i.e., new partners, changes in marketing plans, etc.).

This Plan Can Help You

As you proceed with the writing of your own plan, it may help you to look at Mr. Garcia's business plan to see how he handled each of the corresponding sections. Some of the research material has been condensed and all of his supporting documents are not included. I have also chosen to omit his personal financial history for privacy reasons.

Regarding the Marketing Plan

In the opening page of Chapter 5, "The Marketing Plan," it was stated that smaller start-ups may choose not to address all of the components of a full blown marketing strategy, but should still cover the basic marketing elements.

As you examine the marketing plan section for Marine Art of California, you will see that Mr. Garcia has chosen that path. He does a great job assessing his target market, evaluating his competition, researching his market, and planning his advertising. This is an excellent example of the development of a basic marketing plan. You should especially note how meticulous he has been in the documentation of his resources.

> *Warning! The plan is to be examined for Mr. Garcia's handling of content only. It has been used as an example in the book and software because it is a fine example of a basic business plan. There is no judgment inferred as to appropriateness or financial potential for lenders or investors. Do not use it as a source of research for your own company.*

I am very pleased that I have the opportunity to include this material in *Anatomy of a Business Plan* and **AUTOMATE YOUR BUSINESS PLAN** and hope that it will be of benefit to you. I thank Bob Garcia for being so generous and for allowing me to share his interpretation of business planning with so many small business owners.

MARINE ART OF CALIFORNIA

P.O. Box 10059-251
Newport Beach, CA 92658
714-997-9100

BUSINESS PLAN

Robert A. Garcia, President
P.O. Box 10059-251
Newport Beach, CA 92658
714-997-9100

Plan prepared *
by
Robert A. Garcia
(Private and Confidential)

Copy 1 of 2

* Financial history updated through December 31, 2002, by the developers of AUTOMATE YOUR BUSINESS PLAN. Historical financial statements in this plan show what could have happened in 2002. The 2002 year-end financial statements and financial statement analysis were prepared by **AUTOMATE YOUR BUSINESS PLAN** developers and are intended to be used for educational purposes only. They were not meant to and *do not* reflect the actual financial history of Marine Art of California.

TABLE OF CONTENTS

MARINE ART OF CALIFORNIA

EXECUTIVE SUMMARY

Marine Art of California is a Limited Partnership to be established in 2001. The direct mail-order and showroom company will be located in Newport Beach, California. The company is seeking working capital in the amount of $130,000 for the purpose of start-up operations and to cover estimated operating expenses for a six-month period.

Twenty limited partnerships (2.25% each) are being offered in return investments of $6,500 to be treated as loan funds to be repaid over a 15-year period at the rate of 11%. Limited partnerships will have a duration of four years, at which time the partners' shares will be bought back at the rate of $3,250 for each 2.25% share. At the end of the 15-year loan period, it is projected that the Return on Investment (ROI) for each $6,500 share will amount to $34,084.

The $130,000 in loan funds will enable the company to effectively market its products and services while maintaining proper cash flow. Funding is needed in time for the first catalog issue to be distributed in November 2001 and for a showroom to be operational in the same month for the Christmas buying season. There is a two to three week period between order placement and delivery date.

It is projected that the company will reach its break-even point in the latter part of the second year of operation.

Repayment of the loan and interest can begin promptly within 30 days of receipt of funds and can be secured by the percentage of the business to be held as collateral.

I. ORGANIZATIONAL PLAN
Marine Art of California

SUMMARY DESCRIPTION OF BUSINESS

Marine Art of California is a start-up company in Newport Beach, marketing the works of California artists through a direct mail-order catalog. The product line is a unique combination of art, gift items, and jewelry, all tied together by a marine or nautical theme. This marketing concept is a first! There is no known retailer or catalog company exclusively featuring the works of California artists in either a retail store or by mail-order catalog. I'm targeting a specific genre of the art market that, in terms of marketability, is on the cutting edge.

Having managed Sea Fantasies Art Gallery at Fashion Island Mall in Newport Beach, I was able to discuss my idea personally and collect more than 700 names and addresses of highly interested customers who are marine art lovers. Of these, 90% live in the surrounding communities and the rest are from across the United States and other nations.

Currently, I have begun mailings, taking orders, and making sales. I have a large number of artists and vendors throughout California with marketing agreements already in place.

I have assets of about $10,000 of miscellaneous items. These include framed and unframed originals, lithographs, posters, bronzes, acrylic boats, jewelry, videos, cassettes, CDs, T-shirts, glass figurines, greeting cards, shells, and coral.

Sales will be processed by a four-step marketing plan. First, is a direct mail-order catalog published bimonthly (six times a year). This allows for complete marketing freedom targeting high-income households, interior designers, and other businesses located in coastal areas. The second is to generate sales through a retail showroom where merchandise can be purchased on-site and large high-end pieces (exhibited on consignment) can be ordered by catalog and drop shipped from artist/vendor directly to the customer. Third, a comprehensive advertising campaign targeting the surrounding high-income communities shall be conducted (e.g., yellow pages, high-profile magazines, monthly guest artist shows, grand opening mailings, and fliers with discount coupons). Fourth, is to conduct an ongoing telemarketing program aimed at customers on our mail lists in our local area at minimal cost.

Industry trends have stabilized with the bottoming of the current recession. My plan to counter this situation is to obtain exclusive marketing rights on unique designs and the widest selection in the market of quality items priced affordably under $100.

My plan is to secure my ranking as the number two marine art dealer in Southern California, second only to the Wyland Galleries by the end of 2003, and by 2004, through steadily increasing catalog distribution to more than 150,000 copies per mailing, to rank as the number one dealer in California in gross sales. From 2004 through 2006, projected catalog distribution will increase at a rate of at least 100,000 catalogs per year.

PRODUCTS AND SERVICES

The product line of **Marine Art of California** consists of hand-signed limited editions of bronzes, acrylics, lithographs, and posters with certificates. Included are exclusive designs (covered by signed contracts) of (1) originals and prints, (2) glass figurines, and (3) fine jewelry. Rounding out the line are ceramic figures, videos, cassettes, CDs, marine life books, nautical clocks, marine jewelry (14k gold, sterling silver, genuine gemstones) and many more gift items, as well as a specific line for children. The marketing areas covered are both Northern California and Southern California.

The suppliers are artists and vendors from throughout California. They number over 260. I chose them because they best express, artistically, the growing interest in the marine environment. However, due to catalog space, only 30 to 50 artists/vendors can be represented. The retail showroom will be able to accommodate more.

My framing source for art images is a wholesale operation in Fullerton that services many large accounts including Disney Studios.

With an extremely large artist/vendor pool to draw from, I virtually eliminate any supply shortage that cannot be replaced quickly. Also, my shipping policy specifies a maximum of three weeks delivery time for custom-made pieces, such as limited edition bronzes that need to be poured at foundries. Almost all of my suppliers have been in business for years and understand the yearly marketing trends.

LEGAL STRUCTURE

The structure of the company will consist of one (1) General Partner and up to twenty (20) Limited Partners. The amount of funds needed from the Limited Partners is $130,000, which will equal 45% ownership of the business. Each Limited Partner's investment of $6,500 shall equal 2.25% of the business.

The investment will be treated as a loan and will be paid back over 15 years at 11% interest. The loan repayment amount for each 2.25% share will be $79.03 per month. No Limited Partner shall have any right to be active in the conduct of the Partnership's business or have the power to bind the Partnership with any contract, agreement, promise, or undertaking.

Provisions for Exit and Dissolution of the Company

The duration of the Partnership* is four years. The General Partner will have the option of buying out the Limited Partners at the end of four years for $3,250 for each 2.25% interest. The buyout will not affect the outstanding loan, but the General Partner will provide collateral equal to the loan balance. The value of the business will be used as that collateral.

The distribution of profits shall be made within 75 days of the end of the year. Each Limited Partner will receive 2.25% per share of investment on any profits over and above the following two months' operating expenses (January and February). This amount will be required to maintain operations and generate revenues necessary to keep the company solvent.

In the event of a loss, each Limited Partner will assume a 2.25% liability for tax purposes and no profits will be paid. The General Partner will assume 55% of the loss for tax purposes.

A Key Man Insurance Policy in the amount of $250,000 shall be taken out on the General Partner to be paid to the Limited Partners in the event of the General Partner's death. The policy will be divided among the Limited Partners according to their percentage of interest in the company.

See copy of Proposal for Limited Partnership in Supporting Documents for remainder of details.

MANAGEMENT

At present, I, **Robert A. Garcia**, am sole proprietor. I possess a wealth of business environment experience as indicated on my résumé. My first long-term job was in the grocery industry with Stater Brothers Market. I worked from high school through college, rising to the position of second assistant manager. The most valuable experience I came away with was the ability to work cohesively with a variety of personalities in demanding customer situations. It was at this point that I learned the importance and value of the customer in American business. The customers' needs are placed first! They are the most important link in the chain.

With the opportunity for better pay and regular weekday hours, I left Stater Bros. for employment with General Dynamics Pomona Division. For the next 11 years I was employed in Production Control and earned the title of Manufacturing Coordinator, supervising a small number of key individuals. I was responsible for all printed circuit board assemblies fabricated in off-site facilities located in Arizona and Arkansas. My duties included traveling between these facilities as needed. On a daily basis, I interfaced with supporting departments of Engineering, Quality Assurance, Procurement, Shipping and Receiving, Inspection, Stockroom and Inventory Control, Data Control Center, Electronic Fabrication, Machine Shop, and Final Assembly areas.

The programs involved were the Standard Missile (Surface to Air Weapon System), Phalanx Close I Weapons System, Stinger System, and Sparrow Missile. My group was responsible for all analysis reports for upper management, Naval personnel, and corporate headquarters in St. Louis, Missouri. Duties included: solving material shortages, scheduling work to be released to maintain starts and completions, and driving all support departments to meet final assembly needs for contract delivery. Problem solving was the name of the game. The importance of follow-up was critical. Three key concepts that we used as business guidelines were: (1) production of a *quality product*; (2) at a *competitive price*; and (3) delivered *on schedule*.

I'm currently in contact on a regular basis with eight advisors with backgrounds in marketing, advertising, corporate law, small business start-up, finance, direct mail-order business, and catalog production. Two individuals are college professors with active businesses, one is a publisher of my business plan reference book, and two are retired executives with backgrounds in marketing and corporate law involved in the SCORE program through the Small Business Administration (SBA). I meet with these two executives every week.

Pertinent Courses and Seminars Completed

College Course	Supervisory Training	Mt. San Antonio College
College Course	Successful Business Writing	Mt. San Antonio College
Seminar	Producing a Direct Mail Catalog	Coastline Community College
Seminar	Business Taxes and Recordkeeping	SCORE Workshop
Seminar	Business Plan Road Map	SCORE Workshop

Note: See résumé in Supporting Documents.

Manager Salary Plan. Upon the signing of Limited Partnership agreements, I will maintain the status as managing partner and decision maker. For the duration of the Partnership (planned for four years), as the manager, I will draw a monthly salary of $2,000, as per the agreement. In addition, I will retain 55% ownership of the company.

PERSONNEL

The total number of employees to be hired initially will be four. Interviews have been conducted for each position, and all are tentatively filled. I will be on the premises during all business hours for both retail and catalog ordering operations during the first month of business. It will be the owner's duty to hire the following employees:

1. **Store Manager**: part-time at $11.00 per hour
2. **1st Assistant Manager**: part-time at $9.00 per hour
3. **2nd Assistant Manager**: part-time at $8.00 per hour
4. **Sales Consultant**: part-time at $6.50 per hour
5. **Administrative Assistant**: part-time at $10.00 per hour

Training

1. **All employees** will be cross trained in the following areas:
   a. Knowledge of product line and familiarity with key suppliers
   b. Daily Sales Reconciliation Report (DSR)
   c. Catalog order processing
   d. Company policy regarding customer relations
   e. Charges with VISA or MasterCard

Personnel Duties

1. **Manager**. Reports directly to the Owner.
   a. Open store (key) then dust and vacuum.
   b. Write work schedule.
   c. Verify previous day's sales figures.
   d. Follow up on any problems of previous day.
   e. Head biweekly wall-to-wall inventory.
   f. Reconcile any business discrepancies.
   g. Responsible for store and catalog operations.
   h. Order inventory and process catalog orders.
   i. Have access to safe.
   j. Conduct telemarketing in spare time.
   k. Authorize employee purchase program (EPP).

2. **Administrative Assistant**. Reports to Manager.
   a. Open store (key) and have access to safe.
   b. Write work schedule.
   c. Perform office functions.
      (1) Daily Sales Reconciliation Report (DSR)
      (2) Accounts Receivable and Payable (A/R) (A/P)
      (3) Accounts Payable (A/P)
      (4) Payroll (P/R)
      (5) General Ledger (G/L)
      (6) Typing: 60 wpm
      (7) Computer: WP/Lotus/D-Base
      (8) 10-Key Adding Machine
   d. Process catalog orders.
   e. Authorize employee purchase program (EPP).

Personnel – cont.

3. **1st Assistant Manager**. Reports to Manager
   a. Close store (key).
   b. Order inventory.
   c. Complete Daily Sales Reconciliation Report (DSR).
   d. Follow up on day's problems not yet solved.
   e. Have access to safe.
   f. Process catalog orders.
   g. Conduct telemarketing in spare time.

4. **2nd Assistant Manager**. Reports to 1st Assistant Manager
   a. Is familiar with all 1st Assistant Manager tasks.
   b. Process catalog orders.
   c. Assist in customer relations follow-up.
   d. Dust and vacuum showroom.
   e. Conduct telemarketing in spare time.

5. **Sales Consultant**. Reports to 2nd Assistant Manager.
   a. Cover showroom floor.
   b. Process catalog orders.
   c. Assist in customer relations follow-up.
   d. Dust and vacuum showroom.
   e. Conduct telemarketing in spare time.

Employee Profile

1. Personable, outgoing, reliable, in good health

2. College background

3. High integrity and dedication

4. Neat in appearance

5. Able to take on responsibilities

6. Able to follow directives

7. Demonstrates leadership qualities

8. Previous retail experience

9. Basic office skills

10. Sincere interest in marine art and environment

11. Likes water sports

12. Team worker

LEGAL AND ACCOUNTING

Legal. Lester Smith of Taylor, Smith, Varges & Whelen, a law corporation will be retained for all legal matters. The firm is located in Orange County, California and specializes in business and copyright law. Mr. Smith is one of the firm's original partners.

Accounting. All bookkeeping activities shall be done by the administrative assistant. John Horist, a CPA, has been hired to take care of financial reporting and tax accounting. John brings more than 40 years experience in his field. His hourly fee is very reasonable.

Business software. I would like to point out the key areas of recordkeeping required in the business and explain the software to be used and why. The areas are as follows:

- **Mail Lists.** List & Mail Plus Software from Avery. It stores, sorts, and prints up to 64,000 addresses with no programming required. It contains predefined label formats or I can create my own. Searching and extracting subsets of the mailing list are possible. It also checks for duplicate entries.

- **Labels.** MacLabel Pro Software from Avery. The features include preset layouts for Avery laser labels and dot matrix labels, drawing tools and graphic sizing, built-in clip art, and easy mail merge.

- **Accounting.** Sybiz Windows Accounting Software. This program automatically updates all accounts, customers, payroll, suppliers, inventory, and ledgers in one step. Windows graphics, fonts, and integration make it easy to use.

- **Business Planning.** AUTOMATE YOUR BUSINESS PLAN software will be used to analyze and update the company's strategy and financial plan.

The simplicity and power of these reasonably priced programs make them very attractive.

INSURANCE

Prospective Carrier:	**State Farm Insurance**	
	2610 Avon, Suite C	
	Newport Beach, CA 92660	
	714-645-6000	
Agent:	**Kim Hiller**	
Type of Insurance:	Business/Personal:	$ 150,000.00
	Deductible:	$ 1,000.00
	Liability:	$1,000,000.00
Premium:	Annual Premium:	$ 3,100.00
	Monthly Premium:	**$ 258.00**
	Workers' Compensation:	1.43 per/1K of Gross Payroll

SECURITY

PROBLEM SITUATIONS TO BE CONSIDERED AND PROTECTIVE MEASURES TO BE USED:

1. **Internal Theft**. Employee Dishonesty.

   a. Shoplifting of store merchandise. Two closed-circuit monitoring cameras recording showroom activity each business day.

   b. Cash theft. There is a $400 limit of cash on hand. Timely safe drops and daily maintenance of Daily Sales Reconciliation Report will balance cash with receipts.

   c. Falsifying receipts. DSR will detect discrepancies.

   d. Employee Purchase Plan. This will reduce the inclination to steal. Employee discount is 35% off retail price. Can purchase layaway (20% down, balance over 60 days) or by payroll deduction (deducted from each check over four pay periods). Processed by authorized personnel other than oneself (two signatures required).

   e. Employee Orientation Program. This will stress security procedures and employee integrity.

   f. Biweekly wall-to-wall inventory. Frequent taking of inventory will reveal any losses.

2. **External Theft**. Customer shoplifting or robbery.

   a. Walk-in theft. Two closed-circuit monitoring cameras recording showroom activity each business day should prevent this from happening.

   b. Break-in theft or robbery. Alarm system plus closed circuit monitoring cameras. All fine jewelry is displayed in locked cases and will be removed and stored in the safe each night.

   c. Wall-to-wall biweekly inventory. This will reveal any merchandise loss.

II. MARKETING PLAN
Marine Art of California

TARGET MARKET

Who are my customers?

1. **Profile**

   Economic level—middle to upper class.

   Psychological makeup—art lover, jewelry lover, fashion conscious, ocean lover, eclectic taste, college educated, discriminating buyer, upwardly mobile life-style.

   Age—35 to 55.

   Sex—Male/Female.

   Income level—$75,000 and above.

   Habits—high-expense entertainment, travel, marine-oriented hobbies (shell/dolphin collectors, scuba diver, boat/yacht owner, etc.), patrons of performing arts, concerts, and museums.

   Work—professional, business owners, business executives, middle management, interior designers.

   Shop—middle to high-profile retail establishments.

2. **Location**

   Orange County—coastal areas, homes valued at $500,000 and above.

   San Francisco County, San Diego County, San Bernardino County.

3. **Market size**

   Mail list purchased through wholesale mail list companies. The consumer base will range from 20,000 to 100,000 in the first year of operations.

4. **Competition**

   Minimal due to unique two-pronged marketing concept of marketing exclusively California marine art, custom-designed jewelry, and giftware by way of (1) direct mail-order catalog, and (2) retail showroom. No known operation in either category.

5. **Other factors**

   As acting distributor for several artists I am able to retain exclusive marketing rights and, in most cases, have contracted to purchase at **10 to 15% below published wholesale price lists**.

COMPETITION

The two areas of competition to consider will be (1) competitors to the retail showroom, and (2) competitors to the direct mail-order operation.

1. **Competition to Retail Showroom**

    In the Supporting Documents, you will find a Competition Evaluation Worksheet with information on competitors who operate within a radius of three miles of proposed store site. Retail Stores to be evaluated have at least one of the four categories of my product line: *

    A. Marine Art—Framed (custom) and framed

    B. Marine Sculpting—Cast in bronze and acrylic

    C. Marine and Nautical Gift Items

    D. Marine and Contemporary Jewelry Designs—Fine and fashion

2. **Competition to Direct Mail-Order Catalog**

    After investigating scores of catalog companies across the nation for the past year and speaking to artists and vendors across the state of California, we are aware of only one mail-order company with a similar theme but with a very different line and profile than Marine Art of California.

---

* Supporting documents are not attached to this sample Marketing Plan

MARKET/INDUSTRY TRENDS

Information extracted from: ABI/INFORM DATABASE at UCI Library for Business Research.

Title: ***Sharper Image Revamps Product Line. Sells Items Consumers Can Actually Buy.***

Journal: **Marketing News** Vol.: 26 Issue: 10, Pg.: 2

Summary: Although shoppers will still find upscale items at Sharper Image, the company has doubled the amount of goods that are more affordable. The addition of low-priced items is part of a continuing shift that will last, even if the economy improves.

Title: ***What's Selling, and Why***

Journal: **Catalog Age** Vol.: 9 Issue: 5, Pg.: 5

Summary: Market researcher Judith Langer believes today's mailers must create a value package that combines quality and price. Merchandise is reflecting consumer sentiment about the economy and the desire to buy U.S. goods and services.

Title: ***Tripping the Gift Market Fantastic***

Journal: **Catalog Age** Vol.: 9 Issue: 6, Pg.: 30

Summary: Christmas Fantastic and Celebration Fantastic catalogs feature gifts and decorative accessories and target upscale females age 25 and over. Response has been strong. Average orders of $95 for Christmas Fantastic and $85 for Celebration Fantastic have surpassed company expectations.

Market/Industry Trends – cont.

Title: *Spring Sales Blossom*

Journal: **Catalog Age** Vol.: 9 Issue: 6, Pg.: 36

Summary: Spring sales appear to be much stronger than in 2000. Many mailers believe the latest upturn in sales will be long-lasting.

Title: *Your Catalog's List Is Its Greatest Asset*

Journal: **Target Marketing** Vol.: 15 Issue: 2, Pg.: 44-45

Summary: There are a number of reasons why greater attention should be paid to the customer mail list rather than prospecting for new customers: (1) It is the primary source of profit for the company; (2) It is the cataloger's most valuable asset; and (3) It will outperform a rented list by as much as ten times in response rate and average order.

Note: The above articles have been condensed for brevity.

MARKET RESEARCH RESOURCES

Art Business News (Monthly)

> Monthly trade magazine for art dealers and framers. Foremost business journal in the art industry. It provides readers with a wide range of art industry news, features, sales and marketing trends, and new product information. Reports on trade shows nationally and internationally.

National Jeweler (Monthly)

> Dealer magazine. Provides jewelry industry news, features, sales and marketing trends, fashions, and styles. Lists major manufacturers and wholesalers.

Catalog Age (Monthly)

> Monthly journal featuring articles on mail-order companies. Provides inside information on statistics for mail-order business. Highly informative.

Target Marketing (Monthly)—Monthly trade journal.

Orange County Business Journal (Weekly)

U.S. Small Business Administration

> Free Publications: *Selling by Mail Order*
> *Tax and Regulatory Requirements in Orange County*
> *Partnership Agreements - Planning Checklist*
> *Understanding Cash Flow*
> *How to Write a Business Plan*
> *Insurance Checklist for Small Business*

Anatomy of a Business Plan—Pinson (Dearborn)

AUTOMATE YOUR BUSINESS PLAN 9.0—Pinson (Out of Your Mind...and Into the Marketplace)

Market Research Resources – cont.

Direct Marketing Handbook—Edward L. Nash (McGraw-Hill)

The Catalog Handbook—James Holland

Direct Marketing Association—Membership organization for catalogers.

Orange County Demographic Overview
Demographic reports, charts and maps provided by the market research department of the Orange County Register.

ABI/INFORM Data Base - University of California, Irvine (see Industry Trends section)
Online database located in the library. Contained in this database are abstracts and indexes to business articles that are published in more than 800 different journals. ABI/INFORM is an excellent source of information on:

Companies	Trends	Marketing
Products	Corporate Strategies	Advertising
Business Conditions	Management Strategies	

METHODS OF SALES AND DISTRIBUTION

Two-Way Distribution Program

A. Direct Mail-Order Catalog

1. Catalog mailings are distributed through target marketing.

2. Orders are processed via telephone (1-800 #) or by return mail-order forms, accepting checks, VISA/MC, or American Express.

3. Shipping in most cases is done by the artist or vendor directly to the customer per my instructions. All other shipping is done by **Marine Art of California**.

4. Shipping costs are indicated in the catalog for each item. The customer is charged for shipping costs to reimburse the vendor.

5. UPS shipping is available throughout the United States.

B. Retail Showroom

1. All items shown in the catalog will be available for purchase in the retail store.

2. High-ticket items will be carried on consignment with previous agreements already made with individual artists.

3. General Catalogs will be displayed on an order counter for all products not stocked in the store and and that can be shipped on request.

4. All large items will be delivered anywhere in Orange County at no charge.

Methods of Sales and Distribution – cont.

Since I am dealing with more than 260 artists and vendors across the state there should be no problem with the availability of merchandise. I am only able to carry about 55 artists and vendors in the catalog. Most items can be ordered for the store and be in stock within a two to three day turnaround.

For more detailed information on shipping arrangements, please see copy of Terms and Conditions for Participants in Supporting Documents section.

ADVERTISING

Pacific Bell	Yellow/white pages one line No charge	
	Bold—$5.00 extra each line	
Pac Bell/Sammy	Sales order # N74717625 (8/21)	
740-5211	Business line installation	$70.45
	Monthly rate DEADLINE—August 19th	$11.85
	Cannot change without $18.00 per month rate increase	
	Display—1/4 column listing (per month)	$49.00
	(Yearly cost $588.00)	
	Disconnect w/message (new #) 1 year No charge	
Donnelly	White pages—1 line	No charge
1-800-834-8425	Yellow pages—2 lines	No charge
	3 or more	$10.00
	1/2 add (per month)	$27.00
	DEADLINE—August 21 (30 days to cancel)	
	Change deadline—September 10	
	Deposit due September 11	$183.00
	Monthly rate	$91.50
	(Yearly cost $1098.00)	
Metropolitan	Circulation 40,000	
Magazine:	Monthly rate	$129.00
757-1404		
Kim Moore		
4940 Campus Drive		
Newport Beach,		
CA 92660		
California Riveria:	1/6 page (per month)	$300.00
494-2659	Art charge—one time	$50.00
Leslie	40% discount—new subscriber	
Box 536	Can hold rate for 6 months (Reg. $575.00)	
Laguna Beach,	Color (per month)	$600.00
CA 92652	Articles	No charge
	Print month end	
	Circulation: 50,000	29K High Traffic
		21K Direct Mail (92660 - 92625)

Advertising – cont.

Grand Opening:	4 x 6 Postcard—color	$400.00
	Catering $200.00	
	Artist show	
	Discount coupons	
	Fliers	
	Newspaper ads OC Register—one time cost - $100	
Orange County News 714-565-3881	Will get advertising estimates after 6 months in business.	
Orange County Register	Monthly rate	$100.00

Donnelly Listings

Five Categories:
1. **Art Dealer, Galleries**
2. **Interior Designers and Decorators**
3. **Framers**
4. **Jewelers**
5. **Gift Shops**

1. **ART DEALERS, GALLERIES:**
   Original Art, Lithos, Posters, Custom Framing, Bronze and Acrylic Sculptings, Int. Designer Prices, Ask for Catalog

2. **INTERIOR DECORATORS AND DESIGNERS:**
   Original Art, Lithos, Posters, Custom Framing, Bronze and Acrylic Sculptings, Dealer Prices, Ask for Catalog

3. **FRAMERS:**
   Large Selection of California Marine Art, Coastal Scenes, Custom Framing, Matting, Ask for Mail-Order Catalog

4. **JEWELERS:**
   Specialty, Marine/Nautical Custom Designs by California Artists, 14K Gold, Sterling, Gemstones, Ask for Catalog

5. **GIFT SHOPS:**
   Unique Line of Marine/Nautical Gifts, Glass Figurines, Acrylic Boats, Clocks, Art, Jewelry, Bronzes, Ask for Catalog

PRICING

A. Purchasing

As stipulated in my Terms and Conditions, I request a 10 to 15% discount off published wholesale prices from artists and vendors in lieu of a participation fee. In about 95% of all agreements made, I am receiving this important discount!

B. Catalog Pricing

- Non-Jewelry Items—To recover publication costs, I have "keystoned" (100% markup) all items plus an additional 10 to 50%. Keystoning is typical in the retail industry. The added margin will cover any additional shipping charges that may not be covered by the indicated shipping fee paid by the customer.
- Jewelry Items—Typical pricing in the industry is "Key" plus 50% (150% markup) to triple"Key" (200% markup). My markup is "Key" plus 10 to 30% to stay competitive.

C. Store Pricing

All items "Keystone" plus 10 to 20% to allow a good margin for sales on selected items.

D. Wholesale

Mailings and advertising will target Interior Decorators and Designers. To purchase wholesale, one must present a copy of an ASID or ISID license number and order a minimum purchase of $500.00 or more. The discount will be 20% off retail price.

Below is a sample of the computer database with 16 fields of information on each item in inventory and how the retail price is computed.

File: Price List—Record 1 of 4 49

Item:	Fisherman's Wharf	Image Pr:	$5.00	Disc:	50% IM
Make:	Poster	Type:	Poster	Adj. Whsl:	$36.50
Vendor:	Chrasta	Frame:	PT4XW	Key+:	10%
Exclusive:	So. California	Frame Price:	$31.50	Retail Price:	$79.50
Size:	21.5 26 Sq.	Whsl. Price:	$36.50	Group:	1
Vendor #:	NAC102WM				

LOCATION

The prime business location targeted for **Marine Art of California** retail showroom is 1,000 square feet at 106 Bayview Circle, Newport Beach, California 92660. This site was chosen because of large front display windows, excellent visibility and access for the showroom, as well as adequate floor space to house inventory for catalog shipping. Both operations require certain square footage to operate successfully. Demographics and surrounding stores are extremely favorable.

Proposed site: Newport Beach, California

Features:
- Retail shop space of 1000 sq. ft.
- Located in the primary retail and business sector of Newport Beach, Orange County's most affluent and growing community.
- Excellent visibility and access.
- Median household income in one mile radius is $90,000.

Location – cont.

Demographics*	1 Mile	3 Miles	5 Miles
Population:	1,043	111,983	308,906
Income:	$90,000	$61,990	$59,600

Private Sector Employment (Daytime population)

	1 Mile	3 Miles	5 Miles
	43,921	113,061	306,313

Socio-Economic Status Indicator (SESI)

	1 Mile	3 Miles	5 Miles
	73	79	79

Population by Age

	1 Mile		3 Miles	5 Miles
	25–29		9.2%	8.4%
	30–34		9.4%	9.9%
	35–44		16.1%	18.6%
	45–54		12.3%	12.1%
	25–54	TOTAL	47.0%	49.0%

Leasing Agent. Chuck Sullivan, CB Commercial, 4040 MacArthur Blvd., Newport Beach, California 92660

Donnelly Marketing Information Service

GALLERY DESIGN

After managing Sea Fantasies Gallery at Fashion Island Mall in Newport Beach, I have decided to recreate its basic layout. My goal is to create the most stunning and unique showroom design in Orange County with a product line that appeals to the high-profile customer's taste.

The design theme is to give the customer a feeling of being underwater when they enter. This would be accomplished by the use of glass display stands, and live potted tropical plants to simulate lush, green underwater vegetation. Overhead curtains 18-inches wide would cleverly hide the track lighting while reflecting the light on the curtain sides, creating the illusion of an underwater scene with sunlight reflecting on the ocean surface.

A large-screen TV would continuously play videos of colorful underwater scenes with mood music playing on the store's sound system. A loveseat for shoppers to relax in would face the screen. Along with creating a soothing and relaxing atmosphere, the videos, CDs, and cassettes would be available for sale. All fine art pieces (bronzes and framed art) would be accented with overhead track lighting, creating a strong visual effect.

Large coral pieces would be used for display purposes, such as for jewelry. Others would be strewn around the showroom floor area for a natural ocean floor effect. Certain end displays would be constructed of glass with ocean floor scenes set inside consisting of an arrangement of coral, shells, and brightly painted wooden tropical fish on a two-inch bed of sand. All display stands would be available for sale.

This design concept was generally considered to be the most outstanding original store plan in Fashion Island as expressed by mall customers and the Management Office. By incorporating these tried and proven concepts with my own creative designs, this gallery will have the most outstanding and unique appearance of any gallery from Long Beach to San Clemente. The showroom area will be approximately 800-square feet. The rear and stock area is about 200-square feet.

TIMING OF MARKET ENTRY

Considering the fact that most of my product line could be viewed as gift items, the upcoming holiday season is of **CRITICAL IMPORTANCE.** This is typically the peak sales period in the retail industry. Catalogs from large retailers and mail-order houses are already appearing in the mail for the holidays. These are the dates to consider:

1. **OCTOBER 8:**   Camera-ready artwork goes to film separator.

    Turnaround time is three days.

2. **OCTOBER 11:**   All slides and artwork must be ready to be delivered to the printer, Bertco Graphics, in Los Angeles.

    Turnaround time is 11 working days.

3. **OCTOBER 22:**   Printed catalogs must be delivered to Towne House Marketing in Santa Ana.

    Turnaround time is three days.

4. **OCTOBER 29:**   Catalogs shipped to Santa Ana Main Post Office.

    Turnaround time is two working days.

5. **NOVEMBER 1:**   **CUSTOMER RECEIVES CATALOG** - Ordering begins.

6. **DECEMBER 4:**   Last ordering date to ensure Christmas delivery! Can send all stocked items and all stocked items at vendors via Federal Express.

    Problem Items:
      a) High-end cast bronzes
      b) Hand-made glass figurines
      c) Original paintings

    Turnaround time is three weeks.

III. FINANCIAL DOCUMENTS

Marine Art of California

SOURCES AND USES OF LOAN FUNDS

2002 FINANCIAL PROJECTIONS

2002 HISTORICAL STATEMENTS

FINANCIAL STATEMENT ANALYSIS

SUMMARY OF FINANCIAL NEEDS

I. **Marine Art of California**, a limited partnership, is seeking equity capital for start-up purposes.
   A. Direct Mail-Order Catalog
   B. Retail/Wholesale Showroom

II. **Funds needed to accomplish above** goal will be $130,000. See Loan Fund Dispersal Statement below for distribution of funds and backup statement.

LOAN FUND DISPERSAL STATEMENT

I. **Dispersal of Loan Funds**
   Marine Art of California will utilize funds in the amount of $130,000 for start-up of two retail functions: (1) a direct mail-order catalog, and (2) a retail showroom to conduct related functions.

II. **Backup Statement**
   Direct mail-order catalog: a) 24 pages
   b) two editions

c) Quantities:	20K	$20,000
	30K	23,300
Start-up expense of warehouse – One Time Cost:		25,275
Three Months Operating Expense:		58,364
Three Month Total Loan Repayment Cost @ $1,560:		3,161
	TOTAL	**$130,000**

Pro Forma Cash Flow Statement
Page 1 (Pre-Start-Up and January thru May)
Marine Art of California

For the Year 2002	Start-Up Nov-Dec	Jan	Feb	Mar	Apr	May	Jun
BEGINNING CASH BALANCE	0	75,575	65,312	50,837	49,397	37,807	43,559
CASH RECEIPTS							
A. Sales/revenues	41,620	22,065	16,040	42,350	30,300	67,744	47,696
B. Receivables (credit accts.)	0	0	0	0	0	0	0
C. Interest income	0	0	0	0	0	0	0
D. Sale of long-term assets	0	0	0	0	0	0	0
TOTAL CASH AVAILABLE	41,620	97,640	81,352	93,187	79,697	105,551	91,255
CASH PAYMENTS							
A. Cost of goods to be sold							
Inventory purchases	29,900	12,213	9,200	22,375	16,375	35,122	25,123
B. Variable expenses							
1. Advertising/marketing	1,042	221	221	221	521	521	521
2. Car delivery/travel	200	100	100	100	100	100	100
3. Catalog expense	27,600	9,600	10,800	10,800	14,600	14,600	16,400
4. Gross wages	5,120	2,560	2,560	2,560	2,560	3,520	3,520
5. Payroll expense	384	192	192	192	192	269	269
6. Shipping	800	400	400	400	400	400	400
7. Misc. var. exp.	3,000	500	500	500	500	500	500
Total variable expenses	38,146	13,573	14,773	14,773	18,873	19,910	21,710
C. Fixed expenses							
1. Accounting and legal	820	160	160	160	160	160	160
2. Insurance + workers' comp	904	302	302	302	302	320	320
3. Rent	3,900	1,300	1,300	1,300	1,300	1,300	1,300
4. Repairs and maintenance	60	30	30	30	30	30	30
5. Guaranteed pay't (mgr. partner)	4,000	2,000	2,000	2,000	2,000	2,000	2,000
6. Supplies	600	300	300	300	300	300	300
7. Telephone	1,050	600	600	700	700	1,000	1,000
8. Utilities	630	290	290	290	290	290	290
9. Misc. (inc. licenses/permits)	175	0	0	0	0	0	0
Total fixed expenses	12,139	4,982	4,982	5,082	5,082	5,400	5,400
D. Interest expense	1,192	1,192	1,192	1,192	1,192	1,192	1,192
E. Federal/state income tax	0	0	0	0	0	0	0
F. Capital purchases (office)	9,000	0	0	0	0	0	0
G. Capital purchases (showroom)	5,300	0	0	0	0	0	0
H. Loan payments	368	368	368	368	368	368	368
I. Equity withdrawals	0	0	0	0	0	0	0
TOTAL CASH PAID OUT	96,045	32,328	30,515	43,790	41,890	61,992	53,793
CASH BALANCE/DEFICIENCY	(54,425)	65,312	50,837	49,397	37,807	43,559	37,462
LOANS TO BE RECEIVED	130,000	0	0	0	0	0	0
EQUITY DEPOSITS	0	0	0	0	0	0	0
ENDING CASH BALANCE	75,575	65,312	50,837	49,397	37,807	43,559	37,462

1. $130,000 15-year loan. 20 limited partners @ $6,500 in exchange for 2.5% equity (each) in company (see proposal in Supporting Documents)
2. Cash business: Prepaid orders and paid on-site purchases only; no open accounts or receivables.

Pro Forma Cash Flow Statement

Page 2 (May thru December + 6 and 12-month Totals)

Marine Art of California

6-MONTH TOTALS	Jul	Aug	Sep	Oct	Nov	Dec	12-MONTH TOTALS
75,575	37,462	48,996	46,287	47,992	37,772	80,527	75,575
226,195	83,508	58,672	67,950	47,700	154,200	105,700	743,925
0	0	0	0	0	0	0	0
0	0	0	0	0	0	0	0
0	0	0	0	0	0	0	0
301,770	120,970	107,668	114,237	95,692	191,972	186,227	819,500
120,408	43,054	30,661	35,275	25,150	78,375	54,125	387,048
2,226	521	521	521	521	521	521	5,352
600	100	100	100	100	100	100	1,200
76,800	16,400	18,200	18,200	20,000	20,000	20,000	189,600
17,280	3,520	3,520	3,520	3,520	3,520	3,520	38,400
1,306	269	269	269	269	269	269	2,920
2,400	400	400	400	400	400	400	4,800
3,000	500	500	500	500	500	500	6,000
103,612	21,710	23,510	23,510	25,310	25,310	25,310	248,272
960	160	160	160	160	160	160	1,920
1,848	320	320	320	320	320	320	3,768
7,800	1,300	1,300	1,300	1,300	1,300	1,300	15,600
180	30	30	30	30	30	30	360
12,000	2,000	2,000	2,000	2,000	2,000	2,000	24,000
1,800	300	300	300	300	300	300	3,600
4,600	1,250	1,250	1,500	1,500	1,800	1,800	13,700
1,740	290	290	290	290	290	290	3,480
0	0	0	0	0	0	0	0
30,928	5,650	5,650	5,900	5,900	6,200	6,200	66,428
7,152	1,192	1,192	1,192	1,192	1,190	1,190	14,300
0	0	0	0	0	0	0	0
0	0	0	0	0	0	0	0
0	0	0	0	0	0	0	0
2,208	368	368	368	368	370	370	4,420
0	0	0	0	0	0	0	0
264,308	71,974	61,381	66,245	57,920	111,445	87,195	720,468
37,462	48,996	46,287	47,992	37,772	80,527	99,032	99,032
0	0	0	0	0	0	0	0
0	0	0	0	0	0	0	0
37,462	48,996	46,287	47,992	37,772	80,527	99,032	99,032

Quarterly Budget Analysis
Marine Art of California

For the Quarter Ending: December 31, 2002

BUDGET ITEM	THIS QUARTER			YEAR-TO-DATE		
	Budget	Actual	Var.	Budget	Actual	Var.
Sales/revenues	**307,600**	**300,196**	**(7,404)**	**743,925**	**730,379**	**(13,546)**
a. Catalog sales	285,500	275,238	(10,262)	672,920	647,380	(25,540)
b. Showroom sales	15,300	16,382	1,082	46,325	53,805	7,480
c. Wholesale sales	6,800	8,576	1,776	24,680	29,194	4,514
Less cost of goods	**159,650**	**146,315**	**13,335**	**375,048**	**369,502**	**5,546**
a. Purchases	167,650	154,172	13,478	387,048	380,914	6,134
Catalog products	152,750	137,619	15,131	336,460	323,690	12,770
Showroom products	10,650	11,191	(541)	35,163	38,903	(3,740)
Wholesale products	4,250	5,362	(1,112)	15,425	18,321	(2,896)
b. Less change in ending inventory	8,000	7,857	143	12,000	11,412	588
Gross profits	**147,950**	**153,881**	**5,931**	**368,877**	**360,877**	**(8,000)**
Variable expenses						
1. Advertising/marketing	1,563	4,641	(3,078)	5,352	16,431	(11,079)
2. Car delivery/travel	300	268	32	1,200	1,193	7
3. Catalog expense	60,000	54,852	5,148	189,600	172,263	17,337
4. Gross wages	10,560	10,560	0	38,400	38,400	0
5. Payroll expense	807	807	0	2,920	2,920	0
6. Shipping	1,200	1,732	(532)	4,800	5,591	(791)
7. Miscellaneious selling expense	1,500	1,328	172	6,000	4,460	1,540
8. Depreciation (showroom assets)	265	265	0	1,060	1,060	0
Fixed expenses						
1. Accounting and legal	480	450	30	1,920	2,035	(115)
2. Insurance + workers' comp	960	960	0	3,768	3,768	0
3. Rent	3,900	3,900	0	15,600	15,600	0
4. Repairs and maintenance	90	46	44	360	299	61
5. Guaranteed pay't (mgr. partner)	6,000	6,000	0	24,000	24,000	0
6. Supplies	900	500	400	3,600	2,770	830
7. Telephone	5,100	5,134	(34)	13,700	13,024	676
8. Utilities	870	673	197	3,480	2,447	1,033
9. Miscellaneous admin. expense	0	197	(197)	0	372	(372)
10. Depreciation (office equip)	450	450	0	1,800	1,800	0
Net income from operations	**53,005**	**61,118**	**8,113**	**51,317**	**52,444**	**1,127**
Interest income	0	0	0	0	0	0
Interest expense	3,858	3,858	0	14,300	14,300	0
Net profit (loss) before taxes	**49,147**	**57,260**	**8,113**	**37,017**	**38,144**	**1,127**
Taxes (partnership*)	0	0	0	0	0	0
(Partners taxed individually according to distributive shares of profit/loss)						
PARTNERSHIP: NET PROFIT (LOSS)	**49,147**	**57,260**	**8,113**	**37,017**	**38,144**	**1,127**

NON-INCOME STATEMENT ITEMS

	Budget	Actual	Var.	Budget	Actual	Var.
1. Long-term asset repayments	0	0	0	0	0	0
2. Loan repayments	1,104	1,104	0	4,420	4,420	0
3. Equity withdrawals	0	0	0	0	0	0
4. Inventory assets	8,000	7,857	143	12,000	11,412	588

BUDGET DEVIATIONS

	This Quarter	Year-to-Date
1. Income statement Items:	$ 8,113	$ 1,127
2. Non-income statement items:	$ 143	$ 588
3. Total deviation	$ 8,256	$ 1,715
Cash Position Year-To-Date:	Projected = $99,032	Actual = $100,747

Three-Year Income Projection
Marine Art of California

Updated: September 26, 2001	Nov-Dec 2001 Pre-Start-Up	YEAR 1 2002	YEAR 2 2003	YEAR 3 2004	TOTAL 3 YEARS
INCOME					
1. Sales/revenues	41,620	743,930	2,651,856	4,515,406	7,952,812
Catalog sales	33,820	672,925	2,570,200	4,421,500	7,698,445
Showroom sales	4,600	46,325	53,274	61,266	165,465
Wholesale sales	3,200	24,680	28,382	32,640	88,902
2. Cost of goods sold (c − d)	23,900	375,048	1,329,476	2,261,783	3,990,207
a. Beginning inventory	6,000	6,000	18,000	25,000	6,000
b. Purchases	23,900	387,048	1,336,476	2,268,783	4,016,207
Catalog	19,600	336,460	1,285,100	2,210,750	3,851,910
Showroom (walk-in)	2,300	35,163	33,637	37,633	108,733
Wholesale	2,000	15,425	17,739	20,400	55,564
c. C.O.G. avail. sale (a + b)	29,900	393,048	1,354,476	2,293,783	4,022,207
d. Less ending inventory (12/31)	6,000	18,000	25,000	32,000	32,000
3. Gross profit on sales (1 − 2)	17,720	368,882	1,322,380	2,253,623	3,962,605
EXPENSES					
1. Variable (selling) (a thru h)	38,146	249,332	734,263	1,316,291	2,338,032
a. Advertising/marketing	1,042	5,352	5,727	6,127	18,248
b. Car delivery/travel	200	1,200	1,284	1,374	4,058
c. Catalog expense	27,600	189,600	670,400	1,248,000	2,135,600
d. Gross wages	5,120	38,400	41,088	43,964	128,572
e. Payroll expenses	384	2,920	3,124	3,343	9,771
f. Shipping	800	4,800	5,280	5,808	16,688
g. Miscellaneous selling expenses	3,000	6,000	6,300	6,615	21,915
h. Depreciation (showroom assets)	0	1,060	1,060	1,060	3,180
2. Fixed (administrative) (a thru h)	12,139	68,228	71,609	75,268	227,244
a. Accounting and legal	820	1,920	2,054	2,198	6,992
b. Insurance + workers' comp	904	3,768	4,032	4,314	13,018
c. Rent	3,900	15,600	16,692	17,860	54,052
d. Repairs and maintenance	60	360	385	412	1,217
e. Guaranteed pay't (mgr. partner)	4,000	24,000	24,000	24,000	76,000
f. Supplies	600	3,600	3,852	4,123	12,175
g. Telephone	1,050	13,700	15,070	16,577	46,397
h. Utilities	630	3,480	3,724	3,984	11,818
i. Miscellaneous fixed expense	175	0	0	0	175
j. Depreciation (Office Assets)	0	1,800	1,800	1,800	5,400
Total operating expenses (1 + 2)	50,285	317,560	805,872	1,391,559	2,565,276
Net income operations (GPr − Exp)	(32,565)	51,322	516,508	862,064	1,397,329
Other income (interest income)	0	0	0	0	0
Other expense (interest expense)	1,192	14,300	13,814	13,274	42,580
Net profit (loss) for partnership	(33,757)	37,022	502,694	848,790	1,354,749
Taxes: (partnership)*	0	0	0	0	0
(partners taxed individually according to	0	0	0	0	0
distributive shares of profit or loss)	0	0	0	0	0
PARTNERSHIP: NET PROFIT (LOSS)	(33,757)	37,022	502,694	848,790	1,354,749

Projected Balance Sheet

Business Name:

Marine Art of California

Date of Projection: September 30, 2001

Date Projected for: December 31, 2002

ASSETS

		% of Assets
Current assets		
Cash	$ 98,032	73.96%
Petty cash	$ 1,000	0.75%
Sales tax holding account	$ 4,067	3.07%
Accounts receivable	$ 0	0.00%
Inventory	$ 18,000	13.58%
Short-term investments	$ 0	0.00%
Long-term investments	$ 0	0.00%
Fixed assets		
Land (valued at cost)	$ 0	0.00%
Buildings	$ 0	0.00%
1. Cost 0		
2. Less acc. depr. 0		
Showroom improvements	$ 4,240	3.20%
1. Cost 5,300		
2. Less acc. depr. 1,060		
Office improvements	$ 4,160	3.14%
1. Cost 5,200		
2. Less acc. depr. 1,040		
Office equipment	$ 3,040	2.29%
1. Cost 3,800		
2. Less acc. depr. 760		
Autos/vehicles	$ 0	0.00%
1. Cost 0		
2. Less acc. depr. 0		
Other assets		
1.	$ 0	0.00%
2.	$ 0	0.00%
TOTAL ASSETS	$ 132,539	100.00%

LIABILITIES

		% of Liabilities
Current liabilities		
Accounts payable	$ 0	0.00%
Notes payable	$ 4,906	3.79%
Interest payable	$ 0	0.00%
Taxes payable (partnership)		
Federal income tax	$ 0	0.00%
Self-employment tax	$ 0	0.00%
State income tax	$ 0	0.00%
Sales tax accrual	$ 4,067	3.15%
Property tax	$ 0	0.00%
Payroll accrual	$ 0	0.00%
Long-term liabilities		
Notes payable to investors	$ 120,306	93.06%
Notes payable others	$ 0	0.00%
TOTAL LIABILITIES	$ 129,279	100.00%

NET WORTH (EQUITY)

		% of Net Worth
Proprietorship	$ 0	0.00%
or		
Partnership		
1. Bob Garcia, 55% equity	$ 1,793	55.00%
2. Ltd. Prtnrs., 45% equity	$ 1,467	45.00%
or		
Corporation		
Capital stock	$ 0	0.00%
Surplus paid in	$ 0	0.00%
Retained earnings	$ 0	0.00%
TOTAL NET WORTH	$ 3,260	100.00%

Assets – Liabilities = Net Worth

and

Liabilities + Equity = Total Assets

1. See Financial Statement Analysis for ratios and notations.

Break-Even Analysis
Marine Art of California

Date of Analysis: September 29, 2002

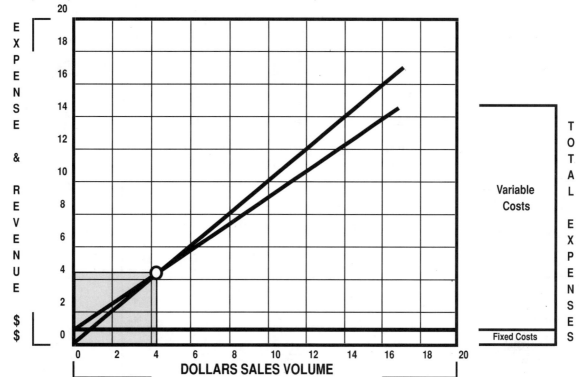

NOTE: Figures shown in 2 hundreds of thousands of dollars (Ex: 2 = $ 400,000)

Marine Art of California
Break-Even Point Calculation

B-E POINT (SALES) = Fixed costs + [(Variable costs/Est. revenues) X Sales]

B-E Point (Sales) = $ 181,282.00 + [($ 2,750,165.00 / $ 3,437,406.00) X Sales]

B-E Point (Sales) = $ 181,282.00 + [.8001 X Sales]

S - .8001S = $181,282.00   S - .8001S = $181,282.00   .19992S = $181,282.00

S = $181,282.00/.1999

Break-Even Point
S = $906,700*

*rounded figure

FC **(Fixed costs)** =	(Administrative expenses + Interest)	$	181,282
VC **(Variable costs)** =	(Cost of goods + Selling expenses)	$	2,750,165
R **(Est. revenues)** =	(Income from sale of products and services)	$	3,437,406
BREAK-EVEN POINT =		$	906,727

The financial figures below in no way represent an actual Profit & Loss Statement for Mr. Garcia's business. This statement is for illustrative purposes only and is an example of what "might have happened" during Marine Art of California's first year of business.

Profit and Loss (Income) Statement
Marine Art of California

Page 1 (January thru June + 6-Month Totals)

For the Year: 2002	Jan	Feb	Mar	Apr	May	Jun	6-MONTH TOTALS AMOUNT	% of Total Revenues PERCENT
INCOME								
1. Sales/revenues	**21,073**	**17,916**	**40,640**	**31,408**	**66,858**	**50,034**	**227,929**	**100.00%**
a. Catalog sales (60%-40%)	16,700	13,700	34,786	24,600	61,540	42,846	194,172	85.19%
b. Showroom sales (walk-in)	1,825	2,356	3,900	4,670	3,170	4,648	20,569	9.02%
c. Wholesale sales	2,548	1,860	1,954	2,138	2,148	2,540	13,188	5.79%
2. Cost of goods sold	**10,622**	**9,960**	**22,799**	**16,417**	**35,137**	**25,580**	**120,515**	**52.87%**
a. Beginning inventory	6,000	7,234	7,465	6,230	6,784	6,345	6,000	2.63%
b. Purchases	**11,856**	**10,191**	**21,564**	**16,971**	**34,698**	**26,335**	**121,615**	**53.36%**
(1) Catalog goods (50%)	8,350	6,850	17,393	12,300	30,770	21,423	97,086	42.59%
(2) Showroom (50%+$1Kp/m)	1,913	2,178	2,950	3,335	2,585	3,324	16,285	7.14%
(3) Wholesales (x.625)	1,593	1,163	1,221	1,336	1,343	1,588	8,244	3.62%
c. C.O.G. available for sale	17,856	17,425	29,029	23,201	41,482	32,680	127,615	55.99%
d. Less ending inventory	7,234	7,465	6,230	6,784	6,345	7,100	7,100	3.12%
3. Gross profit	**10,451**	**7,956**	**17,841**	**14,991**	**31,721**	**24,454**	**107,414**	**47.13%**
EXPENSES								
1. Variable (selling) expenses								
a. Advertising/marketing	836	836	836	1,547	1,547	1,547	7,149	3.14%
b. Car delivery/travel	94	126	78	83	112	97	590	0.26%
c. Catalog expense	9,600	10,770	10,770	11,960	11,960	11,960	67,020	29.40%
d. Gross wages	2,560	2,560	2,560	2,560	3,520	3,520	17,280	7.58%
e. Payroll expense	192	192	192	192	269	269	1,306	0.57%
f. Shipping	385	432	391	406	389	391	2,394	1.05%
g. Miscell. variable expenses	538	147	268	621	382	211	2,167	0.95%
h. Deprec. (showroom)	88	88	89	88	88	89	530	0.23%
Total variable expenses	**14,293**	**15,151**	**15,184**	**17,457**	**18,267**	**18,084**	**98,436**	**43.19%**
1. Fixed (admin) expenses								
a. Accounting and legal	150	150	150	385	150	150	1,135	0.50%
b. Insurance + workers' comp	302	302	302	302	320	320	1,848	0.81%
c. Rent	1,300	1,300	1,300	1,300	1,300	1,300	7,800	3.42%
d. Repairs and maintenance	0	12	56	0	0	72	140	0.06%
e. Guar. pay't (mgr. partner)	2,000	2,000	2,000	2,000	2,000	2,000	12,000	5.26%
f. Supplies	287	246	301	223	259	172	1,488	0.65%
g. Telephone	542	634	556	621	836	872	4,061	1.78%
h. Utilities	287	263	246	164	168	172	1,300	0.57%
i. Misc. fixed expenses	23	17	0	46	39	0	125	0.05%
j. Deprec. (office equip)	150	150	150	150	150	150	900	0.39%
Total fixed expenses	**5,041**	**5,074**	**5,061**	**5,191**	**5,222**	**5,208**	**30,797**	**13.51%**
Total operating expense	**19,334**	**20,225**	**20,245**	**22,648**	**23,489**	**23,292**	**129,233**	**56.70%**
Net income from operations	(8,883)	(12,269)	(2,404)	(7,657)	8,232	1,162	(21,819)	-9.57%
Other income (interest)	0	0	0	0	0	0	0	0.00%
Other expense (interest)	1,192	1,192	1,192	1,192	1,192	1,192	7,152	3.14%
Net profit (loss) before taxes	(10,075)	(13,461)	(3,596)	(8,849)	7,040	(30)	(28,971)	-12.71%
Taxes: partnership*	0	0	0	0	0	0	0	0.00%
*(partners taxed individually on	0	0	0	0	0	0	0	0.00%
distributive shares of profits)	0	0	0	0	0	0	0	0.00%
PARTNERSHIP: NET PROFIT (LOSS)	**(10,075)**	**(13,461)**	**(3,596)**	**(8,849)**	**7,040**	**(30)**	**(28,971)**	**-12.71%**

The financial figures below in no way represent an actual Profit & Loss Statement for Mr. Garcia's business. This statement is for illustrative purposes only and is an example of what "might have happened" during Marine Art of California's first year of business.

Profit and Loss (Income) Statement
Marine Art of California

Page 2 (July thru December + 12-Month Totals)

For the Year: 2002

	Jul	Aug	Sep	Oct	Nov	Dec	12-MONTH TOTALS AMOUNT	of Total Revenues PERCENT
INCOME								
1. Sales/revenues	81,092	57,014	64,148	67,684	127,390	105,122	730,379	100.00%
a. Catalog sales (60%-40%)	72,740	47,890	57,340	57,468	120,550	97,220	647,380	88.64%
b. Showroom sales (walk-in)	5,490	6,734	4,630	6,340	4,280	5,762	53,805	7.37%
c. Wholesale sales	2,862	2,390	2,178	3,876	2,560	2,140	29,194	4.00%
2. Cost of goods sold	41,819	28,641	32,212	33,942	63,689	48,684	369,502	50.59%
a. Beginning inventory	7,100	7,256	8,421	9,555	10,940	12,267	6,000	0.82%
b. Purchases	41,975	29,806	33,346	35,327	65,016	53,829	380,914	52.15%
(1) Catalog goods (50%)	36,370	23,945	28,670	28,734	60,275	48,610	323,690	44.32%
(2) Showroom (50%+$1Kp/m)	3,745	4,367	3,315	4,170	3,140	3,881	38,903	5.33%
(3) Wholesales (x.625)	1,860	1,494	1,361	2,423	1,601	1,338	18,321	2.51%
c. C.O.G. available for sale	49,075	37,062	41,767	44,882	75,956	66,096	386,914	52.97%
d. Less ending inventory	7,256	8,421	9,555	10,940	12,267	17,412	17,412	2.38%
3. Gross profit	39,273	28,373	31,936	33,742	63,701	56,438	360,877	49.41%
EXPENSES								
1. Variable (selling) expenses								
a. Advertising/marketing	1,547	1,547	1,547	1,547	1,547	1,547	16,431	2.25%
b. Car delivery/travel	136	107	92	96	84	88	1,193	0.16%
c. Catalog expense	15,125	17,633	17,633	18,284	18,284	18,284	172,263	23.59%
d. Gross wages	3,520	3,520	3,520	3,520	3,520	3,520	38,400	5.26%
e. Payroll expense	269	269	269	269	269	269	2,920	0.40%
f. Shipping	516	467	482	534	617	581	5,591	0.77%
g. Miscell. variable expenses	459	184	322	721	265	342	4,460	0.61%
h. Deprec. (showroom)	88	88	89	88	88	89	1,060	0.15%
Total variable expenses	21,660	23,815	23,954	25,059	24,674	24,720	242,318	33.18%
1. Fixed (admin) expenses								
a. Accounting and legal	150	150	150	150	150	150	2,035	0.28%
b. Insurance + workers' comp	320	320	320	320	320	320	3,768	0.52%
c. Rent	1,300	1,300	1,300	1,300	1,300	1,300	15,600	2.14%
d. Repairs and maintenance	0	0	113	46	0	0	299	0.04%
e. Guar. pay't (mgr. partner)	2,000	2,000	2,000	2,000	2,000	2,000	24,000	3.29%
f. Supplies	164	231	387	143	164	193	2,770	0.38%
g. Telephone	1,164	1,287	1,378	1,422	1,943	1,769	13,024	1.78%
h. Utilities	159	148	167	193	217	263	2,447	0.34%
i. Misc. fixed expenses	41	9	0	22	0	175	372	0.05%
j. Deprec. (office equip)	150	150	150	150	150	150	1,800	0.25%
Total fixed expenses	5,448	5,595	5,965	5,746	6,244	6,320	66,115	9.05%
Total operating expense	27,108	29,410	29,919	30,805	30,918	31,040	308,433	42.23%
Net income from operations	12,165	(1,037)	2,017	2,937	32,783	25,398	52,444	7.18%
Other income (interest)	0	0	0	0	0	0	0	0.00%
Other expense (interest)	1,192	1,192	1,192	1,192	1,190	1,190	14,300	1.96%
Net profit (loss) before taxes	10,973	(2,229)	825	1,745	31,593	24,208	38,144	5.22%
Taxes: partnership*	0	0	0	0	0	0	0	0.00%
*(partners taxed individually on	0	0	0	0	0	0	0	0.00%
distributive shares of profits)	0	0	0	0	0	0	0	0.00%
PARTNERSHIP: NET PROFIT (LOSS)	10,973	(2,229)	825	1,745	31,593	24,208	38,144	5.22%

Balance Sheet

Business Name:

Marine Art of California   Date: December 31, 2002

ASSETS			% of Assets
Current assets			
Cash	$	100,102	75.43%
Petty cash	$	645	0.49%
Sales tax holding account	$	3,107	2.34%
Accounts receivable	$	0	0.00%
Inventory	$	17,412	13.12%
Short-term investments	$	0	0.00%
Long-term investments	$	0	0.00%
Fixed assets			
Land (valued at cost)	$	0	0.00%
Buildings	$	0	0.00%
1. Cost 0			
2. Less acc. depr. 0			
Showroom improvements	$	4,240	3.20%
1. Cost 5,300			
2. Less acc. depr. 1,060			
Office improvements	$	4,160	3.13%
1. Cost 5,200			
2. Less acc. depr. 1,040			
Office equipment	$	3,040	2.29%
1. Cost 3,800			
2. Less acc. depr. 760			
Autos/vehicles	$	0	0.00%
1. Cost 0			
2. Less acc. depr. 0			
Other assets			
1.	$	0	0.00%
2.	$	0	0.00%
TOTAL ASSETS	$	132,706	100.00%

LIABILITIES			% of Liabilities
Current liabilities			
Accounts payable	$	0	0.00%
Notes payable	$	4,906	3.82%
Interest payable	$	0	0.00%
Taxes payable			
Federal income tax	$	0	0.00%
Self-employment tax	$	0	0.00%
State income tax	$	0	0.00%
Sales tax accrual	$	3,107	2.42%
Property tax	$	0	0.00%
Payroll accrual	$	0	0.00%
Long-term liabilities			
Notes payable to investors	$	120,306	93.76%
Notes payable others	$	0	0.00%
TOTAL LIABILITIES	$	128,319	100.00%

NET WORTH (EQUITY)			% of Net Worth
Proprietorship	$	0	0.00%
or			
Partnership			
1. Bob Garcia, 55% equity	$	2,413	55.00%
2. Ltd. Prtnrs., 45% equity	$	1,974	45.00%
or			
Corporation			
Capital stock	$	0	0.00%
Surplus paid in	$	0	0.00%
Retained earnings	$	0	0.00%
TOTAL NET WORTH	$	4,387	100.00%

Assets - Liabilities = Net Worth

and

Liabilities + Equity = Total Assets

Financial Statement Analysis Summary

The following is a summary of the 2002 financial statement analysis information developed on the next three pages of spreadsheets (pages 30–32):

Writer must research industry forstandards.

2002	PROJECTED	ACTUAL	INDUSTRY* STANDARD
1. Net working capital	$112,126	$113,253	$100,000 +
2. Current ratio	13.5	15.1	2.0 +
3. Quick ratio	11.5	13.0	1.0 +
4. Gross profit margin	49.60%	49.4%	45.0%
5. Operating profit margin	6.9%	7.2%	6.8%
6. Net profit margin	5.0%	5.2%	12.4%
7. Debt to assets	97.5%	96.7%	33.0%
8. Debt to equity	39.7:1	29.3:1	1.0:1 +
9. ROI (return on investment)	28.0%	28.7%	11% +
10. Vertical income statement analysis **			
Sales/revenues	100.0%	100.0%	
Cost of goods	50.4%	50.6%	50.0% -
Gross profit	49.6%	49.4%	40.0% +
Operating expense	42.7%	42.2%	35.0% +
Net income operations	6.9%	7.2%	15.0% +
Interest income	0/0%	0.0%	N/A
Interest expense	1.9%	2.0%	Variable
Net profit (pre-tax)	5.0%	5.2%	10.0% +

** All items stated as % of total revenues

11. Vertical balance sheet analysis ***			
Current assets	91.2%	91.4%	85.0%
Inventory	13.6%	13.1%	28.0%
Total assets	3.7%	96.7%	
Current liabilities	3.7%	3.7%	20.0% -
Total liabilities	97.5%	96.7%	
Net worth	2.5%	3.3%	50.0% +
Total liabilities + Net worth	100.0%	100.0%	

*** All Asset items stated as % of Total Assets;
Liability & Net Worth items stated as % of Total Liabilities + Net Worth

Notes:

Marine Art of California has an excessively high debt ratio (96.7%). However, the company has survived the first year of business, maintained its cash flow ($100,000+), and returned a higher amount than originally promised to its investors. Sales for the first year were less than projected (-2%), but the net profit was still in excess of projections by 0.2%. Good management of the company by Mr. Garcia plus a timely product with a solid niche would seem to be a good indicator that this company's profits will continue to increase rapidly and that the company will be more than able to fulfill its obligations to its limited partners/investors.

Financial Statement Analysis
Marine Art of California

For the Year: 2002

Type of Analysis	Formula	Projected: Year 1		Historical: Year 1	
1. Liquidity Analysis	**Balance Sheet**				
	Current Assets	Current Assets	121,099	Current Assets	121,266
a. Net Working Capital	— Current Liabilities	Current Liabilities	8,973	Current Liabilities	8,013
		Net Working Capital	**$112,126**	**Net Working Capital**	**$113,253**
	Balance Sheet	Current Assets	121,099	Current Assets	121,266
b. Current Ratio	Current Assets	Current Liabilities	8,973	Current Liabilities	8,013
	Current Liabilities	**Current Ratio**	**13.50**	**Current Ratio**	**15.13**
	Balance Sheet	Current Assets	121,099	Current Assets	121,266
c. Quick Ratio	Current Assets minus Inventory	Inventory	18,000	Inventory	17,412
	Current Liabilities	Current Liabilities	8,973	Current Liabilities	8,013
		Quick Ratio	**11.49**	**Quick Ratio**	**12.96**
2. Profitability Analysis	**Income Statement**				
a. Gross Profit Margin	Gross Profits	Gross Profits	368,882	Gross Profits	360,877
	Sales	Sales	743,930	Sales	730,379
		Gross Profit Margin	**49.59%**	**Gross Profit Margin**	**49.41%**
b. Operating Profit Margin	Income from Operations	Income From Ops.	51,322	Income From Ops.	52,444
	Sales	Sales	743,930	Sales	730,379
		Op. Profit Margin	**6.90%**	**Op. Profit argin**	**7.18%**
c. Net Profit Margin	Net Profits	Net Profits	37,022	Net Profits	38,144
	Sales	Sales	743,930	Sales	730,379
		Net Profit Margin	**4.98%**	**Net Profit Margin**	**5.22%**
4. Debt Ratios	**Balance Sheet**	Total Liabilities	129,279	Total Liabilities	128,319
	Total Liabilities	Total Assets	132,539	Total Assets	132,706
a. Debt to Assets	Total Assets	**Debt to Assets Ratio**	**97.54%**	**Debt to Assets Ratio**	**96.69%**
	Total Liabilities	Total Liabilities	129,279	Total Liabilities	128,319
b. Debt to Equity	Total Owners' Equity	Total Owners' Equity	3,260	Total Owners' Equity	4,387
		Debt to Equity Ratio	**3965.61%**	**Debt to Equity Ratio**	**2924.98%**
4. Measures of Investment	**Balance Sheet**	Net Profits	37,022	Net Profits	38,144
a. ROI	Net Profits	Total Assets	132,539	Total Assets	132,706
(Return on Investment)	Total Assets	**ROI (Ret. on Invest.)**	**27.93%**	**ROI (Ret. on Invest.)**	**28.74%**
	Balance Sheet	**NOTE:**		**NOTE:**	
	1. Each asset % of Total Assets				
5. Vertical Financial	2. Liability & Equity % of Total L&E	*See Attached*		*See Attached*	
Statement Analysis		**Balance Sheet and**		**Balance Sheet and**	
	Income Statement				
	3. All items % of Total Revenues	**Income Statement**		**Income Statement**	
	Balance Sheet				
	1. Assets, Liab & Equity measured	**NOTE:**		**NOTE:**	
	against 2nd year. Increases and				
6. Horizontal Financial	decreases stated as amount & %	**Horizontal Analysis**		**Horizontal Analysis**	
Statement Analysis		**Not Applicable**		**Not Applicable**	
	Income Statement				
	2. Revenues & Expenses measured				
	against 2nd year. Increases and	**Only one year in business**		**Only one year in business**	
	decreases stated as amount & %				

The financial figures below in no way represent an actual Profit & Loss (Income) Statement for Mr. Garcia's business.

This statement is for illustrative purposes only and is an example of what "might have happened" during Marine Art of California's first year of business.

Vertical Income Statement Analysis
Marine Art of California

Historical For the Year: 2002	Begin: January 1, 2002 End: December 31, 2002

	AMOUNT		% Total Revenues
INCOME			
1. Sales/revenues		$ 730,379	100.00%
a. Catalog sales	647,380		88.64%
b. Showroom sales	53,805		7.37%
c. Wholesale sales	29,194		4.00%
2. Cost of goods sold (c – d)		369,502	50.59%
a. Beginning inventory	6,000		0.82%
b. Purchases	380,914		52.15%
(1) Catalog products	323,690		44.32%
(2) Showroom (walk-in) products	38,903		5.33%
(3) Wholesale products	18,321		2.51%
c. C.O.G. avail. sale (a+b)	386,914		52.97%
d. Less ending inventory (12/31)	17,412		2.38%
3. Gross profit on sales (1 – 2)		$ 360,877	49.41%
EXPENSES			
1. Variable (selling) (a thru l)		242,318	33.18%
a. Advertising/marketing	16,431		2.25%
b. Car delivery/travel	1,193		0.16%
c. Catalog expense	172,263		23.59%
d. Gross wages	38,400		5.26%
e. Payroll expense	2,920		0.40%
f. Shipping	5,591		0.77%
g. Miscellaneous variable selling expense	4,460		0.61%
h. Depreciation (prod/serv assets)	1,060		0.15%
2. Fixed (administrative) (a thru l)		66,115	9.05%
a. Accounting and legal	2,035		0.28%
b. Insurance and workers' comp	3,768		0.52%
c. Rent	15,600		2.14%
d. Repairs and maintenance	299		0.04%
e. Guaranteed payment (mgr. partner)	24,000		3.29%
f. Supplies	2,770		0.38%
g. Telephone	13,024		1.78%
h. Utilities	2,447		0.34%
i. Miscellaneous fixed (admin) expenses	372		0.05%
j. Depreciation (administrative assets)	1,800		0.25%
Total operating expenses (1 + 2)		308,433	42.23%
Net income from operations (GP – Exp)		$ 52,444	7.18%
Other income (interest income)	0		0.00%
Other expense (interest expense)	14,300		1.96%
Net profit (loss) before taxes		$ 38,144	5.22%
Taxes: (partnership)			
	0		0.00%
* (partners taxed individually according to	0	0	0.00%
distributive shares of profit or loss)	0		0.00%
PARTNERSHIP: NET PROFIT (LOSS)		$ 38,144	5.22%

This financial statement is for illustrative purposes only and the figures in no way represent an actual Balance Sheet for Mr. Garcia's business.
The example below represents a "possible scenario" for the asset, liability, and net worth positions of Marine Art of California after one year of business.

Vertical Balance Sheet Analysis

(All Asset %'s represent % of Total Assets; All Liability or Equity %'s represent % of Total Liabilities + Total Equity)

Analysis of Historical Balance Sheet			Date of Balance Sheet: December 31, 2002		
Marine Art of California					

ASSETS		% of Total Assets	LIABILITIES		% of Total L + NW
Current assets			**Current liabilities**		
Cash	$ 100,102	75.43%	Accounts payable	$ 0	0.00%
Petty cash	$ 645	0.49%	Notes payable	$ 4,906	3.70%
Sales tax holding account	$ 3,107	2.34%	Interest payable	$ 0	0.00%
Accounts receivable	$ 0	0.00%			
Inventory	$ 17,412	13.12%	Taxes payable		
Short-term investments	$ 0	0.00%	Federal income tax	$ 0	0.00%
			Self-employment tax	$ 0	0.00%
Long-term investments	$ 0	0.00%	State income tax	$ 0	0.00%
			Sales tax accrual	$ 3,107	2.34%
Fixed assets			Property tax	$ 0	0.00%
Land (valued at cost)	$ 0	0.00%			
			Payroll accrual	$ 0	0.00%
Buildings	$ 0	0.00%			
1. Cost 0			**Long-term liabilities**		
2. Less acc. depr. 0			Notes payable to investors	$ 120,306	90.66%
			Notes payable others	$ 0	0.00%
Showroom improvements	$ 4,240	3.20%			
1. Cost 5,300					
2. Less acc. depr. 1,060			**TOTAL LIABILITIES**	$ 128,319	96.69%
Office improvements	$ 4,160	3.13%			
1. Cost 5,200					
2. Less acc. depr. 1,040			**NET WORTH (EQUITY)**		
Office equipment	$ 3,040	2.29%			
1. Cost 3,800			**Proprietorship**	$ 0	0.00%
2. Less acc. depr. 760			or		
			Partnership		
Autos/vehicles	$ 0	0.00%	1. Bob Garcia, 55% equity	$ 2,413	1.82%
1. Cost 0			2. Ltd. Prtnrs., 45% equity	$ 1,974	1.49%
2. Less acc. depr. 0			or		
			Corporation		
			Capital stock	$ 0	0.00%
Other assets			Surplus paid in	$ 0	0.00%
1.	$ 0	0.00%	Retained earnings	$ 0	0.00%
2.	$ 0	0.00%			
			TOTAL NET WORTH	$ 4,387	3.31%
TOTAL ASSETS	$ 132,706	100.00%	**LIABILITIES + NET WORTH**	$ 132,706	100.00%
			Assets – Liabilities = Net Worth -or- Liabilities + Equity = Assets		

IV. SUPPORTING DOCUMENTS

Marine Art of California

Personal Résumé

Catalog Cost Analysis

Competition Comparison Analysis

Proposal for Limited Partnership

Terms and Conditions for Participants

Letter of Reference

ROBERT A. GARCIA

P.O. Box 10059-251
Newport Beach, CA 92658

714-722-6478

Manufacturing Management

Record of accomplishments in 12+ years in manufacturing and distribution. Experience in start-up and turn-around operations. In-depth understanding of multi-facility high-tech production systems/methods. Strengths in project management, problem solving, and coordinating/managing critical manufacturing functions: purchasing, engineering, inventory control, tracking, scheduling, and quality assurance developed with General Dynamics.

PROFILE

Hands-on management style: coordinated five support groups in Arizona, Arkansas, and California facilities in production of 57 complex assemblies, each having up to 100 components per circuit board.

- Experience in product development for target markets; multi-product experience.

- Set priorities, provided clear direction, energized others, got positive results.

- Enthusiastic rapport builder, analytical self-starter, persistent, persuasive.

ACHIEVEMENT OVERVIEW

Turnaround Operations

Production of systems seven months behind schedule, inventory control unreliable, purchasing not aggressively seeking critical components from vendors.

- Procured materials for electronic circuit card assemblies in support of off-site and final assembly of missile systems.

- Created, along with other members of special task team, procedures and internal tracking system to show how specific part shortages would impact production schedules up to six months ahead.

- Chaired weekly inventory status meetings with Purchasing and Quality Assurance representatives.

- Supervised five analysts.

- Coordinated sub-assembly activities between offsite facilities in Arizona and Arkansas and final assembly in California in order to deliver product to customers against tight time constraints.

- Trained new hires.

- Provided data analysis to upper management for review.

Results Achieved: Corrected inventory accuracy from 70% to 97% within nine months.

cont. next page

Robert A. Garcia – Page 2

Start-up Production/Distribution - Part-time Operation (secondary income)

- Researched market, found great potential for product (Bonsai trees).

- Studied plant propagation methods, built large greenhouse, implemented methods learned, marketed product.

- Participated in various home and garden shows, county fairs, three major shows/year.

- Employed staff of eight, wholesaled products to nurseries in Los Angeles and Orange Counties.

Results Achieved: Grew and operated business successfully for eight years, increased net profit from $4500 to $12,000 within four years.

CAREER HISTORY

Marine Art of California *Owner/President and Freelance Photographer*	1992–Current
Sea Fantasies Gallery *Store Manager*	1991–1992
General Dynamics Corporation *Manufacturing Coordinator*	1980–1989
Casa Vallarta Restaurant *Controller (part -time)*	1986–1987
B & D Nursery (secondary income) *Operations Manager*	1973–1981
Stater Bros Markets *Journeyman Clerk*	1969–1980

EDUCATION

Completed course work in History, California State Polytechnic University. Independent studies in Psychology of Supervision, Written Communication.

AFFILIATIONS/INTERESTS

Coordinator on Service Board for Orange County
Alanon and Alateen Family Groups, 1988–1990.
Regularly cast in musical productions.
Have appeared at Orange County Performing Arts Center and Fullerton Civic Light Opera.

Catalog Cost Analysis

PRINTING QUANTITY	20,000	30,000	40,000	50,000	60,000
CATALOG ITEMS					
24-page: Price per 1000	521.37	413.92	360.07	336.11	306.49
Weight - 2.208 OZ.					
Extended cost	10,427.40	12,417.60	14,402.80	16,305.50	18,389.40
Prep and delivery	756.00	970.00	1,235.00	1,500.00	1,765.00
Mail list costs - $50.00 per/1000	1,000.00	1,500.00	2,000.00	2,500.00	3,000.00
Postage - $170 per/1000	3,200.00	4,800.00	6,400.00	8,000.00	9,600.00
Film separations - $64 per/page	3,600.00	2,500.00	2,500.00	2,500.00	2,500.00
Art work	1,000.00	1,000.00	1,000.00	1,000.00	1,000.00
TOTAL COSTS	**19,983.40**	**23,187.60**	**27,537.80**	**31,805.50**	**36,254.40**
Rounded numbers	20,000.00	23,200.00	27,600.00	32,000.00	36,500.00
Unit costs	1.00	0.77	0.69	0.64	0.61
Costs per page	0.04	0.03	0.03	0.03	0.03
Costs per/1000	999.17	772.92	688.44	636.11	604.24

PRINTING QUANTITY	70,000	80,000	90,000	100,000	
CATALOG ITEMS					
24-page: Price per 1000	291.72	280.29	268.85	261.00	
Weight - 2.208 OZ.					
Extended cost	20,420.40	22,423.20	24,196.50	26,100.00	
Prep and delivery	2,030.00	2,295.00	2,560.00	2,825.00	
Mail list costs - $50.00 per/1000	3,500.00	4,000.00	4,500.00	5,000.00	
Postage - $170 per/1000	11,900.00	13,600.00	15,300.00	17,000.00	
Film separations - $64 per/page	2,500.00	2,500.00	2,500.00	2,500.00	
Art work	1,000.00	1,000.00	1,000.00	1,000.00	
TOTAL COSTS	**41,350.40**	**45,818.20**	**50,056.50**	**54,425.00**	
Rounded numbers	41,500.00	46,000.00	50,500.00	55,000.00	
Unit costs	0.59	0.57	0.56	0.54	
Costs per page	0.02	0.02	0.02	0.02	
Costs per/1000	590.72	572.73	556.18	544.25	

FOREIGN PRINTING QUANTITY	40,000.00	50,000.00	60,000.00	70,000.00	
NOTE: 20% will be deducted for foreign printing. Prices are reflected in Profit Analysis	27,600.00	32,000.00	36,500.00	41,500.00	
	0.80	0.80	0.80	0.80	
FOREIGN PRINTING COSTS	**22,080.00**	**25,600.00**	**29,200.00**	**33,200.00**	

FOREIGN PRINTING QUANTITY	80,000.00	90,000.00	100,000.00		
	46,000.00	50,500.00	55,000.00		
	0.80	0.80	0.80		
FOREIGN PRINTING COSTS	**36,800.00**	**40,400.00**	**44,000.00**		

Competition Comparison Analysis

	Price Range	Total Retail Prices	% of Total Prices	# of Items	Item RNG %		
COMPANY NAME							
Wild Wings	-50.00	2,092.35	3%	68	19%		
Spring	-100.00	5,269.50	7%	68	19%	-100.00	38%
32 Pages	-200.00	11,302.00	15%	78	22%		
	-500.00	39,905.00	54%	124	35%		
	-999.00	11,045.00	15%	19	5%		
	$1,000.00	4,745.00	6%	2	1%		
		$74,358.85	100%	359	100%		
						Avg item price	$207.13
			(Based on keystone pricing)			Avg item profit	$103.56
Sharper Image	-50.00	1,580.65	9%	47	39%		
Jul/Aug	-100.00	2,418.45	14%	31	26%	-100.00	64%
24 of 60 Pages	-200.00	3,898.75	23%	25	21%		
	-500.00	4,879.45	29%	13	11%		
	-999.00	2,797.85	17%	4	3%		
	$1,000.00	1,195.00	7%	1	1%		
		$16,770.15	100%	121	100%		
						Avg item price	$138.60
			(Based on keystone pricing)			Avg item profit	$69.30
Sharper Image	-50.00	2,223.60	10%	73	42%		
Jul/Aug	-100.00	3,227.95	15%	41	24%	-100.00	66%
32 of 60 Pages	-200.00	5,088.35	23%	33	19%		
	-500.00	7,129.10	33%	20	12%		
	-999.00	4,047.75	19%	6	3%		
	$1,000.00	0.00	0%	0	0%		
		$21,716.75	100%	173	100%		
						Avg item price	$125.53
			(Based on keystone pricing)			Avg item profit	$62.77
Marine Art of California	-50.00	2,826.95	13%	108	54%		
Nov/Dec	-100.00	3,587.65	17%	46	23%	-100.00	77%
40 Pages	-200.00	3,461.85	16%	23	12%		
	-500.00	4,528.25	21%	15	8%		
	-999.00	4,281.00	20%	6	3%		
	$1,000.00	2,600.00	12%	1	1%		
		$21,285.70	100%	199	100%		
						Avg item price	$106.96
			(Based on keystone pricing)			Avg item profit	$53.48

PROPOSAL FOR LIMITED PARTNERSHIP

Borrow $130,000.00 from private investors as limited partners as outlined:
- $130,000.00 = 45% of Marine Art of California
- $130,000.00 = 20 shares @ $6,500.00 each
- 1 share = 2.25% of Marine Art of California

Limited Partners will own 2.25% of the business for each $6,500.00 invested. The investment will be treated as a loan and paid back at 11% interest over 15 years at approximately $78.00 per month per shareholder.
- 1 share = $78.00 per month for 15 years
- 20 shares = $1,560.00 per month

The General Partner, Robert A. Garcia, will own 55% of the business. The Limited Partners will own 45% of the business for the duration of the partnership.

The duration of the partnership is four years. The General Partner will have the option of buying out the Limited Partners at the end of four years for $3,250.00 for each 2.25% interest. The buyout will not affect the outstanding loan, but the General Partner will provide collateral equal to the loan balance. The value of inventory will be used as that collateral.

Return on Investment (ROI) for each $6,500.00 share:

A.

Principal (15 years)		Interest (15 years)		Buy-out (4 years)		Total (15 years)
$6,500.00	+	$7,540.00	+	$3,250.00	=	$17,290.00

B. PROJECTED Annual Profits (Loss) for 1 share (2.25%):

2001	2002	2003	2004		4 Year Total
($759.53)	$833.00	$11,310.62	$19,097.78	=	$30,481.87

- Principal and Interest (15 years) $14,040.00
- Buy-Out (4 years) $ 3,250.00
- Projected Profits/loss (4 years) $30,481.87

Total Projected Return on Investment **$47,771.87**

or

$$\frac{\text{Net Profits}}{\text{Assets}} = \frac{\$41,271}{\$6,500} = 635\%$$

Contract Highlights

1. **First Right of Refusal.** Limited Partners agree to extend the First Right of Refusal to the General Partner, Robert A. Garcia, in the event the Limited Partner desires to sell, grant, or trade his/her share of the business.
2. **Key Man Insurance:** A life insurance policy valued at $250,000.00 shall be taken out on General Partner, Robert A. Garcia, which is approximately double the amount of the $130,000.00 loan needed. In the event of the death of Robert A Garcia, the payments of the full policy amount will be divided among the Limited Partners equal to the amount invested (e.g., 2.25% investment would equal a 1/20th layout of $12,500.00).
3. **Limited Partner Purchase Program:** General Partner, Robert A. Garcia, agrees to grant **at cost buying privileges** on all product line items for the purchase of three or more shares. For one to two shares, a 45% discount shall be extended. These shall be in effect for the life of the Limited Partnership contract (minimum four years before exercising buy-out option). For remainder of the loan contract (two years), a discount of 35% off retail price will be extended. At the completion of the loan repayment, a **Lifetime Discount of 20%** off retail will be extended to Limited Partners. These privileges are nontransferable.

MARINE ART OF CALIFORNIA

Robert A. Garcia
P.O. Box 10059-251, Newport Beach, CA 92658
714-722-6478

TERMS AND CONDITIONS FOR PARTICIPANTS

1. **Artist/Vendor** agrees to drop ship stocked items within 48 hours of notification to indicated customer with Instructions for Shipping provided by **Marine Art of California**. A time schedule is needed for custom-made pieces such as bronzes, acrylics, or original art works requiring longer delivery. Customer will pay shipping.

2. **Artist/Vendor** agrees to provide 48 hour Federal Express Delivery with added shipping charges for all stocked items.

3. **Artist/Vendor** agrees to use only shipping labels provided by **Marine Art of California.**

4. **Artist/Vendor** guarantees that all items shipped will be free of any business names, logos, addresses, phone numbers, or any other printed material referencing said **Artist/Vendor** (engravings or signatures of **Artist** on pieces not included).

5. Each **Artist** shall include a pre-approved autobiographical sheet with each shipment.

6. **Artist/Vendor** shall include required Certificates of Authenticity on all Limited Edition pieces shipped.

7. Exclusive marketing rights for a selected art item made for **Marine Art of California** shall be covered in a separate contract.

8. **Artist/Vendor** agrees to fax a copy of the shipping manifest or phone in shipping information and date of pickup on same day of transaction.

9. **Artist/Vendor** guarantees insurance coverage for the full retail value.

10. **Artist/Vendor** shall agree to ten-day full refund period beginning from the date customer receives shipped merchandise.

11. **Artist/Vendor** agrees to extend 30 days net payment plan to **Marine Art of California**.

12. **Artist/Vendor** shall not record names nor addresses of buyers for purposes of any sales or marketing contact within 24 months of shipment of the order.

13. In lieu of any participation fee, **Artist/Vendor** agrees to extend a 15% discount on published wholesale prices to **Marine Art of California**. This is justifiable due to advertising, printing, mailing, and target marketing costs and projected volume sales.

14. Each **Artist/Vendor** shall be notified 2 weeks prior to the mailing of the first catalog issue.

15. **Artist/Vendor** agrees to provide goods and services as stated above for a minimum duration of 60 days after publication date.

I hereby acknowledge and accept these terms and conditions set forth by **Marine Art of California.**

_____   _____
(Company)   (Signature and Title of Authorized Representative)

Date
_____   _____
(Print Name and Title)

Powell and Associates
Marketing Consultants

1215 West Imperial Highway • Suite 103 • Brea, CA 92621 • Keith Powell • President Tel: 714-680-8306

Dear Prospective Investor:

It is indeed a pleasure to write a reference letter for Bob A. Garcia.

I have known Bob over the past five years and have found him to be an extremely creative and enthusiastic individual. I have been associated with Bob through several community and civic organizations for which he is an active participant. He has also held office in several of these organizations and has always fulfilled his duties with aplomb.

Bob approached me well over a year ago to meet with him on a regular basis to become a "mentor" of a then dream, now a reality, his company MARINE ART OF CALIFORNIA. Along with several other mentors that he has been seeking advice from, I have had the privilege of reviewing, commenting, and assisting in the development of his plan. He has evidenced great discipline, follow-through, creativity, and a willingness to do his homework on this business venture.

I would most highly recommend he be given the consideration he seeks. Bob has evidenced the qualities needed to succeed in any business venture; those of commitment, dedication, optimism, and follow-through.

If you have any further questions, please do not hesitate to contact me. My direct line is 714-680-8306.

Cordially,

Keith P. Powell
President

DAYNE LANDSCAPING, INC. BUSINESS PLAN

The Dayne Landscaping, Inc. business plan presented on the following pages is based on research for a landscaping and snow removal business in New Hampshire. It was developed by international marketing specialist, Robin Dayne, President of rtd Marketing International, Inc. in Nashua, New Hampshire. Robin wrote this plan specifically for you (the readers of *Anatomy of a Business Plan* and the users of the **AUTOMATE YOUR BUSINESS PLAN** software). It will show you how you can follow the format and write a winning business plan for your own company.

DAYNE LANDSCAPING, INC. SCENARIO

Dayne Landscaping, Inc. is a fictitious one-year old business that provides landscaping and snow removal services in Nashua, New Hampshire. The business had a successful first year (2001) and is planning to expand its customer base and purchase its present site (currently leased) for $375,000. In order to purchase the location, Dayne Landscaping, Inc. will use $100,000 of its own funds and seek a loan for the remaining $275,000.

How Is this Business Plan Organized?

The Organizational and Marketing Plans for Dayne Landscaping, Inc. reflect the company's current status and its plans for future expansion. It is important that the marketing plan provide convincing evidence supporting the feasibility of the loan. The lender needs to know that the company has the ability to increase its market share (and revenues) enough to ensure that it can repay the loan and interest and still maintain its profitability.

Financial documents need to reflect the company's history and project its future. This company has been in business for one year (2001) and is seeking a loan. Therefore, the financial documents need to begin with a summary of financial needs and dispersal of loan funds statement. The next section includes projections and historical financial statements for the 2001 business year. They will show how well the company met its original projections and what its current financial status is. The third area to be covered in financial documents will address the company's projections for the future—projected cash flow, three-year income projection, and projected balance sheet. The closing pages of the financial section contain a financial statement analysis of the company's history and future projections. Utilizing the financial information developed previously, ratios are computed and matched against industry standards.

Of Special Note

I found two things of particular interest in Robin's Dayne Landscaping, Inc. Plan. The Organizational Plan very effectively addressed Personnel in terms of who they are, training, duties, profile, and salaries/benefits. In the Marketing Plan, Robin did not address the full gamut of marketing considerations. However, I liked her treatment of the target market and her example of the marketing promotion of target market #1.

As you proceed with the writing of your own plan, it may help you to look at Dayne Landscaping, Inc.'s business plan to see how Robin handled each of the corresponding sections. Some of the research material has been condensed and we have not included all of the necessary supporting documents. We have also chosen to omit any business or personal financial history that the writer or lender may wish to include in copies of the business plan.

> ***Warning!*** *This plan is to be examined for Ms. Dayne's handling of content only. It has been used as an example in the book and software because it clearly illustrates business plan organization. There is no judgment inferred as to appropriateness or financial potential for lenders or investors. Do not use it as a source of research for your own company.*

I am pleased that Robin Dayne has provided us with this excellent example of a business plan for inclusion in *Anatomy of a Business Plan* and **AUTOMATE YOUR BUSINESS PLAN**. I thank Robin for being so generous and for allowing us to share her interpretation of business planning with readers.

Robin Dayne is an international marketing consultant who specializes in creating increased revenues through Customer Base Management™. If you would like to contact Robin for information on her services, you can write to her at: rtd Marketing International, Inc., 81 Walden Pond Drive, Nashua, New Hampshire 03060 Telephone 603-880-0136.

DAYNE LANDSCAPING, INC.

22 San Carlos Dr.
Nashua, New Hampshire 03060
603-335-8200

Robin T. Dayne, President
22 San Carlos Dr.
Nashua, NH 03060
603-335-8200

Joe Sanborn, Vice-President
56 Gingham St.
Nashua, NH 03990
603-446-9870

Fred Ryan, Treasurer
98 Canon St.
Nashua, NH 06223
603-883-0938

Trudy St. George, Secretary
31 Mill St.
Nashua, NH 08876
603-595-3982

Business Plan Prepared January 2002
by the Corporate Officers

(Private and Confidential)

Copy 1 of 5

TABLE OF CONTENTS

* Note: *We have included only part of the supporting documents in this sample business plan.*

DAYNE LANDSCAPING, INC.

Executive Summary

Dayne Landscaping, Inc. is a one-year-old landscaping and snow-removal company established in January of 2001. The company is located at 22 San Carlos Ave., Nashua, New Hampshire. The currently leased location is available for sale at $375,000. Dayne Landscaping, Inc. has $100,000 to invest and is seeking a $275,000 loan to complete the purchase. By owning the facility, the company can increase its equity for an amount equivalent to the current rental expense.

Dayne Landscaping has established its niche in the landscaping and snow removal business during 2001. Projections for 2002 show that it is reasonable to expect expansion of customer base to new markets and territories. Cash flow projections support the assumption that the company will have sufficient funds to purchase equipment and hire additional employees to support implementation of the marketing programs.

Management. Dayne Landscaping is managed by Robin Dayne. She has five years of prior experience in the landscaping business, working for a local competitor. Previously she worked in a variety of service industries selling and marketing products and services. Robin has established a strong team of very dedicated people who love to work with nature. As manager her role is to identify new business, develop and implement marketing activities, and negotiate and close new contracts.

Current Market. Today the business services 100 residential accounts, 15 small business accounts, and currently no large corporate accounts. The services include: landscaping and design, lawn care and maintenance, snow plowing and removal, and tree maintenance and removal. The success of the company has been a direct result of our ability to provide personal service at a competitive rate, thus creating a dedicated customer base. Currently, the average cost for lawn maintenance of a residential home is $25 to $30 per hour, small business accounts $50 to $100 per hour, and large corporate accounts will be negotiated on a per contract basis. Due to the seasonal changes in New Hampshire, snow removal becomes an important part of the business to maintain the company's revenues during the slower winter months of December, January, February, and March.

Projected Market. The projected growth rate for the landscaping industry, based the previous years is 28%. We will be expanding our business with new equipment, marketing, and additional employees to meet and exceed that demand. We are expecting to grow our customer base by 50% based on our first year's track record, our unique offering, and planned marketing activities.

Loan Repayment. The $275,000 in loan funds will be required for April 2002 closing. Repayment of the 15-year loan, plus interest, can begin promptly in May. Early retirement of the loan is anticipated, possibly by the end of tax year 2007. In addition to the property and facility, itself, the loan can further be secured by the owner's home equity, which is currently $167,000.

DAYNE LANDSCAPING, INC.

Part I. The Organizational Plan

Summary Description of the Business

Dayne Landscaping, Inc., established in January 2001 as a corporation, handles landscaping, lawn maintenance, and snow removal of residential homes and small businesses in New Hampshire. It began with 20 residential accounts and two small business accounts. As of January 2002, the company has grown to 100 residential accounts and 15 small business accounts, totaling $750,000 in revenue, a growth of 520%.

Mission

The company has been very successful due to the high standard of service and care provided to the customer and because of its reputation for quick response times during snow storms.

Business Model

The company also offers a unique service of oriental garden design landscaping, the only one in the tri-state area. Today that service is offered in New Hampshire only. Twenty-five of the 115 accounts have contracted for these unique gardens. Our plan is to open markets in Connecticut and Massachusetts over the next three years. It is important to note that these gardens are not only a unique service; they are also our premium high ticket service and provide a larger profit margin, directly impacting the company's bottom line.

Strategy

The company's growth strategy is to buy out smaller landscaping companies as we expand the business in to Massachusetts and Connecticut and increase our large corporate accounts for snow removal. Currently, with local corporations downsizing, out-sourcing these services to local businesses has become prevalent.

Facility

The company currently leases a 20,000-square foot area, which includes a 4,000-square foot building for the main office, a large attached garage for trucks, maintenance equipment, and supplies, two large lots, one fenced in for parking equipment, plows, flatbeds, and storage of trees, shrubs, and plants.

Products and Services

Dayne Landscaping offers three categories of landscaping services to three varieties of customers. The customers consist of residential homes, small businesses, and large corporations. Each group has the option of purchasing the same types of services. Lawn care includes mowing, weeding, planting, re-sod, pest control, and tree and shrub maintenance. Customized landscape design can be purchased on a contract basis, including specialties in oriental gardens, tree sculpture, and complete landscape design. The third service offered is snow plowing and removal.

All the plantings are high quality and purchased from a local nursery that has been in the business for over 35 years. We also have an arrangement to use the nursery as a consultant when there is a need for it.

Customer Profiles

The following are descriptions of the three types of customer and the services that are typically purchased by each.

1. **Residential homeowners.** In mid- to high-income areas, residential homeowners typically purchase lawn care that consists of mowing, weeding, pest control, and tree/shrub maintenance. There are two people assigned per job: two part-time college students, overseen by a supervisor. This job can take an average of two hours to complete. Each home receives a contract for two visits per month unless there is a special need, which is an additional cost to the basic contract. These lawn contacts run from March through November. Additionally, 50% of the residential customers also purchase winter snow removal for their driveways, and these customers are charged a minimal flat fee and a per call fee, with an upfront deposit to insure they get priority service.

2. **Small business account or office park.** This is the second type of customer. They typically consist of banks or small office buildings and require shrub and landscaping care, weed and pest control, and minimal lawn mowing. The average time required to service this type of account is three to four hours with one supervisor and two or three part-time employees. All the small business accounts have a contract for snow removal. A predetermined amount for the contract is negotiated in October for the four months November through February, with a per call fee for the month of March, which can have unpredictable snow storms. These customers require quick response times and are charged for that level of service, as they need to accommodate their own customers during business hours.

3. **Large corporate account or condo complex.** This third type of customer requires the same services as the small corporate account, but many more hours, employees, and equipment. Additionally, included in their lawn maintenance is routine watering. The accounts that are being targeted will require an average of one week of maintenance per month. This is the area to be expanded over the next three years. To support the watering needed every other day during the summer months, one part-time worker is hired and dedicated to watering for every two companies. Corporate account contracts are negotiated individually, and range from $60K to $350K per year depending on the amount of square footage and specific landscaping requirements. These customers also require immediate response times, especially in winter during the snow season.

Legal Structure

Dayne Landscaping, Inc. is a corporation filed under the same name. The legal and financial advisors recommended a corporation as the most efficient structure based on the plan to purchase pre-existing small landscaping companies in the tri-state area over the next two years. There have been 300 shares of stock applied for, and 100 issued to the sole shareholder (President) at the time of incorporation. This will leave the flexibility of having additional shares on hand should we need to use them in negotiations of larger landscaping company buy-outs.

Corporate Officers

The corporate officers are: Robin Dayne, President

Bob Sanborn, Vice President and Accountant

(see résumés in   Fred Ryan, Treasurer

Supporting Documents)   Trudy St. George, Secretary and Legal Counsel

The officers of the company determine the direction of the corporation through its board meetings. Additionally, there is an incentive plan for board members to acquire company stock based on set profit goals.

It should be noted that the President is the only officer working in the day-to-day business. All other officers interact at the monthly board meetings as well as on an "as needed" basis. This allows the company to have access to expertise and advice at large cost savings, which has a direct impact on the bottom line and growth of the company.

Management and Personnel

Management

At present, Robin Dayne is the President and sole shareholder in Dayne Landscaping, Inc. Robin has five prior years of experience in the landscaping business, working for a local competitor. Previously she worked in a variety of service industries selling and marketing products and services.

Dayne Landscaping, Inc. has been incorporated for almost one year, realizing a 520% growth rate between January to November. The growth rate is attributed to high standards set for customer service. Many customers shifted from the prior company because of their loyalty to Robin Dayne. She has set up an incentive plan for her employees that rewards them for outstanding customer service, based on year-end survey results, or when contracts are renewed or new business is obtained.

Under Ms. Dayne's management, a strong team of very dedicated people who love to work with nature has been formed. As manager her role is to identify new business, develop and implement marketing activities, and negotiate and close new contracts.

The four supervisors manage the accounts and part-time workers. They also determine staffing and equipment needed to maintain the account. There are also two design specialists, one of which is specifically trained in oriental garden design and tree topiaries.

Personnel

There are three full-time office employees—one office manager and two administrative assistants. Four supervisors and two design specialists work in the field. The remainder are part-time workers, numbering from 4 to 25 or more, depending on the time of the year and work load.

1. Owner-President. 2001 Guaranteed Salary $65,000 with yearly increases justified by profitability.
2. Design Specialists. 2 in 2002; Salaries @ $25,000 + 5% commission on new business contracts.
3. Four Supervisors. Salaries @ $15,000 + 3% bonus per contract for excellent year-end customer surveys.
4. Office Manager. Salary @ $22,000 per year.
5. Administrative Assistants. One in 2001, two in 2002: Salaries @ $15,000 per year.
6. Part-time workers. 5-25 @ $7 per hour; (more added as volume increases).

Training

All employees receive training from the President and the Supervisor in the following areas:

Given by the President
    a. Company policies and procedures regarding the customers and company standards
    b. Landscaping orientation at the time they are hired
    c. Liability and safety procedures
    d. Equipment care and theft policies

Given by the Supervisors
    a. Overview of each account assignment
    b. Equipment assignment and training—operation of mowers, tools, and supplies
    c. Chemicals precautions

Personnel Duties
1. **President/Owner**
    a. Sets company policies and trains all new employees
    b. Solicits, interviews, and hires new employees
    c. Assigns accounts to supervisors
    d. Negotiates new and large contracts
    e. Approves the purchases of equipment and supplies
    f. Handles customer service issues that can not be satisfied by supervisors
    g. Reviews and signs all checks
    h. Follows up on supervisor sales leads

2. **Four Supervisors—report to the President**
    a. Manages on average 25 residential accounts and four small business accounts
    b. Will be managing one to two large corporate accounts
    c. Responsible for training part-time help on account profiles and equipment
    d. Forecasts supplies needed for each account
    e. Forecasts and manages work schedules
    f. Conducts second round of interviews of part-timers and approves
    g. Handles account problems related to service and quality issues
    h. Solicits new business leads to president
    i. Responsibility for inventory and equipment assigned to their team

3. **Office Manager—reports to the President**
   a. Manages account scheduling
   b. Supports supervisors—back-up supplies misc.
   c. Takes account calls and passes to supervisors
   d. Performs yearly customer survey
   e. Answers phone
   f. Dispatches and is in "beeper" contact with supervisors
   g. Assigns and maintains equipment for supervisors

4. **Administrative Assistant—reports to the President**
   a. Responsible for bookkeeping functions of:
      - Daily sales reconciliation
      - Accounts receivable and accounts payable
      - Payroll
      - General ledger
   b. Computer typing—60 WPM, with software knowledge - WP/Excel/D-Base
   c. Ten-key adding machine
   d. Access to safe
   e. Tracks orders placed for equipment and supplies

5. **Part-time Employees—report to the Supervisor**
   a. Assigned to work specific accounts
   b. Mows, weeds, does manual labor
   c. Identifies any problems
   d. Follows instructions from supervisor
   f. Manages inventory of supplies

Employee Profile

All employees must be:
   a. Hard working and neat in appearance
   b. Like working outdoors
   c. Good communicators
   d. Team workers
   e. Educated for full-time work with a minimum high school degree, or in college
   f. Able to follow directives and be a quick learner
   g. Dedicated to doing an outstanding job
   h. Responsible, regarding safety

Accounting and Legal

Accounting

All bookkeeping is kept on computer on a regular basis by the Administrative Assistant on the software "QuickBooks Pro" from Intuit. At the end of the year the files are printed and passed to the accountant Bob Sanborn, CPA who has been a personal friend for many years and has 35 years experience as a CPA. His fees are reasonable and there is a high level of trust in his input to the business as he is the Vice President for the corporation as well.

The customer base and prospect database is kept on the software ACT from Contact Software International, that allows us to keep precise timelines of our scheduling and manage our accounts accurately. Microsoft Office allows us to perform word processing, develop customized spreadsheets, and create proposals and presentations to larger accounts. All the above programs are off-the-shelf and easy to get support for at very reasonable prices.

Legal

All contracts and other legal matters are handled by Trudy St. George, corporate officer and board member. Trudy is the senior partner of a 20-year old law firm specializing in business contracting.

Insurance

Carrier: Primercia   **Agent:** Sam Bickford
111 Shoe St, Manchester, New Hampshire

Type of Insurance:

Business/personal	600,000
Deductible	4,000
Liability	1,000,000
Equipment	40,000
Deductible	500
Liability	2,000,000
Vehicles	150,000
Deductible	1,000
Liability	1,000,000
Annual Premium	**$8,000**
Monthly Premium	670
Workers' Compensation	1.43 per/1k gross Payroll

Security

Problem situations to be considered and protective measures to be taken:

1. **Internal theft—Employee Dishonesty**
   a. Shoplifting of supplies. Four closed circuit cameras in garage recording 24 hours
   b. Cash theft. Petty cash limit of $600. Daily receipt drop-off to bank of all receivable
   c. Falsifying signatures. All checks signed by president at the end of the day
   d. Employee orientation. To reduce theft and stress security procedures
   e. Monthly Inventory. Responsibility of the supervisors

2. **External theft**
   a. Walk-in theft. Cameras at each doorway exits (2)
   b. Cameras in garage and parking area, and fenced in plant lot
   c. Break-in theft/robbery. Alarms set nightly and connected directly to local police station

DAYNE LANDSCAPING, INC.

Part II. Marketing Plan

Author Note: *The Marketing Plan for Dayne Landscaping, Inc. focuses on three of the basic elements presented in our marketing chapter for a smaller business—Market Analysis (Target Markets and Competition), Sales Strategy, and Advertising. This marketing plan has a special strength in the target marketing area in that the company planned its strategy for each of its market segments by evaluating the target in terms of who they are, what the company will do to approach the target, when the campaign will take place, and where the campaign will be positioned. Also, the Target Market Worksheet for Target #1 at the end of this section is a great tool for analyzing and planning your own target marketing.*

It is my suggestion that the marketing plan for your company should address the components in a way that more closely follows the marketing plan outline in Chapter 5. However, I think this marketing plan may provide you with an organized means for developing your strategy for individual market segments.

Target Markets with Sales Strategies

Target #1

Large Corporate Facilities and Condominiums

Who. Corporations that are "outsourcing" the landscaping maintenance of their facilities to outside vendors, and condominium complexes. There are approximately 75 accounts that are potential customers within a 50-mile radius. Our goal is to secure five in 2002.

What. Telemarket for background information, and send a direct mail with telemarketing follow-up. Describe landscaping, lawn maintenance, pest control, and all other landscaping services, such as tree removal and replacement, landscaping design and care, and snow plowing and removal from their parking lots and driveways. Provide a guarantee for the services and show competitive comparison pricing from local companies.

When. Begin January to determine the bidding process and RFP schedule to determine the timing of proposals. Call each account to determine the timing and arrange for an on-site inspection, to evaluate the amount of work needed and any special needs to develop an estimate. If possible inquire what the previous years costs were and if the customer was satisfied with the work of their current landscaper.

Where. Position joint services with local garden stores for promotions and advertising.

Target #2
Small Businesses or Office Parks

Who. All small businesses and office parks with outdoor grounds that want to save money or are unhappy with their present landscaping company. In the 50-mile radius there are approximately 125 accounts that are potential customers. Our goal is to add 15 new contracts in this category in 2002.

What. Telemarket for background information and send a direct mail with telemarketing follow-up. Describe all the same landscaping and snow plowing services, referencing existing satisfied customers. Provide a guarantee for services rendered, show the cost savings using Dayne Landscaping, Inc., and develop a plan for continued snow and landscape maintenance. Offer the company's quality guarantee and comparison chart of competitive pricing.

When. Begin January to determine when existing contracts expire and provide information on the company and services. Request an on-site evaluation to determine costs and uncover any problem areas needing work.

Where. Position joint services with local garden stores for promotions and advertising. Advertise in the local papers, Yellow Pages, and Business-to-Business Directory.

Target #3
Residential Homes

Who. Target all residential homes in the 50-mile radius that are in mid to high income areas and over three-plus acres. Contact all existing customers with satisfaction survey, and solicit at the same time for:

  a. Additional business—renew contracts for next year.
  b. New customers—referrals.

What. Develop and send company brochure that targets the residential homes supplying them with information on all services offered by Dayne Landscaping, Inc. with price comparisons.

When. Develop brochure in January and mail in February prior to spring and summer contracts. Follow-up with existing customers and potential customers in September for the snow plowing contracts.

Where. Position joint services with local garden stores for promotions and advertising.

Competition

Dayne Landscaping, Inc. currently has two competitors in the local area: The Garden Shop and Landscaping Plus. While they have been in the New Hampshire area for several years, they are family-owned businesses that have a limited number of clients and the same number of accounts year after year. They also have no type of Landscaping specialty. Only the Garden Shop offers snow removal. Landscaping Plus has only three snow plows that are active during the winter months.

Methods of Distribution

Dayne Landscaping sells directly to the customer, and is primarily a service business, with the exception of selling the landscaping plants and shrubs, which come from a local nursery wholesaler.

Advertising Strategy

Paid Advertising

We currently participate in several forms of advertising.

1. **Newspaper ads**. All ad copy is identical and includes information required by the newspaper.

   a. **Ad information**:
      1. Ad size. The ad is two columns by three inches.
      2. Timing. Monthly
      3. Section. Garden section

   b. **Ad location, contact and fees:**

Nashua Telegraph	Contact: Mark Potts
P.O. Box 1008	Circulation: 50,000
Nashua, NH 03061-1008	Fee: $126.00
Manchester Union Leader	Contact: Ken Coose
100 William Loeb Drive	Circulation: 125,000
Manchester, NH 03109	Fee: $171.99
Lowell Sun	Contact: Carol McCabe
15 Kearney Square	Circulation; 75,000
Lowell, MA 01852-1996	Fee: $153.00
Hartford Daily News	Contact: Sue Betz
100 Main St.	Circulation: 150,000
Hartford, CT 10002	Fee: $190.00

2. **Phone books—Yellow pages and directories.**

   a. **NYNEX Phone Book - Yellow Pages**
     Ad Information:

Coverage:	So. NH area
Yearly Fee:	$650.00
Ad Size:	¼ page
Renewal date:	February 1st
Contact:	Sam Moore

   b. **Business to Business Directory (NH only)**
     Ad Information

Coverage:	All NH
Yearly Fee:	$250.00
Ad Size:	¼ page
Renewal Date:	January 1st
Contact:	Karl Hess

3. **Local Cable Channels**

   a. **Channel 13—Local Nashua station reaching all of Southern New Hampshire**
     Ad Information:

Length of ad "spot":	60 seconds
Development costs:	$250.00 (one time fee)
Length of campaign:	3 months
Runs per month:	Three times per day, everyday
Cost for 3 mos.:	$300
Total campaign cost:	**$550**

   b. **Weather Channel "tag line"—reaching 400,000 homes**
     Ad Information:

Length of ad "spot":	15 seconds
Development costs:	$100 (one time fee)
Length of campaign:	3 months
Runs per month:	20 times per day, everyday
Cost for 3 months:	$900
Total campaign cost:	**$1,000**

Direct Mail

Note: There was no direct mail done in the first year of business. With the development of the marketing plan, two direct mail pieces will need to be developed to target our three potential customer bases for 2002 (see detailed plan of this activity).

Direct mail #1

Designed for: Target market #1—large corporations and condominiums
Target market #2—small business and office parks.

Creative Strategy: Design needs to be glossy, appropriate for corporate, professional environment.

Highlight: Customer service—testimonials
Quick response time
All services
Guarantee
Free evaluation

Direct mail #2

Designed for: Target market #3—residential homes

Creative Strategy: Design should be a tri-fold brochure "self-mailer" (no envelope required). Direct highlights for the homeowner.

Highlight: Customer service—testimonials
Quick response time
All services
Guarantee
Free evaluation

Community Involvement

Member of the Chamber of Commerce in Nashua. Board Member of the local Garden Club, involved with teaching kids about plants and nature, as well as the "Beautification of Nashua" program.

Note: *In this sample plan, we have included the promotion for target market #1 only. All target markets would have their own separate plan using the same format.*

Worksheet for Individual Marketing Promotion

Target Market #1: Large Corporate or Condo Landscaping   **Date:** 02/02

Program Name: Corporate Promo   **Media:** Direct Mail and Telemarketing

Program Objectives:

- Generate a minimum of $500k in additional revenue in 2002
- Increase corporate account base by five new accounts
- Establish Dayne Landscaping as a landscaping provider to large corporations and condominiums

Audience

Direct Mail

> **Who.** The 70 identified accounts consisting of condominiums and large corporations.

> **What.** Send direct mail (company brochure) to corporate and condo contacts listing services and benefits of Dayne Landscaping. Position money-back guarantee as an added promotion.

> **Where.** In the New Hampshire and Massachusetts areas (50-mile radius).

> **When.** Drop in mail by mid-January.

Telemarketing (prior to mailing)

> **Who.** Call all accounts to identify landscaping contact in the large corporation, or property management company of the condominium.

> **What.** Find out the contract renewal dates and bid submission dates for each prospect.

> **When.** Make phone calls first two weeks of January.

> **Where.** NA

Telemarketing (post direct mail)

> **Who.** Call all contacts and confirm bid dates

> **What.** Ask if they received the direct mail and offer a free landscaping consultation.

> **When.** Calling begins 5 to 8 working days after the direct mail is received.

> **Where.** NA

List Source

The list was taken from the library in the "New Hampshire Corporate Directory" and "Massachusetts Corporate Directory" as well as the Realty listing of Condominiums.

Creative Strategy for Direct Mail

- Position Dayne Landscaping, Inc. as a leader in quality service
- Position guarantee
- Leverage existing customer base with success stories
- Position against the competition
- Position "free" consulting offer
- The telemarketing call back in a week

Creative Strategy for Telemarketing

- Develop script with the same messages as the direct mail will have
- If possible position—Company and Promotional offer

Components of mailing: Tri-fold brochure components

- Self-mailer, with reply card
- Address hand written on the backside

Timing

Premailing Telemarketing

% Called	Location	Call dates
50%	New Hampshire	1/2–1/9
50%	Massachusetts	1/9–1/18

Direct Mail

% Mailed	Location	Mail date
50%	New Hampshire	Jan. 1/12
50%	Massachusetts	Jan. 1/19

Post-Mailing Telemarketing

% Called	Location	Call dates
50%	New Hampshire	1/22
50%	Massachusetts	1/29

Call to action: Reply card to be sent to office or an 800 number can be called.

Lead Criteria

"Hot" leads are classified as anyone getting a proposal, evaluation, or call back from the mailing or telemarketing. They have the potential of closing in 2002.

"Warm" leads are any accounts that are interested and cannot do anything until 2003 due to their current contracts.

"Cold" leads are those accounts who are not interested at all, and have no revenue potential in the future.

Training

Employees in the field will be given an overview of the entire promotion to prepare them for customers asking questions, while on the job.

Office staff will receive training and instructions on how to answer the phone and track the responses from the #800 and mailer. They will also be assisting on the pre and post telemarketing activities.

Expenses will not exceed $3,000 for the entire promotion.

Measurement

Revenue Goal	500k
Expenses	3K
Total # (list)	70
# of responses	TBD
# of leads	TBD
Cost per response	TBD
Cost per lead	TBD
Revenue/expense ratio	TBD

*TBD = To be determined at the end of the program.

Assumptions

- Average value per contract = 100K
- Response rate = 2.0% on the direct mail and 15 to 20% on the telemarketing or 1.5 responses on the direct mail, and 10 to 14 on the telemarketing.
- "Hot" lead rate = 0.5% on the direct mail and 5 to 7% on the telemarketing or 3.5 leads on the direct mail and 3.5 to 5 leads on the telemarketing

Lead Tracking Process

- All direct mail responses will be tracked
- All phone calls will be logged when responding on the 800 number.
- All regular calls will be screened "are you calling regarding our direct mail promotion?"

Program review: 30 days after last telemarketing follow-up call.

DAYNE LANDSCAPING, INC.

Part III. Financial Documents

Sources and Uses of Loan Funds

2001 Financial Statements (Projected and Historical)

2002 Financial Projections

Financial Statement Analysis

Business Plan Financial Assumptions

Summary of Financial Needs

I. Dayne Landscaping, Inc. is seeking a loan to increase its equity capital through real estate investment:

   A. By purchasing the buildings currently being leased by the company.

   B. By purchasing the parcel of land on which the buildings now stand.

II. Dayne Landscaping, Inc. has $100,000 in cash to invest. An additional amount of $275,000 in loan funds is needed to complete the purchase.

Loan Fund Dispersal Statement

1. Dispersal of Loan Funds

Dayne Landscaping, Inc. will utilize the anticipated loan in the amount of $275,000 to purchase the facility (land and buildings) that it currently leases. The full purchase price is $375,000. The present owner of the premises is John S. Strykker. The parcel and accompanying buildings located at 22 San Carlos Drive in Nashua, New Hampshire are currently owned by John S. Strykker.

2. Back-Up Statement

   a. The land is currently appraised at $200,000. Attached buildings appraise at $175,000. The owner, Mr. John S. Strykker, is agreeable to close of escrow on or about April 15, 2002.

   b. Dayne Landscaping, Inc. has appropriated $100,000 in retained earnings to be used as a capital investment in the facility. The additional $275,000 in loan funds will make up the full purchase amount of $375,000.

   c. The buildings sit on a 20,000-square-foot parcel of land, centrally located in Nashua, New Hampshire. The land is currently appraised at $200,000 and the buildings at $175,000. There are two large lots. One is fenced in for parking equipment and also serves as a storage area for trees, shrubs, and plants. There is a 4,000-square-foot building that serves as the main office and a large attached garage to house trucks, maintenance equipment, and supplies.

   d. The $275,000 in loan funds are needed by April 1st in order to proceed with escrow. Loan repayment can begin promptly on May 1st for a 15-year period. The company has a strong cash flow and a rapidly-growing market. Early payoff is anticipated.

   e. Dayne Landscaping is currently paying $2,850 in monthly rental expense. Payments on the anticipated $275,000, 15-year loan @ 9% would amount to $2,789. Purchase of the land and buildings will enable Dayne Landscaping, with no additional expense, to repay the loan plus interest and to divert the current rental expense into equity growth.

2001 Cash Flow Statement
One-Year Cash Flow Projection and Cash Flow History
Dayne Landscaping, Inc.

For the Year 2001	Projected for: 2001	Historical for: 2001
BEGINNING CASH BALANCE (January 1, 2001)	0	0
CASH RECEIPTS		
A. Sales/revenues	**$573,000**	**$777,864**
1. Landscaping — residential	185,000	216,000
2. Landscaping — small business	65,000	160,700
3. Landscaping — customized	174,000	199,374
4. Snow removal — residential	15,000	18,250
5. Snow removal — small business	125,000	167,100
6. 5% Snow removal contracts	5,000	8,500
7. Sale of miscellaneous accessories	4,000	7,940
B. Receivables	0	0
C. Interest income	1,250	1,250
D. Sale of long-term assets	0	0
TOTAL CASH AVAILABLE	**$574,250**	**$779,114**
CASH PAYMENTS		
A. Cost of goods to be sold		
1. Fertilizer	20,000	19,000
2. Pesticide	10,000	11,000
3. Plants/shrubs	18,000	23,000
4. Salt/sand	5,000	8,030
5. Seed	45,000	45,000
Total cost of goods	**$98,000**	**$106,030**
B. Variable expenses (selling)		
1. Design specialist salary/payroll taxes	20,000	20,000
2. Machinery, tools, equipment	11,500	11,000
3. Marketing	5,411	5,400
4. Part-time worker salaries/payroll taxes	150,000	182,000
5. Sales bonuses	1,500	2,000
6. Sales commissions	8,000	10,800
7. Supervisor salaries/payroll taxes	60,000	60,000
8. Travel expense	9,500	10,400
9. Miscellaneous selling expense	1,000	1,200
Total variable expenses	**$266,911**	**$302,800**
C. Fixed expenses (administrative)		
1. Administrative fees (legal/accounting)	3,050	3,050
2. Insurance (liability, casualty, fire, theft)	11,600	11,600
3. Licenses and permits	4,200	4,200
4. Office equipment	5,700	7,700
5. Office salaries/payroll taxes	42,000	42,000
6. Owner's guaranteed payment	57,000	65,000
7. Rent expense + security deposit	39,900	39,900
8. Utilities	4,320	4,320
9. Miscellaneous administrative expense	200	500
Total fixed expenses	**$167,970**	**$178,270**
D. Interest expense	1,386	5,535
E. Federal and state income tax	7,196	65,220
F. Other uses	0	0
G. Long-term asset payments	17,334	15,081
H. Loan payments	0	0
I. Capital distributions	0	0
TOTAL CASH PAID OUT	**$558,797**	**$672,936**
CASH BALANCE/DEFICIENCY	15,453	106,178
LOANS TO BE RECEIVED	0	0
CAPITAL CONTRIBUTION	25,000	25,000
ENDING CASH BALANCE (December 31, 2001)	**$40,453**	**$131,178**

2001 Quarterly Budget Analysis
Dayne Landscaping, Inc.

For the Quarter Ending: December 31, 2001

BUDGET ITEM	THIS QUARTER			YEAR-TO-DATE		
	Budget	Actual	Variation	Budget	Actual	Variation
SALES/REVENUES	**95,900**	**121,050**	**25,150**	**573,000**	**777,864**	**204,864**
Landscaping — residential	17,800	24,000	6,200	185,000	216,000	31,000
Landscaping — small business	9,600	14,000	4,400	65,000	160,700	95,700
Landscaping — customized	0	0	0	174,000	199,374	25,374
Snow removal — residential	4,200	3,950	(250)	15,000	18,250	3,250
Snow removal — small business	58,300	70,300	12,000	125,000	167,100	42,100
5% Snow removal contracts	6,000	8,500	2,500	5,000	8,500	3,500
Miscellaneous accessories	0	300	300	4,000	7,940	3,940
Less cost of goods	**3,520**	**(1,000)**	**4,520**	**98,000**	**101,030**	**(3,030)**
a. Fertilizer	0	0	0	20,000	19,000	1,000
b. Pesticide	0	0	0	10,000	11,000	(1,000)
c. Plants/shrubs	0	0	0	18,000	23,000	(5,000)
d. Salt/sand	3,520	4,000	(480)	5,000	8,030	(3,030)
e. Seed	0	0	0	45,000	45,000	0
Less ending inventory (12/31)	0	5,000	0	0	5,000	(5,000)
GROSS PROFITS	**92,380**	**122,050**	**29,670**	**475,000**	**676,834**	**201,834**
VARIABLE EXPENSES						
a. Design specialist salary/taxes	5,000	2,500	2,500	20,000	20,000	0
b. Machinery, tools, equipment	0	0	0	11,500	11,000	500
c. Marketing	1,350	1,000	350	5,411	5,400	11
d. Part-time worker salaries/taxes	18,700	33,000	(14,300)	150,000	182,000	(32,000)
e. Sales bonuses	0	0	0	1,500	2,000	(500)
f. Sales commission	1,450	1,750	(300)	8,000	10,800	(2,800)
g. Supervisor salaries/payroll taxes	15,000	15,000	0	60,000	60,000	0
h. Travel expense	2,000	1,600	400	9,500	10,400	(900)
i. Miscellaneous variable expense	0	0	0	1,000	1,200	(200)
j. Depreciation expense	3,801	3,801	0	15,200	15,200	0
FIXED EXPENSES						
a. Administration fees—legal/acct.	500	501	(1)	3,050	3,050	0
b. Insurance (liability, casualty, fire, theft)	2,900	2,898	2	11,600	11,600	0
c. Licenses and permits	1,050	0	1,050	4,200	4,200	0
d. Office equipment	300	400	(100)	5,700	7,700	(2,000)
e. Office salaries/taxes	10,500	10,500	0	42,000	42,000	0
f. Owner's guaranteed payment	16,250	16,248	2	65,000	65,000	0
g. Rent expense + security deposit	8,550	8,550	0	39,900	39,900	0
h. Utilities	1,080	1,080	0	4,320	4,320	0
i. Miscellaneous fixed expense	0	0	0	200	500	(300)
NET INCOME FROM OPERATIONS	**3,949**	**23,222**	**16,773**	**16,919**	**180,564**	**163,645**
INTEREST INCOME	347	312	(35)	1,250	1,250	0
INTEREST EXPENSE	2,400	348	(2,052)	1,386	5,535	4,149
NET PROFIT (Pretax)	**1,896**	**23,186**	**21,290**	**16,783**	**176,279**	**159,496**
TAXES (federal and state)	1,282	12,549	(11,267)	7,196	65,220	(58,024)
NET PROFIT (After Tax)	**614**	**10,637**	**10,023**	**9,587**	**111,059**	**101,472**

NON-INCOME STATEMENT ITEMS

	Budget	Actual	Variation	Budget	Actual	Variation
1. Long-term asset repayments	4,335	3,883	452	17,333	15,081	2,252
2. Loan repayments	0	0	0	0	0	0
3. Dividend payments	0	0	0	0	0	0
4. Capital contribution	0	0	0	25,000	25,000	0
5. Inventory assets	0	5,000	(5,000)	0	5,000	(5,000)

BUDGET DEVIATIONS	This Quarter		Year-to-Date	
1. Income statement items:	$	10,023	$	101,472
2. Nonincome statement items:	$	(4,548)	$	(2,748)
3. Total deviation	**$**	**5,475**	**$**	**98,724**

2001 Profit & Loss (Income) Statement
Dayne Landscaping, Inc.
Page 1 (January thru June + 6-Month Totals)

For the Year: 2001

	Jan	Feb	Mar	Apr	May	Jun	6-MONTH TOTALS AMOUNT	% of Total Revenues PERCENT
INCOME								
1. Sales/revenues	**71,200**	**39,700**	**139,150**	**90,230**	**77,080**	**71,250**	**488,610**	**100.00%**
Landscaping — residential	0	0	55,000	33,000	28,000	22,000	138,000	28.24%
Landscaping — small business	0	0	37,000	23,000	22,000	22,000	104,000	21.28%
Landscaping — customized	0	0	46,000	32,000	26,000	26,250	130,250	26.66%
Snow removal — residential	8,250	5,550	500	0	0	0	14,300	2.93%
Snow removal — small business	62,850	33,950	0	0	0	0	96,800	19.81%
Miscellaneous accessories	100	200	650	2,230	1,080	1,000	5,260	1.08%
5% Snow removal contracts	0	0	0	0	0	0	0	0.00%
2. Cost of goods to be sold	**2,530**	**500**	**30,800**	**17,700**	**21,000**	**18,500**	**91,030**	**18.63%**
a. Beginning inventory	0	0	0	0	0	0	0	0.00%
b. Purchases	2,530	500	30,800	17,700	21,000	18,500	91,030	18.63%
(1) Fertilizer	0	0	7,000	0	6,000	0	13,000	2.66%
(2) Pesticide	0	0	0	3,500	0	4,500	8,000	1.64%
(3) Plants/Shrubs	0	0	8,800	6,200	5,000	2,000	22,000	4.50%
(4) Salt/Sand	2,530	500	0	0	0	0	3,030	0.62%
(5) Seed	0	0	15,000	8,000	10,000	12,000	45,000	9.21%
c. C.O.G. Available for sale	2,530	500	30,800	17,700	21,000	18,500	91,030	18.63%
d. Less ending inventory	0	0	0	0	0	0	0	0.00%
3. GROSS PROFIT	**68,670**	**39,200**	**108,350**	**72,530**	**56,080**	**52,750**	**397,580**	**81.37%**
EXPENSES								
1. Variable (selling) expenses								
a. Design specialist salary	0	0	2,500	2,500	2,500	2,500	10,000	2.05%
b. Machinery, hand tools, equip.	5,000	0	0	2,000	0	2,000	9,000	1.84%
c. Marketing	315	650	925	650	350	315	3,205	0.66%
d. Part-time worker salaries	12,000	9,000	12,000	12,500	13,000	13,750	72,250	14.79%
e. Sales bonuses	0	0	500	500	500	500	2,000	0.41%
f. Sales commission	600	300	800	2,100	1,000	1,500	6,300	1.29%
g. Supervisor salaries	5,000	5,000	5,000	5,000	5,000	5,000	30,000	6.14%
h. Travel expense	800	700	1,100	1,900	1,150	1,050	6,700	1.37%
i. Miscellaneous selling expense	200	100	250	350	0	0	900	0.18%
j. Depreciation (variable assets)	1,266	1,266	1,266	1,266	1,267	1,267	7,598	1.56%
Total Variable Expenses	**25,181**	**17,016**	**24,341**	**28,766**	**24,767**	**27,882**	**147,953**	**28.23%**
1. Fixed (Administrative) Expenses								
a. Admin. fees — legal/acct.	1,216	166	167	166	167	166	2,048	0.42%
b. Insurance (liab, cas, fire, theft)	967	967	967	967	967	967	5,802	1.19%
c. Licenses and permits	100	200	1,250	2,500	150	0	4,200	0.86%
d. Machinery, tools, equipment	1,500	2,250	750	950	650	600	6,700	1.37%
e. Office salaries	3,500	3,500	3,500	3,500	3,500	3,500	21,000	4.30%
f. Owner's guaranteed payment	5,417	5,417	5,417	5,417	5,417	5,417	32,502	6.65%
g. Rent expense + security dep.	8,550	2,850	2,850	2,850	2,850	2,850	22,800	4.67%
h. Utilities	360	360	360	360	360	360	2,160	0.44%
i. Miscellaneous fixed expense	0	0	100	100	100	100	400	0.08%
j. Depreciation (fixed assets)	0	0	0	0	0	0	0	0.00%
Total Fixed Expenses	**21,610**	**15,710**	**15,361**	**16,810**	**14,161**	**13,960**	**97,612**	**19.98%**
Total Operating Expense	**46,791**	**32,726**	**39,702**	**45,576**	**38,928**	**41,842**	**245,565**	**48.21%**
Net Income From Operations	**21,879**	**6,474**	**68,648**	**26,954**	**17,152**	**10,908**	**152,015**	**33.16%**
Other income (interest)	105	104	104	104	104	104	625	0.13%
Other expense (interest)	507	499	490	482	474	466	2,918	0.60%
Net Profit (Loss) Before Taxes	**21,477**	**6,079**	**68,262**	**26,576**	**16,782**	**10,546**	**149,722**	**32.69%**
Provision for income taxes								
a. Federal	3,222	912	16,694	10,156	6,545	4,113	41,642	8.52%
b. State	1,611	456	5,120	1,993	1,259	791	11,230	2.30%
NET PROFIT (LOSS) AFTER TAXES	**16,644**	**4,711**	**46,448**	**14,427**	**8,978**	**5,642**	**96,850**	**21.87%**

2001 Profit & Loss (Income) Statement
Dayne Landscaping, Inc.

Page 2 (July thru December + 12-Month Totals)

For the Year: 2001	Jul	Aug	Sep	Oct	Nov	Dec	12-MONTH TOTALS	% of Total Revenues
							AMOUNT	PERCENT
INCOME								
1. Sales/revenues	60,330	51,012	56,862	38,200	32,800	50,050	777,864	100.00%
Landscaping — residential	18,000	14,000	22,000	24,000	0	0	216,000	27.77%
Landscaping — small business	16,500	10,900	15,300	14,000	0	0	160,700	20.66%
Landscaping — customized	25,150	24,912	19,062	0	0	0	199,374	25.63%
Snow removal — residential	0	0	0	0	950	3,000	18,250	2.35%
Snow removal — small business	0	0	0	0	23,250	47,050	167,100	21.48%
Miscellaneous accessories	0	0	0	0	8,500	0	8,500	1.09%
5% Snow removal contracts	680	1,200	500	200	100	0	7,940	1.02%
2. Cost of goods to be sold	4,000	6,000	1,000	0	1,000	(2,000)	101,030	12.99%
a. Beginning inventory	0	0	0	0	0	0	0	0.00%
b. Purchases	4,000	6,000	1,000	0	1,000	3,000	106,030	5.79%
(1) Fertilizer	0	6,000	0	0	0	0	19,000	2.44%
(2) Pesticide	3,000	0	0	0	0	0	11,000	1.41%
(3) Plants/shrubs	1,000	0	0	0	0	0	23,000	2.96%
(4) Salt/sand	0	0	1,000	0	1,000	3,000	8,030	1.03%
(5) Seed	0	0	0	0	0	0	45,000	5.79%
c. C.O.G. Available for sale	4,000	6,000	1,000	0	1,000	3,000	106,030	5.79%
d. Less ending inventory	0	0	0	0	0	5,000	5,000	0.64%
3. GROSS PROFIT	56,330	45,012	55,862	38,200	31,800	52,050	676,834	87.01%
EXPENSES								
1. Variable (selling) expenses								
a. Design specialist salary/p.tax	2,500	2,500	2,500	2,500	0	0	20,000	2.57%
b. Machinery, hand tools, equip.	1,000	0	1,000	0	0	0	11,000	1.41%
c. Marketing	206	650	339	400	300	300	5,400	0.69%
d. Part-time worker salaries	25,250	25,250	26,250	10,000	12,500	10,500	182,000	23.40%
e. Sales bonuses	0	0	0	0	0	0	2,000	0.26%
f. Sales commission	400	1,100	1,250	250	1,000	500	10,800	1.39%
g. Supervisor salaries/payroll tax	5,000	5,000	5,000	5,000	5,000	5,000	60,000	7.71%
h. Travel expense	850	650	600	620	480	500	10,400	1.34%
i. Misc. variable expense	100	200	0	0	0	0	1,200	0.15%
j. Depreciation (variable assets)	1,267	1,267	1,267	1,267	1,267	1,267	15,200	1.95%
Total Variable Expenses	36,573	36,617	38,206	20,037	20,547	18,067	318,000	40.88%
1. Fixed (Administrative) Expenses								
a. Admin. fees — legal/acct.	167	167	167	167	167	167	3,050	0.39%
b. Insurance (liab, cas, fire, theft)	967	967	966	966	966	966	11,600	1.49%
c. Licenses and permits	0	0	0	0	0	0	4,200	0.54%
d. Machinery, tools, equipment	100	200	300	200	100	100	7,700	0.99%
e. Office salaries	3,500	3,500	3,500	3,500	3,500	3,500	42,000	5.40%
f. Owner's guaranteed payment	5,417	5,417	5,416	5,416	5,416	5,416	65,000	8.36%
g. Rent expense	2,850	2,850	2,850	2,850	2,850	2,850	39,900	5.13%
h. Utilities	360	360	360	360	360	360	4,320	0.56%
i. Miscellaneous fixed expense	100	0	0	0	0	0	500	0.06%
i. Depreciation (fixed assets)	0	0	0	0	0	0	0	0.00%
Total Fixed Expenses	13,461	13,461	13,559	13,459	13,359	13,359	178,270	22.92%
Total Operating Expense	50,034	50,078	51,765	33,496	33,906	31,426	496,270	63.80%
Net Income From Operations	6,296	(5,066)	4,097	4,704	(2,106)	20,624	180,564	23.21%
Other Income (Interest)	105	104	104	104	104	104	1,250	0.16%
Other Expense (Interest)	457	449	441	432	423	415	5,535	0.71%
Net Profit (Loss) Before Taxes	5,944	(5,411)	3,760	4,376	(2,425)	20,313	176,279	22.66%
Provision for Income Taxes								
a. Federal	2,318	($2,110)	1,466	1,707	($946)	7,922	51,999	6.68%
b. State	446	($406)	282	328	($182)	1,523	13,221	1.70%
NET PROFIT (LOSS) AFTER TAXES	3,180	(2,895)	2,012	2,341	(1,297)	10,868	111,059	14.28%

Balance Sheet

Business Name:

Dayne Landscaping, Inc.   Date: December 31, 2001

ASSETS			% of Assets
Current Assets			
Cash	$	31,178	15.83%
Savings (land and building)	$	100,000	50.77%
Petty cash	$	0	0.00%
Accounts receivable	$	0	0.00%
Inventory	$	5,000	2.54%
Long-Term Investments	$	0	0.00%
Fixed Assets			
Land (valued at cost)	$	0	0.00%
Buildings	$	0	0.00%
1. Cost	0		
2. Less acc. depr.	0		
Improvements	$	0	0.00%
1. Cost	0		
2. Less acc. depr.	0		
Equipment	$	12,800	6.50%
1. Cost	16,000		
2. Less acc. depr.	3,200		
Furniture	$	0	0.00%
1. Cost	0		
2. Less acc. depr.	0		
Autos/Vehicles	$	48,000	24.37%
1. Cost	60,000		
2. Less acc. depr.	12,000		
Other Assets			
1.	$	0	0.00%
2.	$	0	0.00%
TOTAL ASSETS	$	196,978	100.00%

LIABILITIES			% of Liabilities
Current Liabilities			
Accounts payable	$	0	0.00%
Notes payable	$	16,332	26.81%
Interest payable	$	0	0.00%
Pre-paid deposits	$	0	0.00%
Taxes payable			
Accrued federal income tax	$	0	0.00%
Accrued state income tax	$	0	0.00%
Accrued payroll tax	$	0	0.00%
Accrued sales tax	$	0	0.00%
Payroll accrual	$	0	0.00%
Long-Term Liabilities			
Notes payable to investors	$	0	0.00%
Notes payable others	$	44,587	73.19%
TOTAL LIABILITIES	$	60,919	100.00%

NET WORTH (EQUITY)			% of Net Worth
Proprietorship	$	0	0.00%
or			
Partnership			
1. (Name 1), ___% equity	$	0	0.00%
2. (Name 2), ___% equity	$	0	0.00%
or			
Corporation			
Capital stock	$	20,000	14.70%
Surplus paid in	$	5,000	3.67%
Retained earnings, appropriated	$	100,000	73.50%
Retained earnings, unappropriated	$	11,059	8.13%
TOTAL NET WORTH	$	136,059	100.00%

Assets – Liabilities = Net Worth

and

Liabilities + Equity = Total Assets

1. See Financial Statement Analysis for ratios and notations

Break-Even Analysis

Based on 2001 Financial Statements—Not a Projection

Dayne Landscaping, Inc.

Date of Analysis: December 31, 2001

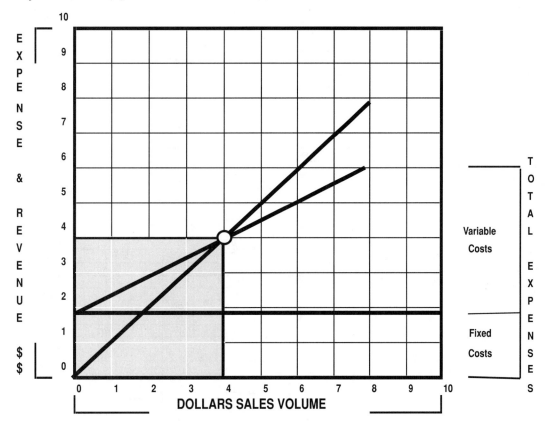

NOTE: Figures shown in hundreds of thousands of dollars (Ex: 1 = $ 100,000)

B-E POINT (SALES) = Fixed costs + [(Variable Costs / Revenues) x Sales]

B-E Point (Sales) = $ 183,805 + [($ 419,030 / $ 777,864) x Sales]

Dayne Landscaping, Inc.

BREAK-EVEN POINT CALCULATION

FC (Fixed Costs) =	(Administrative Expenses + Interest)	$	183,805
VC (Variable Costs) =	(Cost of Goods + Selling Expenses)	$	419,030
R (Revenues) =	(Income from sale of products and services)	$	777,864
BREAK-EVEN POINT =		$	398,444

2002 Pro Forma Cash Flow Statement
Dayne Landscaping, Inc.

Page 1 (January thru June)

For the Year 2002

	Jan	Feb	Mar	Apr	May	Jun
BEGINNING CASH BALANCE	131,178	137,633	140,273	139,746	45,856	115,074
CASH RECEIPTS						
A. Sales/revenues	123,850	89,100	184,400	169,200	200,600	192,900
1. Landscaping — residential	0	0	41,000	21,000	23,000	24,000
2. Landscaping — small business	0	0	56,500	50,500	40,000	39,500
3. Landscaping — large corporations	0	0	73,500	57,200	55,100	51,000
4. Customized landscaping	0	0	13,400	40,500	82,500	78,400
5. Snow removal — residential	11,050	5,700	0	0	0	0
6. Snow removal — small business	66,900	53,000	0	0	0	0
7. Snow removal — large corporations	45,900	30,400	0	0	0	0
8. 5% Snow removal contracts	0	0	0	0	0	0
B. Interest income	108	110	109	110	109	110
C. Sale of long-term assets	0	0	0	0	0	0
TOTAL CASH AVAILABLE	255,136	226,843	324,782	309,056	246,565	308,084
CASH PAYMENTS						
A. Cost of goods to be sold						
1. Fertilizer	0	0	10,700	12,800	9,800	3,100
2. Pesticide	0	0	6,250	2,400	5,500	3,500
3. Plants/shrub	0	0	16,100	13,000	3,500	3,200
4. Salt/sand	5,375	0	0	0	0	0
5. Seed	0	0	21,000	41,500	24,500	5,000
Total cost of goods	5,375	0	54,050	69,700	43,300	14,800
B. Variable expenses						
1. Design specialists (2 w/taxes and benefits)	5,834	5,834	5,834	5,834	5,834	5,834
2. Machinery, tools, equipment	350	6,000	0	500	500	1,000
3. Marketing	3,500	6,500	6,500	3,500	3,500	5,000
4. Part-time worker salaries (w/taxes)	23,500	30,000	37,600	40,000	39,000	38,033
5. Sales bonuses	0	2,000	2,500	500		
6. Sales commissions	0	0	1,100	5,750	2,250	1,500
7. Supervisor salaries (w/taxes and benefits)	7,500	7,500	15,000	15,000	15,000	15,000
8. Travel expense	550	850	1,200	1,300	1,200	860
9. Miscellaneous selling expense	500	500	500	500	500	500
Total variable expenses	41,734	59,184	70,234	72,884	67,784	67,727
C. Fixed expenses						
1. Administration fees — legal/acct.	509	508	508	2,250	508	508
2. Insurance (liability, casualty, fire/theft, w comp)	704	714	735	739	737	736
3. Licenses and permits	100	200	750	2,350	1,300	1,025
4. Office equipment	1,750	8,650	1,100	900	825	525
5. Office salaries (w/taxes and benefits)	5,250	5,250	5,250	5,250	5,250	5,250
6. Owner's guaranteed payment	6,833	6,833	6,833	6,833	6,833	6,833
7. Rent expense	2,850	2,850	2,850	0	0	0
8. Utilities	480	463	360	376	247	378
9. Miscellaneous administrative expense	200	200	200	200	200	200
Total fixed expenses	18,676	25,668	18,586	18,898	15,900	15,455
D. Interest expense (vehicles, equipment)	406	397	389	380	371	362
E. Interest expense (land and buildings)	0	0	0	0	2,062	2,057
F. Federal income tax	0	0	33,249	0	0	33,249
G. State tax	0	0	7,199	0	0	7,199
H. Capital asset purch, cash (land and buildings)*	0	0	0	375,000	0	0
I. Capital asset purch, cash (vehicles, equipment)**	50,000	0	0	0	0	48,000
J. Loan repayment (1996) (land and buildings)	0	0	0	0	727	732
K. Loan repayment (1995) (vehicles, equipment)	1,312	1,321	1,329	1,338	1,347	1,356
TOTAL CASH PAID OUT	117,503	86,570	185,036	538,200	131,491	190,937
CASH BALANCE/DEFICIENCY	137,633	140,273	139,746	(229,144)	115,074	117,147
LOAN TO BE RECEIVED (land and buildings)	0	0	0	275,000	0	0
EQUITY DEPOSITS	0	0	0	0	0	0
ENDING CASH BALANCE	137,633	140,273	139,746	45,856	115,074	117,147

Note: * Building/Land purchased in April for $375,000 ($100,000 cash + bank loan for $275,000)

** Two 4x4 trucks purchased in January and August @ $50,000 cash each. Four U-hauls purchased for cash (July and August) @ $10,000 each

2002 Pro Forma Cash Flow Statement
Dayne Landscaping, Inc.

Page 2 (July thru December + 6 & 12-month Totals)

6-MONTH TOTALS	Jul	Aug	Sep	Oct	Nov	Dec	12-MONTH TOTALS
131,178	117,147	122,610	104,184	100,611	119,509	110,104	131,178
960,050	149,400	138,000	122,000	83,900	67,090	87,760	1,608,200
109,000	24,000	24,000	24,000	24,000	0	0	205,000
186,500	33,400	32,000	30,000	28,000	0	0	309,900
236,800	28,000	35,000	30,500	12,900	0	0	343,200
214,800	64,000	47,000	37,500	9,000			372,300
16,750	0	0	0	0	5,000	6,750	28,500
119,900	0	0	0	0	30,000	42,410	192,310
76,300	0	0	0	0	25,090	38,600	139,990
0	0	0	0	10,000	7,000	0	17,000
656	109	109	109	110	110	110	1,313
0	0	0	0	0	0	0	0
1,091,884	266,656	260,719	226,293	184,621	186,709	197,974	1,740,691
36,400	7,600	4,000	0	0	0	0	48,000
17,650	4,500	1,850	0	0	0	0	24,000
35,800	1,700	2,700	2,300	1,500	0	0	44,000
5,375	0	0	0	0	4,700	5,000	15,075
92,000	2,000	2,000	0	0	0	0	96,000
187,225	15,800	10,550	2,300	1,500	4,700	5,000	227,075
35,004	5,834	5,834	5,834	5,834	5,834	5,834	70,008
8,350	10,000	650	0	0	350	475	19,825
28,500	3,500	3,500	3,500	6,500	6,500	3,500	55,500
208,133	42,000	39,400	38,000	14,000	19,000	21,500	382,033
5,000					500	500	6,000
10,600	500	500	0	2,500	5,000	2,500	21,600
75,000	15,000	15,000	15,000	15,000	15,000	15,000	165,000
5,960	940	1,130	970	400	400	600	10,400
3,000	500	500	500	500	500	500	6,000
379,547	78,274	66,514	63,804	44,734	53,084	50,409	736,366
4,791	508	508	509	508	508	509	7,841
4,365	742	741	739	705	712	716	8,720
5,725	1,175	500	405	295	200	100	8,400
13,750	250	450	350	200	200	200	15,400
31,500	5,250	5,250	5,250	5,250	5,250	5,250	63,000
40,998	6,833	6,833	6,834	6,834	6,834	6,834	82,000
8,550	0	0	0	0	0	0	8,550
2,304	457	432	286	329	360	387	4,555
1,200	250	250	250	250	250	250	2,700
113,183	15,465	14,964	14,623	14,371	14,314	14,246	201,166
2,305	353	344	335	325	316	306	4,284
4,119	2,051	2,046	2,040	2,035	2,029	2,023	16,343
66,498	0	0	33,249	0	0	33,249	132,996
14,398	0	0	7,199	0	0	7,200	28,797
375,000	0	0	0	0	0	0	375,000
98,000	30,000	60,000	0	0	0	0	188,000
1,459	738	743	749	754	760	766	5,969
8,003	1,365	1,374	1,383	1,393	1,402	1,412	16,332
1,249,737	144,046	156,535	125,682	65,112	76,605	114,611	1,932,328
(157,853)	122,610	104,184	100,611	119,509	110,104	83,363	(191,637)
275,000	0	0	0	0	0	0	275,000
0	0	0	0	0	0	0	0
117,147	122,610	104,184	100,611	119,509	110,104	83,363	83,363

Three-Year Income Projection
Dayne Landscaping, Inc.

Updated: December 31, 2001	YEAR 1 2002	YEAR 2 2003	YEAR 3 2004	TOTAL 3 YEARS
INCOME				
1. Sales/revenues	**1,608,200**	**2,010,250**	**2,311,788**	**5,930,238**
a. Landscaping — residential	205,000	256,250	294,688	755,938
b. Landscaping — small business	309,900	387,375	445,481	1,142,756
c. Landscaping — large corporations	343,200	429,000	493,350	1,265,550
d. Customized landscaping	372,300	465,375	535,181	1,372,856
e. Snow removal — residential	28,500	35,625	40,969	105,094
f. Snow removal — small business	192,310	240,388	276,446	709,143
g. Snow removal — large corporations	139,990	174,988	201,236	516,213
h. 5% Snow removal contracts	17,000	21,250	24,438	62,688
2. Cost of goods sold (c – d)	**222,075**	**273,844**	**323,420**	**819,339**
Cost of goods (as a percentage of sales)	13.81%	13.62%	13.99%	13.82%
a. Beginning inventory	5,000	10,000	20,000	5,000
b. Purchases	**227,075**	**283,844**	**326,420**	**837,339**
(1) Fertilizer	48,000	60,000	69,000	177,000
(2) Pesticide	24,000	30,000	34,500	88,500
(3) Plants/shrubs	44,000	55,000	63,250	162,250
(4) Salt/sand	15,075	18,844	21,670	55,589
(5) Seed	96,000	120,000	138,000	354,000
c. C.O.G. avail. sale (a + b)	232,075	293,844	346,420	842,339
d. Less ending inventory (12/31)	10,000	20,000	23,000	23,000
3. Gross profit on sales (1 – 2)	**1,386,125**	**1,736,406**	**1,988,367**	**5,110,898**
Gross profit (as a percentage of sales)	86.19%	86.38%	86.01%	86.18%
EXPENSES				
1. Variable (selling) (a thru j)	**772,933**	**916,341**	**1,027,822**	**2,717,097**
Selling expenses (as a percentage of eales)	48.06%	45.58%	44.46%	45.82%
a. Design specialist salaries/payroll taxes	70,008	77,000	84,700	231,708
b. Machinery, tools, equipment	19,825	15,000	17,000	51,825
c. Marketing	55,500	55,000	55,000	165,500
d. Part-time worker salaries/payroll taxes	382,033	477,541	549,172	1,408,747
e. Sales bonuses	6,000	13,500	18,500	38,000
f. Sales commission	21,600	24,000	27,000	72,600
g. Supervisor salaries/payroll taxes	165,000	181,500	199,650	546,150
h. Travel expense	10,400	12,000	14,000	36,400
i. Miscellaneous selling expense	6,000	8,000	10,000	24,000
j. Depreciation (product/service assets)	36,567	52,800	52,800	142,167
2. Fixed (administrative) (a thru j)	**209,916**	**246,967**	**290,467**	**747,350**
Admin. expenses (as a percentage of sales)	13.05%	12.29%	12.56%	12.60%
a. Administration fees — legal/acct.	7,841	7,800	7,800	23,441
b. Insurance — liability, casualty, fire/theft, w. comp.	8,720	10,500	12,000	31,220
c. Licenses and permits	8,400	10,300	12,200	30,900
d. Office equipment	15,400	30,800	45,200	91,400
e. Office salaries/payroll taxes	63,000	77,000	91,000	231,000
f. Owner's guaranteed payment	82,000	90,000	100,000	272,000
g. Rent expense	8,550	0	0	8,550
h. Utilities	4,555	5,500	6,500	16,555
i. Miscellaneous administrative expense	2,700	3,400	4,100	10,200
j. Depreciation (facility, admin. assets)	8,750	11,667	11,667	32,084
TOTAL OPERATING EXPENSES (1 + 2)	**982,849**	**1,163,308**	**1,318,289**	**3,464,447**
NET INCOME OPERATIONS (GPr – Exp)	**403,276**	**573,098**	**670,078**	**1,646,452**
Net income operations (as a percentage of sales)	25.08%	28.51%	28.99%	27.76%
OTHER INCOME (interest income)	1,313	1,378	1,447	4,138
OTHER EXPENSE (interest expense)	20,627	28,105	25,844	74,576
NET PROFIT (LOSS) BEFORE TAXES	**383,962**	**546,371**	**645,681**	**1,576,014**
Taxes 1. Federal, s-employment	132,996	196,335	235,066	564,397
2. State	28,797	40,978	48,426	118,201
3. Local	0	0	0	0
NET PROFIT (LOSS) AFTER TAXES	**222,169**	**309,058**	**362,189**	**893,416**
Net profit (loss) (as a percentage of sales)	13.81%	15.37%	15.67%	15.07%

Projected Balance Sheet

Business Name:

Dayne Landscaping, Inc.   **Projected for: December 31, 2002**

ASSETS			% of Assets
Current assets			
Cash	$	83,363	12.41%
Petty cash	$	0	0.00%
Accounts receivable	$	0	0.00%
Inventory	$	10,000	1.49%
Short-term investments	$	0	0.00%
Long-term investments	$	0	0.00%
Fixed assets			
Land (valued at cost)	$	200,000	29.77%
Buildings	$	163,050	24.27%
1. Cost	175,000		
2. Less acc. depr.	11,950		
Improvements	$	0	0.00%
1. Cost	0		
2. Less acc. depr.	0		
Equipment	$	92,833	13.82%
1. Cost	104,000		
2. Less acc. depr.	11,167		
Furniture	$	0	0.00%
1. Cost	0		
2. Less acc. depr.	0		
Autos/Vehicles	$	122,600	18.25%
1. Cost	160,000		
2. Less acc. depr.	37,400		
Other assets			
1.	$	0	0.00%
2.	$	0	0.00%
3.	$	0	0.00%
TOTAL ASSETS	$	671,846	100.00%

LIABILITIES			% of Liabilities
Current liabilities			
Accounts payable	$	0	0.00%
Notes payable	$	27,337	8.72%
Interest payable	$	0	0.00%
Pre-paid deposits	$	0	0.00%
Taxes payable			
Accrued federal income tax	$	0	0.00%
Accrued state income tax	$	0	0.00%
Accrued payroll tax	$	0	0.00%
Accrued sales tax	$	0	0.00%
Payroll accrual	$	0	0.00%
Long-term liabilities			
Notes payable to investors	$	0	0.00%
Notes payable others	$	286,281	91.28%
TOTAL LIABILITIES	$	313,618	100.00%

NET WORTH (EQUITY)			% of Net Worth
Proprietorship	$	0	0.00%
or			
Partnership			
1. (Name 1), ___% equity	$	0	0.00%
2. (Name 2), ___% equity	$	0	0.00%
or			
Corporation			
Capital stock	$	20,000	5.58%
Surplus paid In	$	5,000	1.40%
Retained earnings	$	333,228	93.02%
TOTAL NET WORTH	$	358,228	100.00%

Assets – Liabilities = Net Worth

and

Liabilities + Equity = Total Assets

1. See Financial Statement Analysis for ratios and notations

Financial Statement Analysis Summary

The following is a summary of Dayne Landscaping, Inc. 2001 and 2002 financial statement analysis information, as developed on the next three pages of spreadsheets (pages 29–31) :

*Author notation:
Writer must research industry standards.*

	2001 HISTORICAL	2002 PROJECTED	INDUSTRY STANDARD	
1. Net working capital	$119,846	$66,026	$80,000	+ or -
2. Current ratio	8.34	3.42	2.0	+
3. Quick ratio	8.03	3.05	1.0	+ or -
4. Gross profit margin	87.01%	86.19%	85.0%	
5. Operating profit margin	23.21%	25.08%	25.0%	
6. Net profit margin	14.28%	13.81%	14%	
7. Debt to assets	30.93%	46.68%	33.0%	-
8. Debt to equity	44.77%	87.55%	100%	-
9. ROI (return on investment)	56.38%	33.07%	24%	+
10. Vertical income statement analysis *				
Sales/revenues	100.00%	100.0%		
Cost of goods	12.99%	13.81%	15.0%	+ or -
Gross profit	87.01%	86.19%	85.0%	
Operating expense	63.80%	61.11%	62.0%	+ or -
Net income operations	23.21%	25.08%	23.0%	+ or -
Interest income	0.16%	0.08%	N/A	Variable
Interest expense	0.71%	1.28%	4.0%	Variable
Net profit (pre-tax)	22.66%	23.88%	19.0%	+ or -
* All items stated as % of total revenues				
11. Vertical balance sheet analysis *				
Current assets	69.14%	13.90%	18.0%	+
Inventory	2.54%	1.49%	2.0%	
Total assets	100.0%	100.00%		
Current liabilities	8.29%	4.07%	15.0%	-
Total liabilities	30.93%	46.68%	50.0%	-
Net worth	69.07%	53.32%	50.0%	+
Total liabilities + Net worth	100.0%	100.00%		

* All asset items stated as % of total assets;
Liability and net worth items stated as % of Total liabilities + Net worth

Notes:

Dayne Landscaping, Inc. has taken advantage of a rapidly-increasing marketplace, and has also neatly incorporated snow removal services to increase revenues significantly during winter months. The company earned an unusually high 2001 net profit for a start-up service business ($111,059). Debt Ratios (Debt:Assets, 30.93% and Debt:Equity, 44.77%) are better than industry average. A 2002 beginning cash balance of $131,178, with no current liabilities other than $16,332 of notes payable on a previous loan, give the company sufficient marketing funds to expand services into the corporate landscaping and design areas. The purchase of their present facility, currently under a lease agreement (using $100,000 cash + $275,000 loan funds) will not raise the Debt to Equity Ratio (projected at 87.55%) beyond a safe limit. Projections indicate high sales growth with the acquisition of new personnel, vehicles, and equipment to service the increased customer base. The company is experiencing rapid, but controlled growth. Financial projections indicate that the company will be more than able to fulfill its obligations to repay the $275,000 loan with interest and still maintain good cash flow and increased profitability.

Financial Statement Analysis
Ratio Table
Dayne Landscaping, Inc.

Type of Analysis	Formula	Historical: 2001		Projected: 2002	
1. Liquidity Analysis a. Net working capital	**Balance Sheet** Current Assets — Current Liabilities	Current Assets Current Liabilities **Net Working Capital**	136,178 16,332 **$119,846**	Current Assets Current Liabilities **Net Working Capital**	93,363 27,337 **$66,026**
b. Current ratio	**Balance Sheet** Current Assets Current Liabilities	Current Assets Current Liabilities **Current Ratio**	136,178 16,332 **8.34**	Current Assets Current Liabilities **Current Ratio**	93,363 27,337 **3.42**
c. Quick ratio	**Balance Sheet** Current Assets minus Inventory Current Liabilities	Current Assets Inventory Current Liabilities **Quick Ratio**	136,178 5,000 16,332 **8.03**	Current Assets Inventory Current Liabilities **Quick Ratio**	93,363 10,000 27,337 **3.05**
2. Profitability Analysis a. Gross profit margin	**Income Statement** Gross Profits Sales	Gross Profits Sales **Gross Profit Margin**	676,834 777,864 **87.01%**	Gross Profits Sales **Gross Profit Margin**	1,386,125 1,608,200 **86.19%**
b. Operating profit margin	Income From Operations Sales	Income From Ops. Sales **Operating Profit Margin**	180,564 777,864 **23.21%**	Income From Ops. Sales **Operating Profit Margin**	403,276 1,608,200 **25.08%**
c. Net profit margin	Net Profits Sales	Net Profits Sales **Net Profit Margin**	111,059 777,864 **14.28%**	Net Profits Sales **Net Profit Margin**	222,169 1,608,200 **13.81%**
3. Debt Ratios a. Debt to assets	**Balance Sheet** Total Liabilities Total Assets	Total Liabilities Total Assets **Debt to Assets Ratio**	60,919 196,978 **30.93%**	Total Liabilities Total Assets **Debt to Assets Ratio**	313,618 671,846 **46.68%**
b. Debt to equity	Total Liabilities Total Owners' Equity	Total Liabilities Total Owners' Equity **Debt to Equity Ratio**	60,919 136,059 **44.77%**	Total Liabilities Total Owners' Equity **Debt to Equity Ratio**	313,618 358,228 **87.55%**
4. Measures of Investment a. ROI *(Return on Investment)*	**Balance Sheet** Net Profits Total Assets	Net Profits Total Assets **ROI (Return on Invest.)**	111,059 196,978 **56.38%**	Net Profits Total Assets **ROI (Return on Invest.)**	222,169 671,846 **33.07%**
5. Vertical Financial Statement Analysis	**Balance Sheet** 1. Each asset % of Total Assets 2. Liability & Equity % of Total L&E **Income Statement** 3. All items % of Total Revenues	NOTE: See Attached **Balance Sheet and** **Income Statement**		NOTE: See Attached **Balance Sheet and** **Income Statement**	
6. Horizontal Financial Statement Analysis	**Balance Sheet** 1. Assets, Liab & Equity measured against 2nd year. Increases and decreases stated as amount & % **Income Statement** 2. Revenues & Expenses measured against 2nd year. Increases and decreases stated as amount & %	NOTE: **Horizontal Analysis** **Not Applicable** Only one year in business		NOTE: **Horizontal Analysis** **Not Applicable** Only one year in business	

2001 Historical
Vertical Income Statement Analysis

Dayne Landscaping, Inc.	Begin: January 1, 2001　End: December 31, 2001		

	AMOUNT		% Total Revenues
INCOME			
1. Sales/revenues		$　777,864	100.00%
a. Landscaping — residential	216,000		27.77%
b. Landscaping — small business	160,700		20.66%
c. Customized landscaping	199,374		25.63%
d. Snow removal — residential	18,250		2.35%
e. Snow removal — small business	167,100		21.48%
f. 5% Snow removal contracts	8,500		1.09%
g. Miscellaneous accessories	7,940		1.02%
2. Cost of goods sold (c – d)		101,030	12.99%
a. Beginning inventory	0		0.00%
b. Purchases	106,030		13.63%
(1) Fertilizer	19,000		2.44%
(2) Pesticide	11,000		1.41%
(3) Plants/shrubs	23,000		2.96%
(4) Salt/sand	8,030		1.03%
(1) Seed	45,000		5.79%
c. C.O.G. avail. sale (a + b)	106,030		13.63%
d. Less ending inventory (12/31)	5,000		0.64%
3. Gross profit on sales (1 – 2)		$　676,834	87.01%
EXPENSES			
1. Variable (selling) (a thru j)		318,000	40.88%
a. Design specialist salary/payroll taxes	20,000		2.57%
b. Machinery, hand tools, equipment	11,000		1.41%
c. Marketing	5,400		0.69%
d. Part-time worker salaries	182,000		23.40%
e. Sales bonuses	2,000		0.26%
f. Sales commission	10,800		1.39%
g. Supervisor salaries/payroll taxes	60,000		7.71%
h. Travel expense	10,400		1.34%
i. Miscellaneous variable expense	1,200		0.15%
j. Depreciation (product/services assets)	15,200		1.95%
2. Fixed (administrative) (a thru j)		178,270	22.92%
a. Administration fees—legal/accounting	3,050		0.39%
b. Insurance (liability, casualty, fire/theft)	11,600		1.49%
c. Licenses and permits	4,200		0.54%
d. Office equipment	7,700		0.99%
e. Office salaries/payroll taxes	42,000		5.40%
f. Owner's guaranteed payment	65,000		8.36%
g. Rent expense	39,900		5.13%
h. Utilities	4,320		0.56%
i. Miscellaneous fixed expense	500		0.06%
j. Depreciation (administrative assets)	0		0.00%
Total operating expenses (1 + 2)		496,270	63.80%
Net income from operations (GP – Exp)		$　180,564	23.21%
Other income (interest income)	1,250		0.16%
Other expense (interest expense)	5,535		0.71%
Net profit (loss) before taxes		$　176,279	22.66%
Taxes:			
a. Federal	51,999		6.68%
b. State	13,221	65,220	1.70%
c. Local	0		0.00%
NET PROFIT (LOSS) AFTER TAXES		$　111,059	14.28%

2001 Historical
Vertical Balance Sheet Analysis

(All Asset percentages = % of Total Assets; All Liability or Equity percentages = % of Total Liabilities + Total Equity)

Analysis of Historical Balance Sheet			Date of Balance Sheet: December 31, 2001		
Dayne Landscaping, Inc.					

ASSETS		% of Total Assets	LIABILITIES		% of Total L + NW
Current assets			**Current liabilities**		
Cash	$ 131,178	66.60%	Accounts payable	$ 0	0.00%
Petty cash	$ 0	0.00%	Notes payable	$ 16,332	8.29%
Sales tax holding account	$ 0	0.00%	Interest payable	$ 0	0.00%
Accounts receivable	$ 0	0.00%	Pre-paid deposits	$ 0	0.00%
Inventory	$ 5,000	2.54%			
Short-term investments	$ 0	0.00%	Taxes payable		
			Accrued federal income tax	$ 0	0.00%
Long-term investments	$ 0	0.00%	Accrued state income tax	$ 0	0.00%
			Accrued payroll tax	$ 0	0.00%
Fixed assets			Accrued sales tax	$ 0	0.00%
Land (valued at cost)	$ 0	0.00%			
			Payroll accrual	$ 0	0.00%
Buildings	$ 0	0.00%			
1. Cost	0		**Long-term liabilities**		
2. Less acc. depr.	0		Notes payable to investors	$ 0	0.00%
			Notes payable to others	$ 44,587	22.64%
Improvements	$ 0	0.00%			
1. Cost	0				
2. Less acc. depr.	0		**TOTAL LIABILITIES**	$ 60,919	30.93%
Equipment	$ 12,800	6.50%			
1. Cost	16,000				
2. Less acc. depr.	3,200		**NET WORTH (EQUITY)**		
Furniture	$ 0	0.00%	**Proprietorship**	$ 0	0.00%
1. Cost	0		or		
2. Less acc. depr.	0		**Partnership**		
			1. Partner A	$ 0	0.00%
Autos/vehicles	$ 48,000	24.37%	2. Partner B	$ 0	0.00%
1. Cost	60,000		or		
2. Less acc. depr.	12,000		**Corporation**		
			Capital stock	$ 20,000	10.15%
			Surplus paid in	$ 5,000	2.54%
Other assets			Retained earnings, appropriated	$ 100,000	50.77%
1.	$ 0	0.00%	Retained earnings, unappropriated	$ 11,059	5.61%
2.	$ 0	0.00%			
			TOTAL NET WORTH	$ 136,059	69.07%
TOTAL ASSETS	$ 196,978	100.00%	**LIABILITIES + NET WORTH**	$ 196,978	100.00%
			Assets – Liabilities = Net worth -or- Liabilities + Equity = Assets		

Financial Assumptions

Dayne Landscaping, Inc. Business Plan

Seeking Bank Loan

- **Purpose:** To purchase land and facilities currently leased by Dayne Landscaping, Inc.

- **Projected Terms:** $275,000 for 15 Years @ 9%; need funding by April 1, 2002, repayments can begin on May 1, 2002 (see amortization schedule C).

Financial Assumptions

- $25,000 initial capital contribution by owner in corporation (not a loan).

- Required 5% upfront fees for all snow contracts.

- Sales commission of 5% to be paid to sales representatives.

- Bonuses of $500 each to be paid for landing new corporate accounts.

- Salaries for four(4) Supervisors @ $15,000, totaling $60,000 (plus benefits and payroll taxes).

- Salary for the President to be guaranteed @ $65,000 for 2001; projected raise to $82,000 for 2002.

- Salary for the Office Manager @ $22,000 (+ benefits & payroll taxes).

- Salary for Administration Assistants (one in 2001, two in 2002) @ $15000 (plus payroll taxes and benefits).

- Salary for part-time people at $7 per hour. Hired as needed to meet volume.

- Licensing permit fees with city and state during the year.

- Rent deposit at $5,700 for first and last month.

- Heat and electricity at $60 per sq. ft, totaling $360 per month, and $4,320 per year.

- Fire and liability insurance at $50 per square foot, totaling $300 per month, and $3,600 per year.

- All insurance at $8,000 per year. The total cost of insurance at $11,600.

- Two trucks purchased with 2001 loan: $60,000 @ 8%; interest five-year period = $12,995.05 (see amortizing schedule A).

- Four large mowers purchased with 2001 loan: $16,000 @ 8%; interest three-year period = $2049.79 (see amortizing schedule B).

- State income taxes charges at 7.5% of net profits.

- Federal income taxes based on Federal Corporation Tax Schedule (15%-25%-34%-39% of net profits).

- Estimated taxes paid on schedule quarterly, based on actual and projected net profits for 2001 and 2002.

- Ending inventory: 2001 = $5,000; 2002 projected at $10,000.

DAYNE LANDSCAPING, INC.

Part IV. Supporting Documents*

✓ **Competition Comparison**

✓ **Owner's Résumé**

*** Note:** For purposes of brevity, we have chosen to include only a portion of the supporting documents that would be found in Dayne Landscaping, Inc.'s business plan.*

Competition Comparison

Vendor	Garden Shop	Landscaping Plus	Dayne Landscaping
Landscaping			
Design	Yes	Yes	Yes
Oriental design	No	No	Yes
Maintenance	Yes	Yes	Yes
Pest control	No	No	Yes
Snow Services			
Plowing	Yes	Yes	Yes
Removal	No	No	No
Response time	Whenever	Whenever	Designated
Guarantee	No	No	Yes
Servicing	NH only	NH, MA	NH, MA, CT
Price per hour	$25–$30	$30–$35	$20–$30

Robin T. Dayne

181 Thoreaus Landing, Nashua, NH 03060   Tel. 603-888-2020 (W)   603-889-2293 (H)

Summary

Five years' experience in the Landscaping Industry. Skilled in sales, support, and operations of new accounts for an established landscaping company. Managed office of ten employees related to customer service. Proficient in managing and workings of the landscaping service industry. Knowledgeable in landscaping design, and planning.

Experience

Landscaping Plus, Nashua, NH   **1994–2000**

Office Manager, January 1999 to December 2000

Managed ten employees that sold and serviced customer accounts. Responsible for planning scheduling, and managing inventory (equipment and tools) for the ten employees. Implemented the first "customer satisfaction survey" over the phone, to the entire base of customers.

- Developed a tool "check-in" process saving the company $10,000 a year in lost inventory.
- Organized the telemarketing necessary for the customer survey resulting in additional sales revenue of $25,000.
- Implemented and managed service issue "hot line" for dissatisfied customers.
- Responsible for all major accounts and employees that worked at the sites.

Account Supervisor   **December 1997–December 1998**

Managed 20 assigned accounts for landscaping and snow maintenance. Responsible for reporting to the President all account updates and potential revenue opportunities.

- Maintained the 20 accounts by scheduling all part-time workers.
- Trained part-time employees in proper lawn care maintenance.
- Managed the inventory, equipment, and supplies of each worker.
- Managed all customer service issues and received excellence award for all accounts at the end of the year.
- Scheduled all snow removal and coordinated snow emergencies.

Account Landscaping Specialist   **June 1994–November 1997**

- Worked the landscaping contract of a large corporate account.
- Recommended landscaping design changes and secured additional contract with company.
- Provide snow removal during storm and emergencies.
- Learned the operation of all landscaping equipment, tools, and vehicles.

Personal Strengths

Excellent organizational and communication skills   Dedicated to customer service excellence
Strong management training and experience   Strong knowledge of landscaping industry

Education

Completed Bachelors Degree in Horticulture at the University of New Hampshire. Independent studies at the Institute for Higher Learning majoring in Environmental Protection.

Affiliations and Interests

Board member of the Nashua Chamber of Commerce. Committee member of the City's Beautification Program. Volunteer at Community Services of Nashua.

WHOLESALE MOBILE HOMES.COM, INC. BUSINESS PLAN

The business plan presented in Appendix III is an actual business plan developed for *Wholesale Mobile Homes.com, Inc.* using *Anatomy of a Business Plan* and its software companion, **AUTOMATE YOUR BUSINESS PLAN**. Mr. Paul Jarolimek II, President and CEO of the company <www.wmhinc.com> has generously allowed me to publish the plan in the new edition of the book and the new revision of the software.

Wmhinc.com is modeled as an Internet Portal with a primary focus on the housing industry. Their Web site provides consumers the opportunity to design and purchase a home online. *Wmhinc.com*'s vision as an innovative, dynamic start-up company is to provide services that will establish the Company as the premiere online provider of manufactured housing, industry information, and associated services.

The Company is in the process of development and the business plan was written for the purpose of raising venture capital. The Company expects to raise the needed capital by the end of 2001 and begin operations in January 2002.

WORKING WITH A BUSINESS PLAN CONSULTANT

Wmhinc.com's business plan was developed by the owners of the business with professional assistance from a very reputable business plan consultant, Mr. Ndaba Mdhlongwa of Dallas, Texas <nxml673@hotmail.com> or 972-662-9583. I also owe Mr. Mdhlongwa a debt of gratitude because he has put in many extra hours of volunteer time to work with me in preparing the business plan for presentation to my readers and software users.

Many times, the owners of the business either feel too pressed for time to write their plans—or sometimes they feel they would have more confidence in the result—if they could engage the services of a business plan professional. In this case, they found the right person to work with. Before you hire someone yourself, be sure you know what you are getting into. Hiring the wrong person can be very costly both in terms of money and the quality of your business plan. Hiring the right person can be very beneficial.

THIS PLAN IS FOR A MORE AGGRESSIVE BUSINESS

Wmhinc.com is seeking venture capital in the amount of $10 million. As you learned in Chapter 1, investors become equity partners in your company. Because of the risks involved in venturing with a company, they are looking for rapid growth/profitability projections backed by reason. Therefore, you will notice that this business plan is written with a heavy focus on the Summary Description of the Business, Marketing Plan, Sources and Uses of Financing, and Executive Summary.

- **The *Wmhinc.com* marketing plan.** In Chapter 5, "Part II, The Marketing Plan," you were presented with a very comprehensive list of marketing plan components, representing a full spectrum of marketing possibilities. Mr. Jarolimek, with the assistance of Mr. Mdhlongwa, has addressed all of these components in the *Wmhinc.com* marketing plan. It is a good example of a very fine market planning effort.

- **Financial documents.** This is a plan for a start-up company. For this reason, you will note that all of the financial documents are pro forma, or projected, spread-heets. Only after the company has been in business for one accounting period will it have historical financial statements.

- **Note the Executive Summary.** Venture capitalists like to see an exciting Executive Summary. The one in this plan is an example of a more comprehensive one, addressing important highlights of the company and an Income Statement Summary for their Four Phases of Development.

Thank you again, to Mr. Jarolimek and Mr. Ndaba Mdhlongwa for allowing me to share this interpretation of business planning with our readers and software users. I know that it will be a great help to them as they write their plans.

> *Warning! The plan is to be examined for Wmhinc.com's handling of content only. There is no judgment inferred as to appropriateness or financial potential for lenders or investors. Do not use it as a source of research for your own company.*

WHOLESALE MOBILE HOMES.COM, INC.

5300 W Sahara, Suite 101
PO Box 27740
Las Vegas, NV 89146
Telephone 509-663-3876
URL: <www.Wmhinc.com>

Paul Jarolimek II: President and CEO

Mary Lou Jarolimek: CFO

Suzanne Jarolimek: Director of Customer Relations

Mike Gage: CTO

Kerry Lease: Executive VP of Marketing

Plan prepared November 2001
by the Corporate Officers

TABLE OF CONTENTS

* **Note:** *For brevity, only one of Wmhinc.com's Supporting Documents has been included in this plan.*

EXECUTIVE SUMMARY

Wmhinc.com is an innovative, dynamic start-up company providing services that will establish the Company as the premiere online provider of manufactured housing, industry information, and associated services. The Web site provides consumers the opportunity to design and purchase a home online. Additionally, it provides comprehensive industry information, nationwide Associated Services Yellow Pages, and industry and government links.

The Company plans to establish itself as the "next generation provider" of manufactured homes, products, and related services and capture a sizable portion of this market in the next decade. Furthermore, *Wmhinc.com* is modeled as an Internet Portal, constructed and designed after well-known portals such as C/Net (information technology), CNNfn (finance), Showbiz (entertainment), WebMD (health and fitness), and Thrive Online (health and fitness) with primary focus on the housing industry.

HIGHLIGHTS of *Wmhinc.com*

- **Management Experience.** The Management team is highly qualified and knowledgeable in areas of ecommerce, marketing, manufactured home, and housing related services.

- **Industry Knowledge.** *Wmhinc.com* will leverage its knowledge of the industry to establish a dominating presence in its delivery of homes and related services to consumers.

- **Web Site.** The Web site, with its three-click ease of navigation will smoothly transport the consumer from the front page to a state specific choice page. This second page will have multiple directions in which the customer may travel.

- **Diverse Sources of Revenues.** Unlike a number of other transaction-based businesses operating on the Internet, *Wmhinc.com's* business model is not based on click-through advertising revenue nor is it based on subscription, membership dues, or user fees.

- **Aggressive Marketing.** Management is positioning *Wmhinc.com* to grow aggressively through strategic alliances, innovative marketing and branding programs, and first mover initiatives.

- **Growing Market Segment.** Today manufactured homes make up over 25% of new homes in the United States. Sales of new manufactured homes exceeded $16 billion in 1999, an increase of 400% in the last ten years. With new design elements and customizable options, manufactured homes have begun to cross over into the mainstream.

Management has developed a clear and defined path that will help establish the Company as the leading provider of manufactured housing, industry information, and associated services on the Internet. At the forefront of its model is the establishment of departments that will handle various aspects of operations including the sale and distribution of new, factory over-run, and bank-owned homes.

While the Company fully expects competition to materialize in some form, management also believes its business model will mitigate competitive threats and capitalize on the identified opportunity gaps such as geographic specialization/expertise, superior customer service, and usability.

Customers will be the focal point of the *Wmhinc.com* business model and overall strategy. All customers will be treated with respect, their housing choice made simple, and their decision-making process made positive. *Wmhinc.com* will continually develop its customer network, striving to receive referrals from existing customers and visitors.

Wmhinc.com has established strategic relationships with several prominent industry leaders in the areas of financing, decoration, and manufacturing. By the first fiscal year, the Company expects to have set up additional partnerships with major manufacturers, state and national Manufactured Housing Associations, relevant Internet partner suppliers, and other services providers thereby making *Wmhinc.com* a hub for manufactured homes and related services. In addition, these alliances will enable the Company to draw and retain a strong customer base.

Wmhinc.com intends to derive its revenue from various business activities including:

- E-commerce revenues from the sale of new customer-built homes.
- E-commerce revenues from the sale of factory over-run homes through partner suppliers.
- Fees and commissions paid by partner suppliers of Bank-Owned Homes.
- Sales of advertising space to service providers (exclusive, proprietary, Yellow Pages).
- Fees paid by regional and international Internet partner suppliers of *Wmhinc.com* for certain exclusive rights.
- Fees paid by state and municipality commerce and tourism departments for placement referrals.
- E-commerce revenues and fees paid by land and community developers.
- Fees for design, positioning, and management of "Auction Sites" for maximum speed in disposing of large inventory blocks.
- Resale/income stream from company-owned land and community developments.

The Company is seeking venture capital in the amount of $10 million for its four-phase development. The Company's revenue projections for 2002, 2003, and 2004 are $17 million, $77 million, and $136 million, respectively.

Income Statement Summary			
	2001	**2002**	**2003**
Income	$ 17,216,075	$ 77,631,985	$ 136,623,886
Variable Expenses	5,081,104	18,072,884	34,871,019
Fixed Expenses	1,427,176	6,449,120	11,107,191
Income Taxes	5,196,029	23,262,736	40,652,953
Net Income	5,511,766	35,428,528	51,675,986

PART I: ORGANIZATIONAL PLAN

Wholesale Mobile Homes.com, Inc.

Summary Description of the Business

Wmhinc.com is an innovative, dynamic start-up company providing services that will establish the Company as the premiere online provider of manufactured housing, industry information, and associated services.

Mission

At *Wmhinc.com*, our mission is to provide the most innovative and practical Web-based housing solutions. *Wmhinc.com* plans are to become a dominant player in the online marketplace, providing new, factory over-run, and bank-owned homes direct to the consumer.

Business Model

Wmhinc.com has developed a clear and defined path that will help establish the Company as the leading provider of manufactured housing, industry information, and associated services on the Internet. At the forefront of its model, is the establishment of a department that will sell and distribute new, factory over-run, and bank-owned homes, a department the Company believes will be the core of the business. *Wmhinc.com* will leverage its knowledge of the industry to establish a dominant presence in its delivery of homes and related services to consumers. The Web site, with its three-click ease of navigation will smoothly transport the consumer from the front page to a "state specific" choice page. This second page will have multiple directions in which the customer may travel.

At *Wmhinc.com*, consumers are just one click away from building a house online. The *Wmhinc.com* business model is based on strategic alliances with various manufacturing industry leaders. Through these alliances, the Company will showcase floor plans, option books, and color choice catalogs. The Web site will also feature "Factory Special" pages of prebuilt homes, which will allow consumers to find a new, factory over-run home that suites their needs within a specific state. Through the Associate Services Yellow Pages consumers will find help in installing their home, which may be accessed from the second page or from within the information areas. Also, fully integrated with partner suppliers, will be the whole experience of buying, decorating, furnishing, moving in, and setting up a home in a simple, rich, and comfortable environment for consumers.

One of the most innovative and attractive aspects of the *Wmhinc.com* model is the lack of floor planning. Traditional retail outlets rely on loans in order to provide the funds to procure their display models and special order models have long been a risk to manufacturers. This is primarily due to the manufacturer guarantee of a buy-back in the event that a retailer defaults, which is required by the finance companies to secure the loans for a retailer's inventory. By eliminating this, *Wmhinc.com* will virtually eliminate any risk to the manufacturers in our partnership circle.

Upon finalization of the home order, customers will be required to instruct their financing source (or make a cash deposit themselves) to deposit the agreed upon amount for the home into an escrow account that is controlled by *Wmhinc.com*. The Escrow Company will be given instructions to fund the Factory for the home upon the verification of the building of the home and the presentation of the invoice. *Wmhinc.com* will retain the balance of the funds after the payoff to the Factory, to be paid when delivery is completed, thus completing the contractual obligations.

Strategy

The Company plans to establish itself as the "next generation provider" of manufactured homes, products, and related services and capture a sizable portion of this market in the next decade. Furthermore, *Wmhinc.com* is modeled as an Internet Portal, constructed and designed after well-known portals such as C/Net (information technology), CNNfn (finance), Showbiz (entertainment), WebMD (health and fitness), and Thrive Online (health and fitness) with primary focus on the housing industry.

The dual strategy of the selling and distribution of homes and associated products and services as well as developing *Wmhinc.com* as a portal, takes into account that the home buying and installation process takes between three to six months. During this time frame, visitors will make repeated, almost daily, visits in order to gain additional information, services, and a sense of community with others in like situations. This strategy will increase page views, repeat traffic, and value to our advertisers. Furthermore, this portal presence will allow *Wmhinc.com* to cultivate additional advertisers from non-related industries in order to take advantage of the relationship with our customers. To enhance this, the Company plans to install message boards and forums for discussions concerning the purchase and installation of manufactured housing, as well as nonspecific games and varied interest content.

Wmhinc.com intends to become the leader and most creative provider of Web-based housing solutions in the market. The Company aims to create a user-friendly Web site that will be an integral and necessary component in helping consumers meet their housing needs. This will be done by developing an innovative and progressive development and management team. *Wmhinc.com* will also accomplish its goal by using market research, industry and competitive analysis, and customer input to further develop our products and services.

The Company's long-term objective is to dominate the Manufactured Housing Internet sector as well as create a brick and mortar presence in the manufacturing and retailing of homes and associated products. The Company will leverage this new service in the housing industry to dominate the growing manufactured home market. As a Company, we feel that there are a number of opportunities we can capitalize on and they include:

- **B2B Technology.** Resale of exclusive technology to brick and mortar business to facilitate their infrastructure. Customers include the manufactured housing industry, auto industry, RV industry, and others.
- **B2B Government.** Sale of homes and coordination of delivery for FEMA and state disaster relief efforts (these number in the 1,000s of homes annually). VA listed preferred provider of housing for qualified discharged service people. Military housing contractor for current enlisted personnel and officers.
- **B2B Developers.** Sale of homes to land and community developers for resale.
- **B2B Advertising.** Sale of advertising space on the Company's exclusive yellow pages for related service companies.
- **B2B Garages.** Exclusive patentable product in development allowing a fully built two-car garage to be delivered and erected on site within hours. These will be sold to brick and mortar companies on a wholesale level.
- **B2B Motorsports.** Ability to remarket advertising space within our NASCAR Winston Cup Series sponsorship program for a substantial amount more than expenses, allowing a co-branding opportunity for affiliates.

- **B2B Service.** Ability through existing service structure to offer brick and mortar companies a service department for the warranty work of the units sold at a substantial reduction of costs. Also a service for manufacturers in providing warranty work for customers sold by other retailers by an existing recognized centralized team.
- **B2B Online Auctions.** Fees and profits generated by resale of large block of homes within an online auction setting. Primarily for manufacturers and banks who must unload a large amount of houses at once.
- **B2B Manufacturing of *Wmhinc.com*-branded homes.** Ability to refire idle manufacturing plants of partner manufacturers with a split of proceeds of retail sales. Long-term intent of purchase of idle plants to allow for greater profit.
- **B2C New Home sales.** Unique national online sales of manufactured housing to retail customers.
- **B2C Bank-Owned home sales.** Realization of fees and commission for resale of bank-owned homes to customers.
- **B2C Garages.** Unique national online sales of exclusive, patentable, deliverable garages.
- **B2C Parts/Service.** Ability through our online partnerships to provide parts and service to individual homeowners to facilitate the maintenance and remodel of existing homes.
- **B2C listing for sale of customer Homes "Net Listings."** Allows customers to list their homes for sale taking advantage of the traffic on our Web site. A fee will be charged based on the sale price.

Wmhinc.com will become a one-stop destination for consumers seeking manufactured housing, presenting long-term opportunities for its partner suppliers by enabling them to increase their product deliveries and market share. Furthermore, as a result of ongoing investments in search engine placement, Internet advertising, and traditional advertising consisting primarily of the NASCAR Winston Cup Series, print, and television. Management is projecting first year traffic will place *Wmhinc.com* firmly in the Media Metrix top 100 Web sites.

Strategic Relationships

The Company has strategic alliances with several leading housing-related companies. These alliances are valuable because they provide *Wmhinc.com* with established companies in the housing industry and established distribution channels.

Cavalier Homes have agreed to partner with *Wmhinc.com* for their work with developers, the sale of the computer programs, and the promotion of a yet publicly undisclosed financing company, which they are developing. The agreement with Cavalier Homes is expected to be finalized by the end of January. Additionally, an agreement is expected to be reached with Fleetwood Homes by the end of January too. Currently, *Wmhinc.com* has working agreements for 4,000 homes with several developers for an average of $2,000 to $5,000 per house.

Establishing dominance in the Internet market for manufactured housing and further increasing and expanding market share, *Wmhinc.com* will add value to the products and services offered by its partner companies. High overhead, accelerated collapse of retailing outlets, and zero market penetration in some areas (primarily due to extremely high start-up costs for new retail centers) have all combined to provide the overwhelming need for *Wmhinc.com*'s services. Below is a status of key relationships:

Manufacturers	
Established Relationships	**Contacted—Pending Commitment**
Kit Homes – Homes (HUD) and RV's	Wick Building Systems – Homes (Modular)
Ritz-Craft Homes – Homes (Modular & HUD)	Cavco (Cendex corp) – Homes (HUD)
Chariot Eagle Homes – Homes (Park Model, HUD), Domestic & Export American Homestar—Homes (HUD) Patriot Homes – Homes (HUD)	Fairmont/Friendship Homes – Homes (HUD)
Oakwood Homes – Homes (overstock new HUD)	Nobility – Homes (HUD)
Turtle Homes – Homes (HUD) Handicapped Housing	Kent Homes – Homes (Modular)
Maple Homes of Canada – Homes (Modular)	Excel Homes – Homes (Modular)
Banks (For Sales of Bank-Owned Homes)	
Established Relationships	**Contacted—Pending Commitment**
Associates Housing Finance	Conseco
Bombardier	GreenPoint
Content Providers and Associates (Internet)	
Established Relationships	**Contacted—Pending Commitment**
MonsterDaata.com – Neighborhood information	GetConnected.com – Services disconnect/reconnection
Moving.com—Moving resources	iSyndicate.com – Miscellaneous content provider
Reprint and Copyright Permission	
Established Relationships	**Contacted—Pending Commitment**
North Dakota Manufactured Housing Association Web site content	South Carolina Manufactured Housing Association Web site content
Ray Sterner—Johns Hopkins University	Pennsylvania Manufactured Housing Association Web site content

Risks

As with all companies, the opportunity is tempered with certain risks. Important risks to consider are described below according to internal and external risk categories.

Wmhinc.com Associated Risks

- **Early Stage Business.** *Wmhinc.com* was incorporated in August 2000 and has a relatively short operating history. The Management Team has experience in the areas of business management, manufactured housing, e-commerce, and various types of expertise that contribute to managing start-ups. Moreover, the Management Team has considerable expertise in product/service launches as well as marketing and sales. In addition, *Wmhinc.com* and its prospects must be considered in light of the risks, expenses, and difficulties frequently encountered by companies in an early stage of development. This is an especially important consideration to weigh in view of the fact that *Wmhinc.com* is engaged in a new and rapidly evolving market for Internet services.
- **Establishing, Building, Maintaining, and Strengthening Brand.** *Wmhinc.com*'s senior management believes building, strengthening, and maintaining the *Wmhinc.com* brand is important in its ability to attract and retain customers. Moreover, the importance of brand recognition will escalate in proportion to the expected increasing numbers of Internet competitors. Positioning and strengthening *Wmhinc.com*'s brand name is dependent upon the success of the Company's marketing and promotional efforts and *Wmhinc.com*'s ability to provide high-quality, cost-effective content. In addition,

Wmhinc.com plans to undertake certain public relations activities and tasks. These efforts contribute to building a brand name.

Internet Associated Risks

- **Technology.** The market for manufactured homes is constantly undergoing change. Important factors to consider include: (1) Changes in customer requirements and preferences; (2) Frequent new product and service introductions that embody new processes and technologies; and (3) Evolving industry standards and practices that could render *Wmhinc.com*'s existing practices and methodologies obsolete.

- **e-Commerce.** *Wmhinc.com*'s future revenues and profits are substantially dependent upon broad acceptance of customers to use the Internet and other online services as a medium for buying manufactured homes. Interest and use of the Web is a recent phenomenon, and it goes along with the rise of Internet and related online services. There can be no assurance that such acceptance and use will continue in the future. Moreover, there is no assurance that a broad base of consumers will adopt or continue to use the Internet as a medium of commerce.

- **System failures.** *Wmhinc.com*'s success and its ability to facilitate electronic commerce successfully depends on the efficient and uninterrupted operation of its Internet connectivity systems. *Wmhinc.com* obtains its high-speed Internet access through third party Internet Service Providers (ISP). ISPs maintain physical and electronic systems that are vulnerable to failure, damage, or interruption resulting from any number of possibilities, ranging from earthquakes, floods, fire, loss of power, telecommunication failures, break-ins, sabotage, vandalism, and similar events.

- **Database security.** Through its Web site, *Wmhinc.com* will maintain sensitive customer data in its database. To protect customer records, a sophisticated security system has been incorporated into the Web site that relies on a combination of security devices and methods that make the data virtually scrambled to the point that a hacker has an extremely low probability of accessing customer records. Despite this, maintaining customer records on a Web-based system bears certain risks and liability.

Business and Financial Risks

- **Competition.** *Wmhinc.com* operates in highly competitive markets and may not be able to compete effectively. Many of *Wmhinc.com*'s current and potential competitors have longer operating histories and substantially greater financial, technical, marketing, distribution, and other resources than *Wmhinc.com* does and therefore may be able to respond more quickly than *Wmhinc.com* can to new or changing opportunities, technologies, standards, or customer requirements.

- **Dependency on Effective Marketing and Sales.** *Wmhinc.com* expects that its future financial performance will depend in part on sales of its services. *Wmhinc.com* recently published its Web site. Market acceptance of Wmhinc (as a company) depends on the market demand for the specific functionality of such services. If Wmhinc's services fail to meet customer needs or expectations, for whatever reason, *Wmhinc.com*'s reputation could be damaged, or it could be required to upgrade or enhance services, which could be costly and time consuming.

- **Dependency on Sales Force and Distribution.** *Wmhinc.com*'s failure to expand its sales force and distribution channels would adversely affect its revenue growth and financial condition. To increase its revenue, *Wmhinc.com* must increase the size of its sales force and the number of its indirect channel partners, including original equipment manufacturers, value-added resellers, and systems integrators. A failure to do so could have a material adverse effect on *Wmhinc.com*'s business, operating results, and financial condition. There is intense competition for sales personnel in *Wmhinc.com*'s business, and there can be no assurance that *Wmhinc.com* will be successful in attracting, integrating, motivating, and retaining new sales personnel. *Wmhinc.com*'s existing or future channel partners may choose to devote greater resources to marketing and supporting the services of competitors. In addition, *Wmhinc.com* will need to resolve potential conflicts among its sales force and channel partners.

- **Poor results by service providers may damage Wmhinc's reputation.** Wmhinc's business could be adversely affected if its subcontractors/partners fail to perform services to its customer's satisfaction. The occurrence of various unfriendly situations could result in loss of or delay in revenue, loss of market share, failure to achieve market acceptance, diversion of development resources, injury to *Wmhinc.com*'s reputation, or damage to its efforts to build brand awareness, any of which could have a material adverse effect on its business, operating results, and financial condition.

Products and Services

The Company plans to establish itself as the "next generation provider" of manufactured homes, products, and related services. The Company's Web site not only provides the opportunity for the consumer to design and purchase a home online, but also includes comprehensive information, a nationwide Associated Services Yellow Pages, and industry and government links. Designed to be user friendly with a simple three-click system and "state specific" listings of products and services, the Web site enables the consumer to find the home or information needed with ease.

Intellectual Property

Patents, copyrights, and/or trademarks

Wmhinc.com regards its copyrights, trademarks, trade secrets (including methodologies, practices, and tools), and other intellectual property rights as critical to success. To protect its rights, *Wmhinc.com* relies on a combination of trademark and copyright laws, trade secret protection, nondisclosure agreements, and other contractual agreements with its employees, affiliates, clients, strategic partners, acquisition targets, and others.

Legal Structure

Wholesalemobilehomes.com, Inc (*Wmhinc.com*) is a privately-held Nevada C corporation. The Company was formed on August 1st, 2000 and incorporated on August 23rd, 2000. Provided below is a list of the Company's corporate officers and their compensation.

Compensation		
Paul S Jarolimek II	President/CEO	$ 52,500
Michael Gage	CTO	$ 52,500
MaryLou Jarolimek	CFO	$ 52,500
Stephen Massie	EVP Warrenty/Service	$ 52,500
Jim Stephens	EVP Sales	$ 52,500
Suzanne Jarolimek	EVP Customer Service	$ 52,500
Kerry Lease	EVP Marketing	STOCK ONLY
Larry Queen	VP Technology—Graphics	$ 52,500
Leon Jarolimek	VP Customer Service/Warranty	$ 52,500
William Smith	Corporate Counsel	STOCK ONLY

Location

The Company's principal offices are located at 5300 W Sahara, Suite 101, Las Vegas, Nevada 89146. Currently, the Company is paying a monthly rental fee of $1,500. The Company plans to develop a gated compound on 10 to 20 acres of land consisting of two converted manufactured homes (total area 5,000 square-feet) that will serve as the office area. Also on the compound will be a housing development featuring six manufactured homes. In January 2002, the Company will begin its search for potential sites. Site selection is expected to be completed by the middle of February with construction beginning in March.

Management

The Company's management philosophy is based on responsibility and mutual respect. At *Wmhinc.com*, we have an environment that encourages creativity and achievement. *Wmhinc.com* management is highly experienced and qualified. *Wmhinc.com*'s management team provides strong leadership ability, sales and marketing expertise, and extensive knowledge in both Manufactured Housing and the Internet. See résumé in Supporting Documents. Descriptions of the management team and responsibilities are as follows.

- **Paul Jarolimek II, Founder, Chairman, President, and CEO.** Paul Jarolimek II is a veteran in the Manufactured Housing industry who has proven his leadership in both independent retail enterprises and from within the corporate structure. A top salesperson for one of the leading Manufactured Housing companies in the nation prior to taking on management roles, he has the management experience, customer service, and people skills to facilitate his role in this company.

- **MaryLou Jarolimek, Board Member and CFO.** MaryLou Jarolimek has nearly 30 years of business acumen. Having successfully run a number of businesses and trained in financial services, her role as CFO is most suited.

- **Suzanne Jarolimek, Board Member and Director of Customer Relations.** Suzanne Jarolimek brings with her a pragmatic and laser focused vision of the needs of our customers.

- **Mike Gage, Board Member and CTO.** Mike Gage possesses many years of Internet commerce experience and deep understanding of hardware and software applications.

- **Kerry Lease, Board Member and Executive VP of Marketing.** Kerry Lease delivers 25 years of successful business ownership in the highly competitive field of advertising and marketing.

Personnel

Management realizes that the strength of the Company's personnel is key to success. As such, plans include filling staff positions with professionals who have proven success and records in the dotcom world and have an understanding of the housing industry. The Company plans to hire five department managers at an average salary of $40,000 per year each and ten hourly employees at an average wage rate that totals $16,800 per year per employee.

Accounting and Legal

- **Accounting**

  Wmhinc.com will follow Generally Accepted Accounting Principles (GAAP). The Company will use the Accrual Basis for recognition of revenues and handle accounting and bookkeeping internally. The CFO is responsible for the overall financial condition of the Company and managing all financial functions in keeping *Wmhinc.com* a profitable corporation.

  All bookkeeping activities will be handled internally by the Administrative Assistant using Peachtree Accounting. Peachtree Accounting has been selected over other accounting packages because of its powerful business management and Internet tools. An outside CPA firm will provide auditing services and develop financial reports for *Wmhinc.com*.

  The Company will keep its customer database on ACT, a contact management software by Symantec. ACT allows users to create a database, faxing, running reports, mail merge, and has a new feature that allows users to send and receive e-mail messages from within Act's interface.

- **Legal**

  For all legal aspects of the business, the Company has retained the services of the Maryland-based Law Office of Kerwin A. Miller, LLC. Provided below is the company's contact information.

  > Law Office of Kerwin A. Miller, LLC
  > Principal—Kerwin Miller
  > 6905 Rockledge Drive, Suite 600
  > Bethesda, MD 20817
  > Off: 301-896-9421
  > Fax: 301-941-9009

Insurance

Management has assessed insurance requirements and has concluded that the Company will need business liability coverage, industry specific liability insurance coverage, workers' compensation coverage, medical coverage, and key-man coverage. (Note: see Insurance Update Form in supporting documents.)

Security

The Company will maintain sensitive customer data in its database and from transactions on the Internet. To protect customer records, a sophisticated security system will be incorporated into the Web site that relies on a combination of security devices and methods that encrypt the data leaving an extremely low probability of accessing customer records.

PART II: MARKETING PLAN
Wholesale Mobile Homes.com, Inc.

I. Overview and Goals

A. Overview of Marketing Strategy

The Marketing Plan is developed in order to support *Wmhinc.com*'s goals and strategies. It is based on strategic goals as well as knowledge gained during analysis of the industry, competitive intelligence, and what *Wmhinc.com* knows (or assumes) about its customers and partners. Initial marketing tactics will focus on the development of the *Wmhinc.com* promotional material, an efficient public relations campaign, including a strong Internet search engine presence, cold calling, and visits to trade shows and a corporate sales force.

B. Goals of Marketing Strategy

- Creating a Strong Brand
- Building a Strong Customer Base
- Increasing Product/Service Sales

II. Market Analysis

A. Target Market(s)

Customers will be the focal point of the *Wmhinc.com* business model and overall strategy. All customers will be treated with respect, their housing choice will be made simple, and their decision-making process made positive. *Wmhinc.com* will continually develop its customer network, continually striving to receive referrals from existing customers and visitors. *Wmhinc.com* caters to the following customer groups/target markets:

- Individuals *(Wmhinc.com's NASCAR advertising campaign that is explained below, will primarily target this market segment)*
- Government
- Developers
- Manufacturers
- Retail Sale Centers
- Advertisers

Value Propositions

Wmhinc.com offers the following value propositions for each customer group/target market.

Individuals

Ease of Use. Easy navigation through the Web site utilizing a three-click process to find the right section, build and purchase homes, and find information.

Buy Homes Online. Prices posted, options, and features from many different manufacturers allow a greater choice than can be found on a local level. No pricing games normally played by local retailers, where your neighbor paid $5,000 less for the same home because he negotiates better. Ability to self direct the design of the home, and ability to see how the inclusion of certain options affect the home and prices before having to commit to a loan. Ability to compare different manufacturers, options, and colors.

No Pressure. No high-pressure sales tactics so often encountered in retail sales. No issues with untrained sales staff or managers. No push by retailers into a home which may not suit their needs in order for the company to remove the home from their inventory.

Unparalleled Information Sources. Wmhinc.com has access to tens of thousands of pages of information and is developing a joint information venture with FEMA for the prevention of disasters. This program will be exclusive and proprietary and will be protected by intellectual property rights. Additionally, *Wmhinc.com* is in the process of securing the rights to reprint two industry related publications (one of which is used by major universities as a textbook) online for our customers to reference. These publications will be published under an exclusive arrangement. Furthermore, directed information such as checklists, instructions, and explanations of the installation and moving processes will give the customer the ability to oversee their own project instead of relying on a third party to do this for them. Customers will also have the ability to verify that the work being done is in a workmanship fashion and in a timely manner. This is a huge problem facing brick and mortar retailers as evidenced by Web sites such as <http://members.boardhost.com/oakwoodhomes/>.

Sense of Community. With the installation of manufactured housing taking three to six months from start to finish *Wmhinc.com* will offer a sense of community to those who visit the Web site. Regardless of whether the Company sells them a home, visitors will benefit from the message boards and information that will provide them with a starting point for their projects and discussion points with people in similar situations.

Less Cost. While the Company intends to be competitive, it also realizes the customer will save a great deal of money working directly with contractors and other companies in order to facilitate their home installation and moving services. There is commonly a mark-up of these types of services by brick and mortar retailers, which is not generally seen in Internet-based sales.

Government

Disaster Relief Services. Centralized point for FEMA to procure homes in the event of a natural disaster for replacement of destroyed property. Also a joint venture with FEMA for disaster awareness and preventative measures which can be undertaken before or after the home is installed.

Military Housing. Ability to provide a wide range of options at a low bid price for the development of personnel housing on military bases.

VA Preferred Provider of Manufactured Housing. Offer the VA department a definitive provider of housing for post-military personnel. This will be done in such a way that the VA recommends us for those in need of manufactured homes.

Developers

Provide large blocks of housing and support for land and community developers. This program provides a tremendous resource for the developer in availability of many choices of homes with one contact, standardized pricing, reference materials, as well as follow-up marketing opportunities.

Manufacturers

Marketing Their Homes. Through their traditional retail outlets, both company owned and independent manufacturers are having extreme difficulty moving their products. This is primarily due to high overhead, accelerated collapse of retailing outlets, and zero market penetration in some areas (due to extremely high start-up costs for new retail centers).

Reduction of Overstock Homes. Many press releases by the major Manufactured Housing companies, such as Oakwood Homes, American Homestar, Champion, Fleetwood and the like have pointed to overproduction of stock homes in an already over-saturated market, combined with higher than normal repossession rates further returning homes to the marketplace.

Immediate Payment on Sold Homes. One of the most innovative and attractive aspects of the *Wmhinc.com* model is the lack of floor planning. This has long been a risk to manufacturers due to the guarantees required by the finance companies to secure the loans for a retailer's inventory. By eliminating this, *Wmhinc.com* will virtually eliminate any risk to the manufacturers in our partnership circle. Upon finalization of the home order by the customer, they will be required to instruct their financing source (or deposit themselves if paying cash) to deposit the agreed upon amount for the home into an escrow account controlled by *Wmhinc.com*. The Escrow Company will be given instructions to fund the Factory for the home upon the verification of the building of the home and the presentation of the invoice.

Retail Sale Centers and Parent Companies

Technology. The technology of the Company's tracking program, which will be installed on the Web site, will give *Wmhinc.com* the ability to track virtually every aspect of the customer's buying process. Additionally, this will enable the Company to constantly communicate with potential customers. Studies have shown that the decision-making process can take six months or more and the installed program will provide the ability to automatically track and keep in contact with the customer during this decision-making process. Furthermore, this will also track the after sale service allowing *Wmhinc.com* to remain in contact and smoothly facilitate warranty service of the homes. This will enable the Company to continue its follow-up with the customer long after the home purchase and mining referrals of new customers through existing clientele. This technology will be offered in a slightly modified version to others in the industry as well as any industry that deals in large ticket items, such as automobiles, RVs, motorcycles, boats, etc.

Prebuilt Garages. Patentable product in development, which can be sold to industry brick and mortars on a wholesale level for eventual resale. *Wmhinc.com* has procured engineering and design, as well as manufacturing space to facilitate the production of these units.

Advertisers

Copyrighted, Exclusive, Industry Specific Yellow Pages. This is designed to provide companies, both on and off the Internet, in related industries the ability to put their products directly in front of the people who need them the most. High volume specific traffic, needing the services listed, provide huge benefits to this program. Furthermore, the Company's involvement in the NASCAR Winston Cup Series, with their viewers' 73% certified brand loyalty, will translate in a loyalty to the Company's advertisers. Management believes that due to the eschewing of the "banner ad" and instead providing a fixed position advertising format familiar and comfortable to our customers, as well as the community aspect of the Web site, the information resources, and the depth of companies partnering in advertising, *Wmhinc.com* will be the one-stop destination for consumers of manufactured housing, thus bringing greater returns to advertising dollars spent.

B. Competition

1. Description of Major Competitors

Chandler, Inc. Chandler is committed to being number one in the South by offering customers "direct from the builder pricing." Chandler drop ships custom-ordered homes directly to the customers, lot from the manufacturer. This amounts to thousands of dollars in savings to the customer. Chandler offers the above propositions that make it one of the best sites to purchase mobile homes:

> 2254 U.S. 84 West
> Valdosta, Georgia 31601
> Phone: 912-242-5900
> Fax: 912-242-8833
> www.chandlersmfg.com/

Homestore.com, Inc. Homestore.com with its family of sites is one of the leading destinations for home and real estate-related information on the Internet. RealSelect, Inc., is the official Internet site of the National Association of Realtors® and has pioneered the use of the Internet as a channel for buying and selling homes. Each site in the Homestore.com™ family provides definitive resources for both professionals and consumers, including advanced search functions, rich editorial content, marketplaces for related products and services, and tools such as checklists and calculators.

> 225 West Hillcrest Drive, Suite 100
> Thousand Oaks, CA 91360
> Phone: 805-557-2300
> www.factorybuilthousing.com/

MHShopper. MHShopper was founded in 2000 to create a network of market leading manufactured home dealers across the country. Through this united network, MHShopper and the Manufactured Home Shopper Network is able to ensure value pricing and a variety of low-cost financing options—savings that are passed to both dealers and consumers. MHShopper completed its first round of financing in July, 2000 through a private placement with Roth Capital Partners of Newport Beach, California.

> 15282 Newsboy Circle, Huntington Beach, CA 92649
> Phone: 714-373-5001 (6:30 AM to 5 PM PST)
> Fax: 714-373-5006
> http://MHShopper.com

Michael Holigan.com. MH2Technologies makes building easier, more productive, and more profitable. Its service offerings, including MH2Build and MH2Marketing, were developed by builders for builders. MH2Build allows homebuilders and light commercial contractors to save time, reduce overhead, simplify ordering, and schedule efficiently. From any location, builders can use MH2Build for job management, scheduling, and materials ordering. MH2Technologies also provides homebuilders exceptional branding power through MH2Marketing. MH2Technologies' licensees gain the ability to differentiate themselves in the very fragmented national homebuilding industry.

MHConnection.com. MHConnection.com is a privately-held Web-based marketplace for the mobile and manufactured home industry. The company is based in Cedaredge, Colorado. Its principals and advisors have vast industry experience as well as technical expertise.

> MHConnection.com, Inc.
> 1825 2550 Rd.
> Cedaredge, CO 81413
> Phone: (800) 304-2835
> www.MHConnection.com

Mobile Homes Coast 2 Coast. Mobile Homes Coast 2 Coast is the ultimate online resource for consumers to showcase their mobile home or manufactured home to prospective buyers and for people wanting to buy a mobile home in their area. Mobile Homes Coast 2 Coast facilitates the process for buyers and sellers through advertisements on their Web site. When a seller places an ad, prospective buyers can instantly view it and the seller has immediate access to make any changes they want to make to their ads.

Mobile Homes Coast 2 Coast also provides all the necessary information and resources to information that buyers and sellers of mobile homes and manufactured homes will ever need. The company provides services for sellers, dealers, financial institutions, and mobile home communities, and offers all businesses related to this industry a low-cost and effective means of advertising.
http://mobilehomescoast2coast.com/

2. Assessment of Their Strengths/Weaknesses

Competition exists within the industry but not at the level at which *Wmhinc.com* is participating. Individual retailers, information-only sites, and manufacturer sites all have a common denominator and that is none of them actually offer the home to the customer. The closest service competitors are offering is allowing the visitor to request more information which is then sent, sans prices.

While *Wmhinc.com* fully expects additional competition to materialize in some form, management also believes its business model will mitigate competitive threats and capitalize on the identified opportunity gaps such as geographic specialization and expertise, superior customer service, and usability.

C. Market Trends

1. Target Market Trends

Wmhinc.com believes that it provides a natural evolution in the manufactured housing market. While the Company's services have never been directly sold on the Internet, recent studies have shown dramatic increases of Internet usage by consumers for home purchases. A unique marketing channel has been developed as clearly shown in the Internet retailing of vehicles, heavy equipment, boats, and big ticket items. Consumers are becoming increasingly more comfortable with making major purchases online. Internet vehicles sales alone exceeded $670 million for the year ending 1999 says analyst James McQuivey of Forrester Research, and by 2003, it is projected that eight million cars will be purchased with some help from the Internet. That market, and a nationwide figure of over 370,000 manufactured homes delivered in 1998, and over 320,000 delivered in 1999, has given *Wmhinc.com* a clearly defined and workable model.

Demographically *Wmhinc.com* is positioned on the cusp of a major resurgence in manufactured housing. While traditional buyers of manufactured housing have been, and continue to be, first-time homebuyers, which is where *Wmhinc.com*'s primary marketing thrust will center early on, the aging baby boomer section of the population will account for a dramatic increase in manufactured housing sales.

The year ending 1999 saw a downturn in the nationwide delivery in Manufactured Housing, and while there are many reasons for the downturn, facts show that as the baby boomers enter the preretirement stages they will become a burgeoning market for Manufactured Housing. Empty nests, upscale 55 and older communities, the high quality and relative low expense not only in the purchase, but maintenance of Manufactured Housing, as well as other factors, will play a pivotal role in the purchase of Manufactured Housing by baby boomers. This, coupled with the demographics of Internet usage showing adults 55 and older represent the fastest growing group of U.S. Internet users. This is according to International Data Corp., which found the number of seniors online will more than triple from 11.1 million in 1999 to 34.1 million in 2004 account for 20% of all new users, and it will provide *Wmhinc.com* a long-term source of customers.

2. Industry Trends

According to *Statistical Surveys*, the industy's leading information source, there has been a precipitous drop in Manufactured Housing shipments over the last two plus years. In 1998 there were over 370,000 total shipments nationwide. In 1999 that figure dropped to over 320,000. Currently the shipments stand at approximately 120,000 through the month of May 2000.

While there has been much speculation concerning this, the industry is cyclical. Many press releases by the major Manufactured Housing companies such as Oakwood Homes, American Homestar, Champion, and Fleetwood have pointed to overproduction of stock homes in an already over-saturated market, combined with higher than normal repossession rates further returning homes to the marketplace. The shutting down of business by major traditional independent retailers because of the obligations extended by the Manufacturers, resulted in the buying back of millions of dollars of inventory and aided in flooding an already overwhelmed retail structure. These and other factors, while perceived as a negative by many, provide *Wmhinc.com* with a world of opportunity.

Through their traditional retail outlets, both company-owned and independent manufacturers are having extreme difficulty moving products. High overhead, accelerated collapse of retailing outlets, and zero market penetration in some areas (primarily due to extremely high start-up costs for new retail centers) have all combined to provide the overwhelming need for the services offered by *Wmhinc.com*.

The Manufactured Home Market

In 1976, the Federal Manufactured Home Construction and Safety Standards Act, administered by the U.S. Department of Housing and Urban Development (HUD), came into effect. This building code, which is also known as the HUD code, federally regulates the design and construction of manufactured homes. It also sets the standards for home durability and safety.

The implementation of the HUD code was a pivotal point in the manufactured home industry. No longer referred to as mobile homes or trailers, manufactured homes began a revolution in housing. Home construction became consistent industry wide, and manufacturers, lenders, and consumers began to recognize manufactured homes as a viable alternative to site-built homes.

Today, manufactured homes make up over 25% of new homes in the United States. Sales of new manufactured homes exceeded $16 billion in 1999, an increase of 400% in the last ten years. With new design elements and customizable options, manufactured homes have begun to cross over into the mainstream.

The improvement of construction standards and incredible sales growth in the industry have caused many national lenders to reconsider their views of manufactured homes. Manufactured home buyers now have more financing options than those buyers who are considering purchasing site-built homes.

D. Market Research—Additional Factors

Additional highlights of the manufactured home market include:

- Over 19 million people (about 8% of the U.S. population) live full-time in over eight million manufactured homes.

- In 1999, the industry shipped 348,671 homes from 323 manufacturing facilities.

- Satisfaction with the manufactured housing lifestyle is reported by 88% of manufactured home owners.

- A majority of manufactured homes are never moved after they have been installed.

- Manufactured housing retail sales were estimated at $16.3 billion in 1998. In 1999, 20.7% of all new single-family housing starts were manufactured homes.

- According to the Census Bureau, 1999 figures show that 68% of new manufactured homes were located on private property, and 32% of new manufactured homes were located in communities.

- The average sales price of a manufactured home was $43,600 in 1999. Single-section homes average $31,800, while multi-section homes average $50,200.

- In 1999, the estimated economic impact from manufactured housing was $34.5 billion. The economic impact reflects the economic activity generated by the production and sale of a home—this includes salaries, goods purchased, and auxiliary services.

III. Marketing Strategy

A. General Description

The overall marketing plan for *Wmhinc.com* 's service is based on the following fundamentals:

- The segment of the market(s) planned to reach.

- Distribution channels planned to be used to reach market segments: NASCAR, television, print, sales associates, and telemarketing.

- Share of the market expected to capture over a fixed period of time.

Market Responsibilities

Wmhinc.com is committed to an extensive promotional campaign. This will be done aggressively and on a broad scale. To accomplish initial sales goals, the Company will require an extremely effective promotional campaign to accomplish two primary objectives:

- Attract quality sales personnel that have a desire to be successful.
- Attract customers that will constantly look to *Wmhinc.com* for their housing needs.

In addition, *Wmhinc.com* plans to advertise in NASCAR, television, newspapers, and joint direct mail efforts with FEMA

B. Method of Sales and Distribution

Wmhinc.com's sales plan is to seek business that will advance the Company's quest to vertically integrate and become a stronger force in the housing industry. The Company will continue to strive towards procuring sales of its services in the nation.

To accomplish *Wmhinc.com*'s endeavors, the Company will utilize internal and external sales tactics. By aggressively seeking new accounts and taking full advantage of the existing relationships the Company has with current customers and broadening its customer base, the Company will expand and compete with the leading companies in its markets.

C. Pricing

Wmhinc.com sets pricing based on market and competitive rates. Through its alliances with various manufacturers, *Wmhinc.com* is able to order the homes at discounted prices. With its business model, the Company is then able to pass on the direct cost savings to the customer while generating significant profit margins.

D. Sales Strategies

Wmhinc.com plans to use a combination of the following strategies to reach its markets.

- Direct sales
- Direct mail
- E-mail marketing
- Affiliate marketing
- Viral marketing

These channels are most appropriate because of time to market, reduced capital requirements, and fast access to established distribution channels. The sales department will be headed by one general sales manager and one national sales manager who will be initially charged with developing the sales force to consist of several sales teams led by local sales managers.

E. Sales Incentives

As an extra incentive for customers and potential customers to remember *Wmhinc.com*'s name, the Company, through its NASCAR involvement, plans to enable the marketing of die-cast renderings of the sponsored racecar, T-shirts and other clothing, miscellaneous novelties, and other advertising specialties with the Company logo. This multi-billion dollar NASCAR sports merchandising program will produce dramatic branding of the *Wmhinc.com* name as these items will appear in virtually every K-Mart and Wal-Mart in the United States and abroad. Retail sales of NASCAR related merchandise have grown over 1,400% in the last decade. This will be an ongoing program for the Company, when appropriate and where it is identified as beneficial.

F. Advertising Strategies

1. Traditional Advertising

Advertising will focus on building awareness of *Wmhinc.com*'s brand and on marketing (online) services as a better and cost effective way for purchasing manufactured homes. Advertising will be directed at bringing interested prospects to *Wmhinc.com*'s Web site for additional information. Advertising programs will include the following channels:

- Television (network/cable)
- Radio
- Print

2. Web Advertising/New Media

Wmhinc.com plans to contract one or more third parties to handle its Web advertising requirements. *Wmhinc.com* will conduct Internet advertising in the form of Internet banner ads, newsletters, co-branding efforts, search engines, portals, and press releases on Web sites that have high traffic-visitors that match *Wmhinc.com*'s target demographics. Through the Web site, prospective customers can obtain detailed information on the services, request additional information, and opt-in or opt-out to future product/service announcements.

Cost of Advertising	
Nascar Winston Cup	$6,000,000
Internet (Primarily search engine placement)	500,000
Print Advertising	200,000

3. Long-Term Sponsorships

Wmhinc.com will initiate a national advertising campaign in conjunction with the Company's sponsorship of a Winston Cup Series team. The Company's national advertising accounts will receive a full-page advertisement (which could be their home page displayed within the *Wmhinc.com* Web site, see: <http://Wmhinc.com/yp> or <Moving.com> within the "moving" section and FEMA in the "FEMA" section of our site). Additionally, they will receive the following value-added propositions.

- Three associate sponsor placements on a NASCAR Winston Cup racecar; this could be in one race or over three races. Races are first come first serve, and include the Daytona 500 and the Brickyard 400 at the Indy Motor Speedway. The Company has selected Derrike Cope as its driver for the upcoming NASCAR season. Advertising will include mention on television (Fox and/or NBC) and radio. NASCAR boasts a viewership of over 4,500,000 people not including the individual race attendance. Location would be:
  - Leading edge of hood
  - Lower quarter panel front of rear wheel
  - Lower quarter panel rear of rear wheel
  - Trunk lid
  - Rear panel in area between rear lights (TV Panel)

- Permanent placement on the car/equipment hauler (rolling billboard from February to November).

- Invitation for two to the exclusive hospitality tent prior to race. Wine and dine with the crew and officials and meet Kenny Wallace and the crew chief, Barry Dobson (per race).

- Two VIP garage passes (per race).

- Opportunity to be a uniformed crewmember during the race.

- News and other TV placement as sponsor.

- Prominently displayed and mentioned as a FEMA "Project Impact" associate during joint press conferences.

- Prominently displayed within the "Project Impact" joint *Wmhinc.com* and FEMA Web site.

- Opportunity for advertiser's name to be in retail outlets including K-Mart and Wal-Mart (die-cast cars and T-shirts).

Wmhinc.com believes this joint marketing venture will help to increase its customer base as well as produce income from the sale of the advertising well over the amount required for its own marketing efforts. Effectively, this will result in an immediate return on the Company's marketing investment as well as the excellent exposure of the NASCAR association.

NASCAR Statistics: 1998–1999 Total U.S. TV rating (regular season—households)

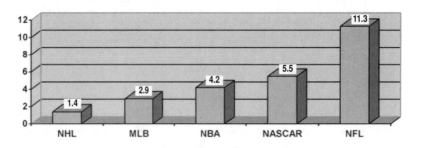

Per event average:
- In-focus time: 9min 04sec
- Sponsor mentions: 5.4
- Value based on cost per :30 ad: $626,330

Other coverage opportunities (no additional cost added):

Television		
NASCAR 2-day (ESPN)	NASCAR 2-day (ESPN)	Inside NASCAR (TNN)
Inside W.C. (Speedvision)	NASCAR Garage (TNN)	Week in NASCAR (Prime)
RPM2Night (ESPN2)		
Radio		
Live coverage MRN&PRN	NASCAR Garage	NASCAR Live
NASCAR Now	NASCAR Today	NASCAR USA
Fast Talk with Benny Parsons		
Publications		
Inside NASCAR	NASCAR Magazine	NASCAR W.C. Scene
NASCAR W.C. Illustrated	NASCAR Racing for Teens	NASCAR Preview
NASCAR Garage	Speedway Scene	National Speed Sport News

Percentage of fans that say sponsorships have an impact on their purchases:

- Somewhat: 48%
- Extreme: 32%
- Very Little: 12%
- None: 8%

Audience brand loyalty

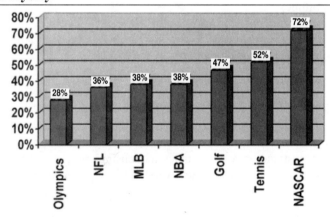

Audience income		Audience age	
>$20,000	15.9%	12–17	12.0%
$20 - $30,000	16.7%	18–24	12.8%
$30 - $50,000	30.2%	25–34	18.7%
$50 - $75,000	20.4%	35– 44	22.6%
$75,000 +	16.8%	35–44	22.6%
		55 +	18.2%

Comparable Value

Throughout the 1999 season, there were 108 broadcasts of Winston Cup Series events, airing on ABC, CBS, ESPN, ESPN2, NBC, TBS, and TNN.

The broadcast season resulted in the collection of 344 hours, 17 minutes, and 53 seconds of exposure time; 20,507 verbal mentions; and $1,438,015,450 of comparable value for 831 sponsors. The average sponsor received $1,732,550 value from their sponsorship involvement in the Winston Cup Series, which was an average of $50,960 per event. The top 25 sponsors received an even greater return averaging $21,285,245 worth of comparable value for the season or $626,330 per event.

Due to *Wmhinc.com*'s NASCAR involvement and FEMA partnership, management clearly expects to drive over one million unique visitors through the Web site every month within the first year. NASCAR's online site generates over 43 million page views by over 4.6 million unique users per month, each averaging 9 minutes per visit. FEMA has over 150,000,000 unique visitors per year on its Web site.

G. Public Relations

As *Wmhinc.com* launches its services, it is extremely important to develop and implement a public relations campaign that creates rapid recognition by the target markets and others who can help the Company build its markets. *Wmhinc.com* plans to establish and promote a favorable relationship with the public by developing communications with non-customers, including labor, public interest groups, government agencies, and press releases. *Wmhinc.com* will also monitor and improve public opinion as well as developing publicity where possible. Wmhinc's public relations campaign will include the following:

- Building an Online Presence
- Communities, Chats, and Message Boards
- Events (online and offline)
- Networking (organization membership, leadership positions)
- Press Releases (print, radio, television, online)
- Interviews (print, radio, television, chat rooms, online events)

H. Networking

Wmhinc.com plans to become a member of state and national manufactured housing associations, the Manufactured Housing Institute <www.manufacturedhousing.org>, the National Manufactured Housing Congress <www.nmhcogress.org> and several industry publications.

IV. Customer Service

The customer service strategy is based on providing high quality service which means having sufficient staffers available to take calls without keeping a customer waiting. *Wmhinc.com* will emphasize through advertising and PR channels that clients will receive personalized service and customer service as needed. *Wmhinc.com* will use automation technology such as FAQ pages on the Web site, message and discussion boards, bulletin boards, an online help desk, and self-service help wherever possible.

One major problem that can arise is if the service is poorly delivered, the Company would require a large customer service department. If such a company is overloaded with customer service calls, eventually we would see an exodus to alternative manufactured housing companies. On the other hand, excellent customer service will enhance the Company's image and boost sales and lead to repeat business, and a high number of sales resulting from referrals.

V. Implementation of Marketing Strategy

A. In-House Responsibilities

Wmhinc.com will develop and execute its marketing strategy in-house. In addition to developing the marketing plan, the Company will set goals, objectives, and propositions.

B. Out-Sourced Functions

Wmhinc.com plans to contract one or more third parties to handle its Web advertising requirements. Additionally, the Company will outsource PR responsibilities to an established public relations company.

VI. Assessment of Marketing Effectiveness

Wmhinc.com, Inc. will evaluate the results of its marketing efforts on a monthly basis. At that time, based on the evaluation, decisions will be made and necessary changes will be implemented to increase marketing effectiveness. Participation in the evaluation process will be required for management + key personnel in the marketing department.

Part III: Financial Documents

Wholesale Mobile Homes.com, Inc.

Wholesale Mobile Homes.com, Inc.

Summary of Financial Needs
and
Dispersal of Investment Funds

Source of Funds

I. *Wmhinc.com* is seeking funding in the amount of $10 million for its four-phase development.

II. Provided below is a breakdown of the use of funds.

Use of Funds

	Use of Funds Based on $10 Million Investment		
Phase I			
	First Quarter of Operations	**Projected Expense**	**% of Gross Proceeds**
1)	Commissions Paid	$ 700,000.00	7.00%
2)	Web site Development	$ 168,750.00	1.69%
3)	Rent Lease and Utilities	$ 81,420.00	0.81%
4)	Connectivity & Installation	$ 5,000.00	0.05%
5)	Executive and Administrative	$ 372,920.00	3.73%
6)	Professional, Legal, Advisory	$ 5,000.00	0.05%
7)	Advertising	$ 1,433,660.00	14.34%
8)	Equipment and Furniture	$ 79,000.00	0.79%
9)	Tech Support	$ 5,000.00	0.05%
10)	Networking Equipment	$ 350,000.00	3.50%
11)	Marketing	$ —	0.00%
12)	Working Capital	$ 175,000.00	1.75%
	Total	**$ 3,375,750.00**	**33.76%**

Phase II

	Second Quarter of Operations	Projected Expense	% of Gross Proceeds
1)	Commissions Paid	$ -	0.00%
2)	Web site Development	$ 168,750.00	1.69%
3)	Rent, Lease, and Utilities	$ 81,420.00	0.81%
4)	Connectivity	$ 10,000.00	0.10%
5)	Executive and Administrative	$ 272,920.00	2.73%
6)	Professional, Legal, Advisory	$ 20,000.00	0.20%
7)	Advertising	$ 1,433,660.00	14.34%
8)	Equipment and Furniture	$ -	0.00%
9)	Tech Support	$ 5,000.00	0.05%
10)	Networking Equipment	$ -	0.00%
11)	Marketing	$ 3,000.00	0.03%
12)	Working Capital	$ 175,000.00	1.75%
	Total	**$ 2,169,750.00**	**21.70%**

Phase III

	Third Quarter of Operations	Projected Expense	% of Gross Proceeds
1)	Commissions Paid	$ -	0.00%
2)	Web site Development	$ 168,750.00	1.69%
3)	Rent, Lease, and Utilities	$ 81,420.00	0.81%
4)	Connectivity	$ 15,000.00	0.15%
5)	Executive and Administrative	$ 272,920.00	2.73%
6)	Professional, Legal, Advisory	$ 20,000.00	0.20%
7)	Advertising	$ 1,433,660.00	14.34%
8)	Equipment and Furniture	$ -	0.00%
9)	Tech Support	$ 5,000.00	0.05%
10)	Networking Equipment	$ 150,000.00	1.50%
11)	Marketing	$ 3,000.00	0.03%
12)	Working Capital	$ 125,000.00	1.25%
	Total	**$ 2,274,750.00**	**22.75%**

Phase IV

	Fourth Quarter of Operations	Projected Expense	% of Gross Proceeds
1)	Commissions Paid	$ -	0.00%
2)	Web site Development	$ 168,750.00	1.69%
3)	Rent, Lease, and Utilities	$ 81,420.00	0.81%
4)	Connectivity	$ 20,000.00	0.20%
5)	Executive and Administrative	$ 272,920.00	2.73%
6)	Professional, Legal, Advisory	$ 20,000.00	0.20%
7)	Advertising	$ 1,433,660.00	14.34%
8)	Equipment and Furniture	$ -	0.00%
9)	Tech Support	$ 5,000.00	0.05%
10)	Network Equipment	$ -	0.00%
11)	Marketing	$ 3,000.00	0.03%
12)	Working Capital	$ 175,000.00	1.75%
	Total	**$ 2,179,750.00**	**21.80%**
	Gross Maximum Proceeds	**$ 10,000,000.00**	**100.00%**

Assumptions for Financial Projections

A summary of the significant accounting policies applied in the preparation of the accompanying projected financial statements. Enclosed are four-year financial projections of *Wmhinc.com* operations, derived from stated projections beginning January 2001.

Initial Funding

The Company is seeking funding in the amount of $10,000,000 from venture capital sources.

Preoperational Expenses/Use of Funds

- Principal Office Development $ 602,480   (Tech Hardware/Software, Communication Support, Office Furniture, Supplies)

- Initial Promotional Budget $6,700,000   (NASCAR, Internet Promo, Print, and Outdoor)

- Working Capital $ 725,840   (Licensing, Vehicle and Equipment Lease, Product Development, R&D, Insurance)

- Cost of Offering $ 200,000

- Offering Commission $1,400,000

Income/Sales

Total revenue of 72 to 75% is generated by business-to-business monthly fee transactions (B2B technology, government, developers, advertising, garages, service, motorsports, online auctions, *Wmhinc.com* branded homes). Total revenues of 25 to 28% are generated by business-to-consumer monthly transactions (new home sales, bank-owned home sales, garages, part/service, net listings of customer home sales).

The Company currently has working agreements for approximately 4,000 homes with several developers for an average of $2,000 to $5,000 per house. Today manufactured homes make up over 25% of new homes in the United States. Sales of new manufactured homes exceeded $16 billion in 1999, an increase of 400% in the last ten years. With new design elements and customizable options, manufactured homes have begun to cross over into the mainstream.

- In 1999, the industry shipped 348,671 homes from 323 manufacturing facilities.

- The average sales price of a manufactured home was $43,600 in 1999. Single-section homes average $31,800, while multi-section homes average $50,200.

- Over 19 million people (about 8% of the U.S. population live full-time in over eight million manufactured homes.

Wmhinc.com Financial Assumptions – page 2

Due to *Wmhinc.com*'s NASCAR involvement and FEMA partnership, management clearly expects to drive over one million unique visitors through the Web site every month within the first year. NASCAR's online site generates over 43 million page views by over 4.6 million unique users per month, each averaging nine minutes per visit. FEMA has over 150,000,000 unique visitors per year on its Web site.

Notes

Four-Year Cash Flow Projections

- **Venture Capital.** The Company's principals are injecting $50,000 into business. In order to fund pre-operational expenses, the Company is seeking venture capital in the amount of $10,000,000.

- **Cash Disbursements.** Dispursements of cash will be determined by the current financial position of the Company. Marketing and Product Development will include focus groups, and product and campaign development. Research & Development will consist of market analysis of viable market opportunities through its hub of Web-based products and services. The company will also commit monthly investments in its corporate community programs in markets that we serve and have a strong presence.

Four-Year Income Projections

- **The annual growth rate.** This is justified by the Company's discipline and ability to establish a Web-based hub of manufactured home resources, long-term strategic alliances, and brand equity in viable markets.

- **Expenses.** Expenses are expected to increase as the Company intensifies its marketing and advertising campaigns. Furthermore, expenses are expected to increase as the Company hires additional staff. The Company plans to hire five department managers at an average salary of $40,000 per year each and ten hourly employees at an average wage rate that totals $16,800 per year. Executive salaries will be as follows:

Paul S Jarolimek II	President/CEO	$ 52,500
Michael Gage	CTO	$ 52,500
MaryLou Jarolimek	CFO	$ 52,500
Stephen Massie	EVP Warrenty/Service	$ 52,500
Jim Stephens	EVP Sales	$ 52,500
Suzanne Jarolimek	EVP Customer Service	$ 52,500
Larry Queen	VP Technology - Graphics	$ 52,500
Leon Jarolimek	VP Customer Service/Warranty	$ 52,500

- **Income Tax Rate.** 19% estimated federal tax; 9% estimated state tax, and 3% estimated local tax.

Three-Year Income Projection

Wholesale Mobile Homes.com, Inc.

Percentages = % of Sales/Revenues
Updated: November 2001

	Year 1: 2002		Year 2: 2003		Year 3: 2004		Total: 3 Years	
	AMOUNT	%	AMOUNT	%	AMOUNT	%	AMOUNT	%
INCOME								
1. SALES/REVENUES (Total)	17,216,075	100.00%	77,631,985	100.00%	136,623,886	100.00%	231,471,946	100.00%
a. B2B Technology	1,705,258	9.91%	7,842,148	10.10%	13,673,847	10.01%	23,221,253	10.03%
b. B2B Government	1,381,258	8.02%	6,330,184	8.15%	11,070,952	8.10%	18,782,394	8.11%
c. B2B Developers	3,752,185	21.79%	17,143,833	22.08%	28,695,395	21.00%	49,591,413	21.42%
d. B2B Advertisers	3,410,510	19.81%	15,551,942	20.03%	27,325,714	20.00%	46,288,166	20.00%
e. B2B Garages	511,577	2.97%	2,330,164	3.00%	4,098,726	3.00%	6,940,467	3.00%
f. B2B Service	136,420	0.79%	621,149	0.80%	1,092,991	0.80%	1,850,560	0.80%
g. B2B Motorsports	204,632	1.19%	931,623	1.20%	1,639,487	1.20%	2,775,742	1.20%
h. B2B Online Auctions	341,121	1.98%	1,552,657	2.00%	2,732,478	2.00%	4,626,256	2.00%
i. B2B Man. Wmhinc.com Homes	1,347,152	7.82%	5,532,123	7.13%	9,725,243	7.12%	16,604,518	7.17%
Total B2B Sales	**12,790,113**	**74.29%**	**57,835,823**	**74.50%**	**100,054,833**	**73.23%**	**170,680,769**	**73.74%**
j. B2C New Home	1,534,732	8.91%	7,375,043	9.50%	13,088,218	9.58%	21,997,993	9.50%
k. B2C Bank Owned Home Sale	1,875,782	10.90%	8,539,519	11.00%	15,805,450	11.57%	26,220,751	11.33%
l. B2C Garages	511,577	2.97%	2,328,960	3.00%	4,800,686	3.51%	7,641,223	3.30%
m. B2C Parts/Service	153,473	0.89%	698,688	0.90%	1,301,162	0.95%	2,153,323	0.93%
n. B2C "Net Listings"	350,398	2.04%	853,952	1.10%	1,573,537	1.15%	2,777,887	1.20%
Total B2C Sales	**4,425,962**	**25.71%**	**19,796,162**	**25.50%**	**36,569,053**	**26.77%**	**60,791,177**	**26.26%**
2. Cost of Goods Sold	0	0.00%	0	0.00%	0	0.00%	0	0.00%
3. GROSS PROFIT ON SALES (1-2)	17,216,075	100.00%	77,631,985	100.00%	136,623,886	100.00%	231,471,946	100.00%
EXPENSES								
1. VARIABLE (Selling) (a thru b)	5,081,104	29.51%	18,072,884	23.28%	34,871,019	25.52%	58,025,007	25.07%
a. Marketing and Advertising	2,046,308	11.89%	12,456,948	16.05%	23,845,694	17.45%	38,348,950	16.57%
b. Communications Support	53,296	0.31%	264,894	0.34%	275,946	0.20%	594,136	0.26%
c. Community Reinvestments	886,733	5.15%	1,250,000	1.61%	2,000,000	1.46%	4,136,733	1.79%
d. Research and Development	1,559,054	9.06%	2,398,512	3.09%	5,200,000	3.81%	9,157,566	3.96%
e. Technical Support	169,762	0.99%	473,955	0.61%	521,658	0.38%	1,165,375	0.50%
f. Travel and Entertainment	341,051	1.98%	492,753	0.63%	1,732,856	1.27%	2,566,660	1.11%
g. Vehicle/Equipment Leases	24,900	0.14%	735,822	0.95%	1,294,865	0.95%	2,055,587	0.89%
2. FIXED (Administrative) (a thru h)	1,427,176	8.29%	6,449,120	8.31%	11,107,191	8.13%	18,983,487	8.20%
a. Company Benefits and Insurance	110,400	0.64%	834,426	1.07%	1,859,465	1.36%	2,804,291	1.21%
b. Executive Salaries	864,996	5.02%	1,648,651	2.12%	2,354,986	1.72%	4,868,633	2.10%
c. Facility Expense	43,680	0.25%	1,469,512	1.89%	3,654,895	2.68%	5,168,087	2.23%
d. General office Expenses	25,939	0.15%	192,645	0.25%	272,698	0.20%	491,282	0.21%
e. Insurance and Licensing	24,000	0.14%	359,485	0.46%	426,595	0.31%	810,080	0.35%
f. Labor/Wages	168,672	0.98%	495,365	0.64%	921,589	0.67%	1,585,626	0.69%
g. Legal	4,256	0.02%	50,000	0.06%	70,000	0.05%	124,256	0.05%
h. Maintenance/Cleaning/Repairs	6,902	0.04%	64,974	0.08%	75,913	0.06%	147,789	0.06%
i. Memberships and Subscriptions	2,779	0.02%	5,139	0.01%	7,968	0.01%	15,886	0.01%
j. Non-Income Taxes	134,376	0.78%	578,624	0.75%	716,945	0.52%	1,429,945	0.62%
k. Utilities	12,071	0.07%	122,698	0.16%	254,658	0.19%	389,427	0.17%
l. Depreciation	14,023	0.08%	42,978	0.06%	64,895	0.05%	121,896	0.05%
m. Misc. Fixed Expense	15,082	0.09%	584,623	0.75%	426,584	0.31%	1,026,289	0.44%
TOTAL OPERATING EXPENSES (1+2)	**6,508,280**	**37.80%**	**19,500,060**	**25.12%**	**45,978,210**	**33.65%**	**77,008,494**	**33.27%**
NET INCOME OPERATIONS (GPr - Exp)	**10,707,795**	**62.20%**	**58,131,925**	**74.88%**	**90,645,676**	**66.35%**	**154,463,452**	**66.73%**
OTHER INCOME (Interest Income)	0	0.00%	0	0.00%	0	0.00%	0	0.00%
OTHER EXPENSE (Interest Expense)	0	0.00%	0	0.00%	0	0.00%	0	0.00%
NET PROFIT (LOSS) BEFORE TAXES	**10,707,795**	**62.20%**	**58,131,925**	**74.88%**	**90,645,676**	**66.35%**	**154,463,452**	**66.73%**
TAXES 1. Federal, S-Employment	3,268,916	18.99%	16,895,236	21.76%	28,694,855	21.00%	48,859,007	21.11%
2. State	1,456,855	8.46%	4,956,265	6.38%	8,956,212	6.56%	15,369,332	6.64%
3. Local	470,258	2.73%	851,896	1.10%	1,318,623	0.97%	2,640,777	1.14%
NET PROFIT (LOSS) AFTER TAXES	**5,511,766**	**32.02%**	**35,428,528**	**45.64%**	**51,675,986**	**37.82%**	**87,594,336**	**37.84%**

Pro Forma Cash Flow Statement

Page 1 (January thru June)

Wholesale Mobile Homes.com, Inc.

For the Year 2002

	Jan	Feb	Mar	Apr	May	Jun
BEGINNING CASH BALANCE	422,040	386,590	584,289	777,245	1,898,144	2,373,465
CASH RECEIPTS						
A. Sales/Revenues B2B	604,681	662,229	691,834	740,481	772,063	875,799
1. B2B Technology	80,624	88,297	92,245	98,731	102,942	116,773
2. B2B Government	65,306	71,521	74,718	79,972	83,383	94,586
3. B2B Developers	177,373	194,254	202,938	217,208	226,472	256,901
4. B2B Advertisers	161,248	176,594	184,489	197,462	205,883	233,546
5. B2B Garages	24,187	26,489	27,673	29,619	30,883	35,032
6. B2B Service	6,450	7,064	7,380	7,898	8,235	9,342
7. B2B Motorsports	9,675	10,596	11,069	11,848	12,353	14,013
8. B2B Online Auctions	16,125	17,659	18,449	19,746	20,588	23,355
9. B2B Man. Wmhinc.com Homes	63,693	69,755	72,873	77,997	81,324	92,251
B. Sales/Revenues B2C	201,561	220,743	230,611	246,827	257,356	291,933
1. B2C New Home	72,562	79,467	83,020	88,858	92,648	105,096
2. B2C Bank Owned Home Sale	88,687	97,127	101,469	108,604	113,236	128,450
3. B2C Garages	24,187	26,489	27,673	29,619	30,883	35,032
4. B2C Parts/Service	7,256	7,947	8,302	8,886	9,265	10,510
5. B2C "Net Listings"	8,869	9,713	10,147	10,860	11,324	12,845
TOTAL CASH AVAILABLE	1,228,282	1,490,305	1,737,345	2,011,380	3,184,919	3,833,130
CASH PAYMENTS						
A. Cost of goods to be sold						
1. (Currently no COG)	0	0	0	0	0	0
Total Cost of Goods	0	0	0	0	0	0
B. Variable (Selling) Expenses						
1. Marketing and Advertising	102,847	113,594	119,143	128,359	134,118	143,482
2. Communications Support	4,200	4,500	4,500	4,750	4,750	4,500
3. Community Reinvestments	41,925	45,914	47,967	51,340	53,530	60,722
4. Research and Development	11,265	16,093	22,990	32,843	46,918	67,026
5. Technical Support	14,000	14,200	14,250	14,250	14,562	14,500
6. Travel and Entertainment	28,000	28,000	29,500	30,000	30,000	30,000
7. Vehicle/Equipment Leases	2,000	2,250	1,875	2,100	1,975	2,000
Total Variable Expenses	204,237	224,551	240,225	263,642	285,853	322,230
C. Fixed (Administrative) Expenses						
1. Company Benefits and Insurance	8,500	8,500	9,000	9,000	9,000	10,500
2. Executive Salaries	72,083	72,083	72,083	72,083	72,083	72,083
3. Facility Expense	3,640	3,640	3,640	3,640	3,640	3,640
4. General office Expenses	2,000	2,050	2,350	2,010	1,989	2,100
5. Insurance and Licensing	2,000	2,000	2,000	2,000	2,000	2,000
6. Labor/Wages	14,056	14,056	14,056	14,056	14,056	14,056
7. Legal	1,000	0	0	0	0	256
8. Maintenance/Cleaning/Repairs	500	500	530	600	520	550
9. Memberships and Subscriptions	200	200	200	200	200	200
10. Non-Income Taxes	9,768	10,012	10,364	10,779	11,085	11,201
11. Utilities	900	900	900	900	1,200	1,200
12. Misc. Fixed Expense	1,250	1,250	1,250	1,250	1,250	1,250
Total Fixed Expenses	115,897	115,191	116,373	116,518	117,023	119,036
D. Interest Expense	0	0	0	0	0	0
E. Federal Income Tax	188,648	197,553	210,945	225,379	237,658	249,985
F. State and Other Taxes	82,975	95,000	106,599	119,251	137,654	158,954
G. Long-term asset payments	0	0	0	0	0	0
H. Marketable Investments	161,248	176,594	184,489	197,462	205,883	233,546
I. Notes Payable to Investors	88,687	97,127	101,469	108,604	113,236	128,450
TOTAL CASH PAID OUT	841,692	906,016	960,100	1,030,856	811,454	1,212,201
CASH BALANCE/DEFICIENCY	386,590	584,289	777,245	1,898,144	2,373,465	2,620,929
LOANS TO BE RECEIVED	0	0	0	0	0	0
EQUITY DEPOSITS	0	0	0	0	0	0
ENDING CASH BALANCE	386,590	584,289	777,245	1,898,144	2,373,465	2,620,929

Note:			Pre-operational Expenses	
	Beginning Cash Balance	50,000		
	Venture Capital	10,000,000	Principal Office Development	602,480
	Total Cash Available	**$10,050,000**	Initial Promotional Budget	6,700,000
			Working Capital	725,480
	Less Pre-operational Expenses (right)	9,627,960	Cost of Offering	200,000
			Offering Commission	1,400,000
	Gross Cash Balance	**$422,040**	**Total Pre-operational Expenses**	**$9,627,960**

Pro Forma Cash Flow Statement

Page 2 (July thru December + 6 & 12-month Totals)

Wholesale Mobile Homes.com, Inc.

6-MONTH TOTALS	Jul	Aug	Sep	Oct	Nov	Dec	12-MONTH TOTALS
422,040	2,620,929	2,937,063	3,335,980	3,755,714	4,406,160	5,825,008	422,040
4,347,087	976,577	1,133,671	1,239,890	1,598,372	1,688,166	1,806,350	12,790,113
579,612	130,128	151,147	165,319	213,116	225,089	240,847	1,705,258
469,486	105,403	122,429	133,908	172,624	182,322	195,086	1,381,258
1,275,146	286,901	332,523	363,701	468,856	495,195	529,863	3,752,185
1,159,222	260,255	302,293	330,637	426,233	450,177	481,693	3,410,510
173,883	39,038	45,344	49,596	63,935	67,527	72,254	511,577
46,369	10,410	12,092	13,225	17,049	18,007	19,268	136,420
69,554	15,615	18,138	19,838	25,574	27,011	28,902	204,632
115,922	26,026	30,299	33,064	42,623	45,018	48,169	341,121
457,893	102,801	119,406	130,602	168,362	177,820	190,268	1,347,152
1,449,031	325,318	377,866	413,298	532,791	564,456	763,202	4,425,962
521,651	117,115	136,032	148,787	191,805	202,580	216,762	1,534,732
637,573	143,140	166,261	181,851	234,428	247,598	264,931	1,875,782
173,883	39,038	45,344	49,596	63,935	67,527	72,254	511,577
52,166	11,711	13,603	14,879	19,180	20,258	21,676	153,473
63,758	14,314	16,626	18,185	23,443	26,493	187,579	350,398
6,218,158	4,248,142	4,826,466	5,402,466	6,419,668	7,223,238	9,157,762	17,638,115
0	0	0	0	0	0	0	0
0	0	0	0	0	0	0	0
741,543	142,178	159,605	167,446	252,396	285,949	297,191	2,046,308
27,200	4,396	4,350	4,350	4,200	4,300	4,500	53,296
301,398	67,666	78,596	85,966	110,821	117,046	125,240	886,733
197,135	95,751	136,787	195,410	279,157	310,175	344,639	1,559,054
85,762	14,000	13,500	13,500	13,500	15,000	14,500	169,762
175,500	24,551	25,000	25,000	25,000	26,000	40,000	341,051
12,200	2,400	2,500	1,500	1,700	2,100	2,500	24,900
1,540,738	350,942	420,338	493,172	686,774	760,570	828,570	5,081,104
54,500	10,500	10,000	9,400	8,000	9,000	9,000	110,400
432,498	72,083	72,083	72,083	72,083	72,083	72,083	864,996
21,840	3,640	3,640	3,640	3,640	3,640	3,640	43,680
12,499	2,700	2,500	1,830	2,310	2,000	2,100	25,939
12,000	2,000	2,000	2,000	2,000	2,000	2,000	24,000
84,336	14,056	14,056	14,056	14,056	14,056	14,056	168,672
1,256	1,000	0	0	0	0	2,000	4,256
3,200	600	600	627	675	600	600	6,902
1,200	264	263	263	263	263	263	2,779
63,209	11,329	11,435	11,754	12,066	12,261	12,322	134,376
6,000	1,200	1,200	971	900	900	900	12,071
7,500	1,257	1,257	1,267	1,267	1,267	1,267	15,082
700,038	120,629	119,034	117,891	117,260	118,070	120,231	1,413,153
0	0	0	0	0	0	0	0
1,310,168	265,481	296,862	324,644	341,552	357,708	272,501	3,168,916
700,433	170,632	185,698	198,557	207,261	224,677	239,855	1,927,113
0	0	0	0	0	0	0	0
1,159,222	260,255	302,293	330,637	426,233	450,177	481,693	3,410,510
637,573	143,140	166,261	181,851	234,428	247,598	264,931	1,875,782
6,048,172	1,311,079	1,490,486	1,646,752	2,013,508	1,398,230	2,207,781	16,876,578
169,986	2,937,063	3,335,980	3,755,714	4,406,160	5,825,008	6,949,981	761,537
0	0	0	0	0	0	0	0
0	0	0	0	0	0	0	0
169,986	2,937,063	3,335,980	3,755,714	4,406,160	5,825,008	6,949,981	761,537

Projected Balance Sheet

Business Name:

Wholesale Mobile Homes, Inc.com

Date of Projection: November, 2001

Date Projected For: December 31, 2002

ASSETS			% of Assets
Current Assets			
Cash	$	6,949,981	35.40%
Petty Cash	$	0	0.00%
Accounts Receivable	$	7,054,432	35.93%
Inventory	$	0	0.00%
Marketable Investments	$	1,875,578	9.55%
Long-Term Investments	$	0	0.00%
Fixed Assets			
Land (valued at cost)	$	0	0.00%
Buildings	$	0	0.00%
1. Cost	0		
2. Less Acc. Depr.	0		
Improvements	$	0	0.00%
1. Cost	0		
2. Less Acc. Depr.	0		
Equipment	$	485,977	2.48%
1. Cost	500,000		
2. Less Acc. Depr.	14,023		
Furniture	$	0	0.00%
1. Cost	0		
2. Less Acc. Depr.	0		
Autos/Vehicles	$	0	0.00%
1. Cost	0		
2. Less Acc. Depr.	0		
Other Assets			
1. Non-Depreciable Assets	$	3,265,874	16.64%
2.	$	0	0.00%
TOTAL ASSETS		19,631,842	100.00%

LIABILITIES			% of Liabilities
Current Liabilities			
Accounts Payable	$	1,166,475	14.16%
Notes Payable	$	0	0.00%
Interest Payable	$	0	0.00%
Taxe Accruals			
Federal Income Tax	$	3,268,916	39.68%
State Income Tax	$	1,456,855	17.68%
Local Income Tax	$	470,258	5.71%
Sales Tax Accrual	$	0	0.00%
Property Tax	$	0	0.00%
Payroll Accrual	$	0	0.00%
Long-Term Liabilities			
Notes Payable to Investors	$	1,875,782	22.77%
Notes Payable Others	$	0	0.00%
TOTAL LIABILITIES	$	8,238,286	100.00%

NET WORTH (EQUITY)			% of Net Worth
Corporation			
Capital Stock	$	10,500,000	92.16%
Surplus Paid In	$	0	0.00%
Retained Earnings	$	893,556	7.84%
TOTAL NET WORTH	$	11,393,556	100.00%

Assets - Liabilities = Net Worth
and
Liabilities + Equity = Total Assets

Break-Even Analysis

Wholesale Mobile Homes.com, Inc.

Date of Analysis: November, 2001

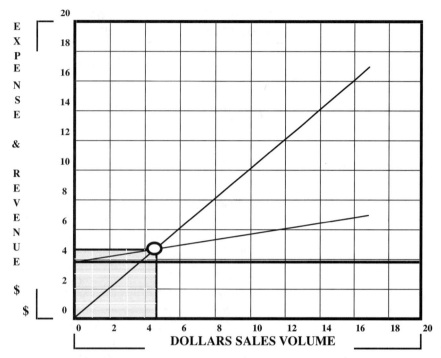

NOTE: Figures shown in (1) millions of dollars (Ex: 2 = $ 2,000 ,000)

B-E POINT (SALES) = Fixed costs + [(Variable Costs/Est. Revenues) x Sales]

B-E Point (Sales) = $ 3,872,963 + [($ 2,635,317 / $ 17,052,654)   x   Sales]

Wholesale Mobile Homes, Inc.com
BREAK-EVEN POINT CALCULATION

FC (Fixed Costs)	=	(Administrative Expenses + Interest)	$	**3,872,963**
VC (Variable Costs)	=	(Cost of Goods + Selling Expenses)	$	**2,635,317**
R (Est. Revenues)	=	(Income from sale of products and services)	$	**17,052,564**
BREAK-EVEN POINT =			$	**4,580,899**

Financial Statement Analysis Summary

The following is a summary of the 2002 financial statement analysis information developed on the next three pages of spreadsheets (pages 35-37) :

		2002 PROJECTED	INDUSTRY STANDARD
1.	Net Working Capital	$9,517,487	$0 + or -
2.	Current Ratio	2.50	1.60 + or -
3.	Quick Ratio	2.5	0.4 + or -
4.	Gross Profit Margin*	100.00%	22.70%
5.	Operating Profit Margin*	62.20%	2.60%
	See explanation below (Notes)		
6.	Net Profit Margin	32.00%	0.0%
7.	Debt to Assets	41.96%	0.0%
8.	Debt to Equity	72.31%	12.5:1 +
9.	ROI (Return on Investment)	28.08%	0.0% +
10.	Vertical Income Statement Analysis *		
	Sales/Revenues	100.00%	
	Cost of Goods	0.0%	0.0% + or -
	Gross Profit	100.00%	22.70% + or -
	Operating Expense	37.80%	20.30% + or -
	Net Income Operations	62.20%	2.40% + or -
	Interest Income	0.0%	N/A
	Interest Expense	0.00%	Variable
	Net Profit (Pre-Tax)	62.20%	2.60% + or -
	All items stated as % of Total Revenues		
11.	Vertical Balance Sheet Analysis *		
	Current Assets	80.90%	77.40%
	Inventory	0.0%	61.50%
	Total Assets	100.00%	100.00%
	Current Liabilities	32.40%	62.30% + or -
	Total Liabilities	42.00%	
	Net Worth	58.00%	26.50% + or -
	Total Liabilities + Net Worth	100.0%	

*All Asset items stated as % of Total Assets;
Liability & Net Worth items stated as % of Total Liabilities + Net Worth*

Notes:

Wholesale Mobile Homes.com, Inc. is entering a rapidly growing marketplace and has developed a business model that will help to keep operating expenses at a minimum. By outsourcing activities related to the development of mobile homes, the Company will initially have zero cost of goods sold. Due to the nature of business activities, management does not anticipate carrying inventory. The operating expenses are higher than industry standards in year one because of the high costs associated with entry into the marketplace. With zero cost of goods sold, *Wmhinc.com* has higher profit margins than RMA figures. Financial projections show that, based on an investment of $10 million, *Wmhinc.com* will maintain good cash flow, increase profitability, and provide a timely and healthy return for investors.

Financial Statement Analysis
Ratio Table

Wholesale Mobile Homes.com, Inc.

Type of Analysis	Formula	Projected: 2002	
1. Liquidity Analysis			
a. Net Working Capital	**Balance Sheet** Current Assets — Current Liabilities	Current Assets Current Liabilities **Net Working Capital**	15,879,991 6,362,504 **$9,517,487**
b. Current Ratio	**Balance Sheet** Current Assets ——————— Current Liabilities	Current Assets Current Liabilities **Current Ratio**	15,879,991 6,362,504 **2.50**
c. Quick Ratio	**Balance Sheet** Current Assets minus Inventory ——————— Current Liabilities	Current Assets Inventory Current Liabilities **Quick Ratio**	15,879,991 0 6,362,504 **2.50**
2. Profitability Analysis			
a. Gross Profit Margin	**Income Statement** Gross Profits ——————— Sales	Gross Profits Sales **Gross Profit Margin**	17,216,075 17,216,075 **100.00%**
b. Operating Profit Margin	Income From Operations ——————— Sales	Income From Ops. Sales **Operating Profit Margin**	10,707,795 17,216,075 **62.20%**
c. Net Profit Margin	Net Profits ——————— Sales	Net Profits Sales **Net Profit Margin**	5,511,766 17,216,075 **32.02%**
3. Debt Ratios	**Income Statement & Balance Sheet**		
a. Debt to Assets	Total Liabilities ——————— Total Assets	Total Liabilities Total Assets **Debt to Assets Ratio**	8,238,286 19,631,842 **41.96%**
b. Debt to Equity	Total Liabilities ——————— Total Owners' Equity	Total Liabilities Total Owners' Equity **Debt to Equity Ratio**	8,238,286 11,393,556 **72.31%**
4. Measures of Investment	**Balance Sheet**		
a. ROI *(Return on Investment)*	Net Profits ——————— Total Assets	Net Profits Total Assets **ROI (Return on Investment)**	5,511,766 19,631,842 **28.08%**
5. Vertical Financial Statement Analysis	**Balance Sheet** 1. Each asset % of Total Assets 2. Liability & Equity % of Total L&E **Income Statement** 3. All items % of Total Revenues	**NOTE:** *See Attached* **Balance Sheet and** **Income Statement**	
6. Horizontal Financial Statement Analysis	**Balance Sheet** 1. Assets, Liab & Equity measured against 2nd year. Increases and decreases stated as amount & % **Income Statement** 2. Revenues & Expenses measured against 2nd year. Increases and decreases stated as amount & %	**NOTE:** **Horizontal Analysis** **Not Applicable** **Projections for End of Year 1**	

2002 Projected
Vertical Income Statement Analysis

(Percentages for all categories are in terms of % of Total Sales/Revenues)

Wholesale Mobile Homes.com, Inc.

Projected For The Year: 2002		Begin: January 1, 2002 End: December 31, 2002	

	AMOUNT		% Total Revenues
INCOME			
1. Sales/Revenues		$ 17,216,075	100.00%
B2B Technology	1,705,258		9.91%
B2B Government	1,381,258		8.02%
B2B Developers	3,752,185		21.79%
B2B Advertisers	3,410,510		19.81%
B2B Garages	511,577		2.97%
B2B Service	136,420		0.79%
B2B Motorsports	204,632		1.19%
B2B Online Auctions\	341,121		1.98%
B2B Man. Wmhinc.com Homes	1,347,152		7.82%
Total B2B Sales	**12,790,113**		**74.29%**
B2C New Home	1,534,732		8.91%
B2C Bank-Owned Home Sale	1,875,782		10.90%
B2C Garage	511,577		2.97%
B2C Parts/Service	153,473		0.89%
B2C "Net Listings"	350,398		2.04%
Total B2C Sales	**4,425,962**		**25.71%**
2. Cost of Goods Sold (c-d)		0	0.00%
3. Gross Profit on Sales (1-2)		$ 17,216,075	100.00%
EXPENSES			
1. Variable (Selling) (a thru l)		5,081,104	29.51%
a. Marketing and Advertising	2,046,308		11.89%
b. Communications Support	53,296		0.31%
c. Community Reinvestments	886,733		5.15%
d. Research and Development	1,559,054		9.06%
e. Technical Support	169,762		0.99%
f. Travel and Entertainment	341,051		1.98%
g. Vehicle/Equipment Leases	24,900		0.14%
2. Fixed (Administrative) (a thru l)		1,427,176	8.29%
a. Company Benefits and Insurance	110,400		0.64%
b. Executive Salaries	864,996		5.02%
c. Facility Expense	43,680		0.25%
d. General Office Expenses	25,939		0.15%
e. Insurance and Licensing	24,000		0.14%
f. Labor/Wages	168,672		0.98%
g. Legal	4,256		0.02%
h. Maintenance/Cleaning/Repairs	6,902		0.04%
i. Memberships and Subscriptions	2,779		0.02%
j. Non-Income Taxes	134,376		0.78%
k. Utilities	12,071		0.07%
l. Miscellaneous Administrative Expense	15,082		0.09%
m. Depreciation (Administrative Assets)	14,023		0.08%
Total Operating Expenses (1+2)		**6,508,280**	**37.80%**
Net Income from Operations (GP-Exp)		$ 10,707,795	62.20%
Other Income (Interest Income)	0		0.00%
Other Expense (Interest Expense)	0		0.00%
Net Profit (Loss) Before Taxes		$ 10,707,795	62.20%
Taxes:			
a. Federal	3,268,916		18.99%
b. State	1,456,855	5,196,029	8.46%
c. Local	470,258		2.73%
NET PROFIT (LOSS) AFTER TAXES		$ 5,511,766	32.02%

2002 Projected
Vertical Balance Sheet Analysis

(All Asset %'s represent % of Total Assets; All Liability or Equity %'s represent % of Total Liabilities + Total Equity)

Date of Projection: November 1, 2001		Date Projected for: December 31, 2002

Wholesale Mobile Homes.com, Inc.

ASSETS		% of Total Assets	LIABILITIES		% of Total L + NW
Current Assets			**Current Liabilities**		
Cash	$ 6,949,981	35.4%	Accounts Payable	$ 1,166,475	5.9%
Petty Cash	$ 0	0.0%	Notes Payable	$ 0	0.0%
Sales Tax Holding Account	$ 0	0.0%	Interest Payable	$ 0	0.0%
Accounts Receivable	$ 7,054,432	35.9%			
Inventory	$ 0	0.0%	**Taxes Payable**		
Marketable Investments	$ 1,875,578	9.6%	Federal Income Tax	$ 3,268,916	16.7%
Total Current Assets	*15,879,991*	*80.9%*	Self-Employment Tax	$ 1,456,855	7.4%
			State Income Tax	$ 470,258	2.4%
L-Term Investments	$ 0	0.0%	Sales Tax Accrual	$ 0	0.0%
			Property Tax	$ 0	0.0%
Fixed Assets					
Land (valued at cost)	$ 0	0.0%	Payroll Accrual	$ 0	0.0%
			Total Current Liabilities	*6,362,504*	*32.4%*
Buildings	$ 0	0.0%			
1. Cost	0		**Long-Term Liabilities**		
2. Less Acc. Depr.	0		Notes Payable to Investors	$ 1,875,782	9.6%
			Notes Payable Others	$ 0	0.0%
Improvements	$ 0	0.0%			
1. Cost	0				
2. Less Acc. Depr.	0		**TOTAL LIABILITIES**	$ 8,238,286	42.0%
Equipment	$ 485,977	2.5%			
1. Cost	500,000				
2. Less Acc. Depr.	14,023		**NET WORTH (EQUITY)**		% of Total L + NW
Furniture	$ 0	0.0%			
1. Cost	0				
2. Less Acc. Depr.	0		**Corporation**		
Autos/Vehicles	$ 0	0.0%	Capital Stock	$ 10,500,000	53.5%
1. Cost	0		Surplus Paid In	$ 0	0.0%
2. Less Acc. Depr.	0		Retained Earnings	$ 893,556	4.6%
Other Assets					
1. Nondepreciable Assets	$ 3,265,874	16.6%			
2.	$ 0	0.0%			
3.	$ 0	0.0%	**TOTAL NET WORTH**	$ 11,393,556	58.0%
TOTAL ASSETS	$ 19,631,842	100.0%	**LIABILITIES + N. WORTH**	$ 19,631,842	100.0%

Assets - Liabilities = Net Worth -or- Liabilities + Equity = Assets

PART IV: SUPPORTING DOCUMENTS

Wholesale Mobile Homes.com, Inc.

- Insurance Update Form

* **Note:** For purposes of brevity, we have chosen to include only one of the supporting documents that would be found in *Wmhinc.com*, Inc.'s business plan.

Insurance Update Form

Insurance Update Form			
Wholesale Mobile Homes.com, Inc.			
Updated as of November, 2001			
Company	Contact Person	Coverage	Cost Per Year
1. HealthWest Insurance 2526 St. John's Street Las Vegas, NV 89247	James Boyd 509-523-9568	Medical and Other	$ 110,400
2. The Insurance Agency 16432 Midway Street Las Vegas, NV 89147	Michael Smith 509-795-7556	Business Liability	$ 4,800
3. The Insurance Agency (Address: see above)	Michael Smith 509-795-7556	Industry Specific	$ 8,100
4. The Insurance Agency (Address: see above)	Michael Smith 509-795-7556	Workers Compensation	$ 6,100
5. The Insurance Agency (Address: see above)	Michael Smith 509-795-7556	Key-man Coverage	$ 3,000
6. Auto Insurance Brokers 4589 Marsh Lane Las Vegas, NV 89146	Gene Hastings 509-465-1235	Auto - Vehicle 1	$ 1,000
7. Auto Insurance Brokers (Address: see above)	Gene Hastings 509-465-1235	Auto - Vehicle 2	$ 1,000
	1. Total Annual Insurance Cost		$ 134,400
	2. Average Monthly Insurance Cost		$ 11,200

BLANK FORMS AND WORKSHEETS

The forms on the following pages have been provided for you to copy and use in the writing of your business plan.

The forms that contain "Variable Expenses" and "Fixed Expenses" have spaces for you to fill in your own categories. They should be customized to your particular business. This will require you to decide on category headings when you begin the financial section of your business plan and follow through with the same headings throughout all financial statements.

The categories are developed by looking at your different accounts in your ledger or by using the categories from your revenue and expense journal. Those expenses that are frequent and sizable will have a heading of their own (i.e., advertising, rent, salaries, etc.). Those expenses that are very small and infrequent will be included under the heading "miscellaneous" in either the variable or fixed expenses section of each of your financial statements.

Cash to Be Paid Out Worksheet

Business Name: _____   **Time Period:** _____ to _____

---

1. START-UP COSTS _____
  Business license _____
  Accounting fees _____
  Legal fees _____
  Other start-up costs: _____
    a. _____
    b. _____
    c. _____
    d. _____

2. INVENTORY PURCHASES
  Cash out for goods intended for resale _____

3. VARIABLE EXPENSES (SELLING)
  a. _____
  b. _____
  c. _____
  d. _____
  e. _____
  f. _____
  g. Miscellaneous variable expense _____
  TOTAL SELLING EXPENSES _____

4. FIXED EXPENSES (ADMINISTRATIVE)
  a. _____
  b. _____
  c. _____
  d. _____
  e. _____
  f. _____
  g. Miscellaneous fixed expense _____
  TOTAL ADMINISTRATIVE EXPENSE _____

5. ASSETS (LONG-TERM PURCHASES) _____
  Cash to be paid out in current period

6. LIABILITIES
  Cash outlay for retiring debts, loans,
  and/or accounts payable _____

7. OWNER EQUITY
  Cash to be withdrawn by owner _____

TOTAL CASH TO BE PAID OUT $ _____

Sources of Cash Worksheet

Business Name: _____

Time Period Covered: _____ ___, _____ to _____ ___, _____

---

1. CASH ON HAND _____

2. SALES (REVENUES)

Product sales income _____

Services income _____

Deposits on sales or services _____

Collections on accounts receivable _____

3. MISCELLANEOUS INCOME

Interest income

Payments to be received on loans _____

4. SALE OF LONG-TERM ASSETS _____

5. LIABILITIES _____

Loan funds (to be received during current period; from banks, through the SBA, or from other lending institutions)

6. EQUITY

Owner investments (sole prop/partners) _____

Contributed capital (corporation) _____

Sale of stock (corporation) _____

Venture capital _____

TOTAL CASH AVAILABLE

A. Without sales = $ _____

B. With sales = $ _____

Pro Forma Cash Flow Statement

Business Name: _____

Year: _____

	Jan	Feb	Mar	Apr	May	Jun	6-MONTH TOTALS	Jul	Aug	Sep	Oct	Nov	Dec	12-MONTH TOTALS
BEGINNING CASH BALANCE														
CASH RECEIPTS														
A. Sales/revenues														
B. Receivables														
C. Interest income														
D. Sale of long-term assets														
TOTAL CASH AVAILABLE														
CASH PAYMENTS														
A. Cost of goods to be sold														
1. Purchases														
2. Material														
3. Labor														
Total cost of goods														
B. Variable expenses														
1.														
2.														
3.														
4.														
5.														
6.														
7. Misc. variable expense														
Total variable expenses														
C. Fixed expenses														
1.														
2.														
3.														
4.														
5.														
6.														
7. Misc. fixed expense														
Total fixed expenses														
D. Interest expense														
E. Federal income tax														
F. Other uses														
G. Long-term asset payments														
H. Loan payments														
I. Owner draws														
TOTAL CASH PAID OUT														
CASH BALANCE/DEFICIENCY														
LOANS TO BE RECEIVED														
EQUITY DEPOSITS														
ENDING CASH BALANCE														

Quarterly Budget Analysis

Business Name: _____   **For the Quarter Ending:** _____ __, _____

BUDGET ITEM	THIS QUARTER			YEAR-TO-DATE		
	Budget	Actual	Variation	Budget	Actual	Variation
SALES REVENUES						
Less cost of goods						
GROSS PROFITS						
VARIABLE EXPENSES						
1.						
2.						
3.						
4.						
5.						
6.						
7. Miscellaneous variable expense						
FIXED EXPENSES						
1.						
2.						
3.						
4.						
5.						
6.						
7. Miscellaneous fixed expense						
NET INCOME FROM OPERATIONS						
INTEREST INCOME						
INTEREST EXPENSE						
NET PROFIT (Pretax)						
TAXES						
NET PROFIT (After Tax)						

NON-INCOME STATEMENT ITEMS

1. Long-term asset repayments						
2. Loan repayments						
3. Owner draws						

BUDGET DEVIATIONS

	This Quarter	Year-to-Date
1. Income statement items:		
2. Non-income statement items:		
3. Total deviation		

Three-Year Income Projection

Business Name: **Updated:** _____ ___, _____

_____	YEAR 1 ____	YEAR 2 20___	YEAR 3 20___	TOTAL 3 YEARS
INCOME				
1. Sales revenues				
2. Cost of goods sold (c – d)				
a. Beginning inventory				
b. Purchases				
c. C.O.G. avail. sale (a + b)				
d. Less ending iventory (12/31)				
3. Gross profit on sales (1-2)				
EXPENSES				
1. Variable (selling) (a thru h)				
a.				
b.				
c.				
d.				
e.				
f.				
g. Miscellaneous selling expense				
h. Depreciation (prod/serv assets)				
2. Fixed (administrative) (a thru h)				
a.				
b.				
c.				
d.				
e.				
f.				
g. Miscellaneous fixed expense				
h. Depreciation (office equipment)				
TOTAL OPERATING EXPENSES (1 + 2)				
NET INCOME OPERATIONS (GPr – Exp)				
OTHER INCOME (interest income)				
OTHER EXPENSE (interest expense)				
NET PROFIT (LOSS) BEFORE TAXES				
TAXES 1. Federal, self-employment				
2. State				
3. Local				
NET PROFIT (LOSS) AFTER TAXES				

Break-Even Analysis Graph

Business Name: _____   **Analysis Date:** _____ __, _____

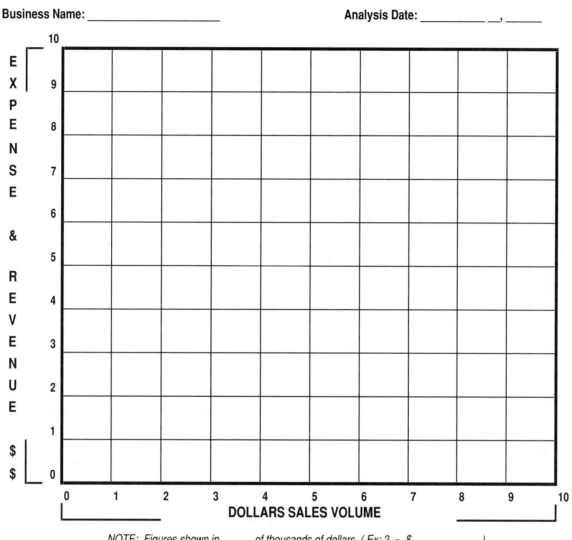

NOTE: Figures shown in _____ of thousands of dollars (Ex: 2 = $ _____)

Break-Even Point Calculation

B-E Point (Sales) = Fixed Costs + [(Variable Costs/Estimated Revenues) x Sales]

1. B-E Point (Sales) = $_____ + [($_____ / $_____) x Sales]

2. B-E Point (Sales) = $_____ + (_____ x Sales)

3. Sales = $_____ + _____ Sales

4. Sales − _____ Sales = $_____

5. _____ Sales = $_____

6. Sales (S) = $_____ / _____

Break-Even Point	
S =	$

Balance Sheet

Business Name: _____   **Date:** _____ ___, _____

ASSETS

Current assets

Cash	$ _____
Petty cash	$ _____
Accounts receivable	$ _____
Inventory	$ _____
Short-term investments	$ _____
Prepaid expenses	$ _____

Long-term investments $ _____

Fixed assets

Land (valued at cost) $ _____

Buildings $ _____
  1. Cost   _____
  2. Less acc. depr.   _____

Improvements $ _____
  1. Cost   _____
  2. Less acc. depr.   _____

Equipment $ _____
  1. Cost   _____
  2. Less Acc. Depr.   _____

Furniture $ _____
  1. Cost   _____
  2. Less acc. depr.   _____

Autos/vehicles $ _____
  1. Cost   _____
  2. Less acc. depr.   _____

Other assets
  1. $ _____
  2. $ _____

TOTAL ASSETS $ _____

LIABILITIES

Current liabilities

Accounts payable	$ _____
Notes payable	$ _____
Interest payable	$ _____

Taxes payable
  Federal income tax $ _____
  Self-employment tax $ _____
  State income tax $ _____
  Sales tax accrual $ _____
  Property tax $ _____

Payroll accrual $ _____

Long-term liabilities
Notes payable $ _____

TOTAL LIABILITIES $ _____

NET WORTH (EQUITY)

Proprietorship $ _____
  or
Partnership
  (name)_____, ___% equity $ _____
  (name)_____, ___% equity $ _____
  or
Corporation
  Capital stock $ _____
  Surplus paid in $ _____
  Retained earnings $ _____

TOTAL NET WORTH $ _____

Assets – Liabilities = Net Worth
and
Liabilities + Equity = Total Assets

Profit & Loss (Income) Statement

Business Name: _____

For the Year: _____

	Jan	Feb	Mar	Apr	May	Jun	6-MONTH TOTALS	Jul	Aug	Sep	Oct	Nov	Dec	12-MONTH TOTALS
INCOME														
1. Net sales (Gr – R&A)														
2. Cost of goods to be sold														
a. Beginning inventory														
b. Purchases														
c. C.O.G. available for sale														
d. Less ending inventory														
3. Gross profit														
EXPENSES														
1. Variable (selling) expenses														
a.														
b.														
c.														
d.														
e.														
f.														
g. Misc. variable expense														
h. Depreciation														
Total variable expenses														
1. Fixed (admin) expenses														
a.														
b.														
c.														
d.														
e.														
f.														
g. Misc. fixed expense														
h. Depreciation														
Total fixed expenses														
Total operating expense														
Net Income From Operations														
Other Income (Interest)														
Other Expense (Interest)														
Net Profit (Loss) Before Taxes														
Taxes: a. Federal														
b. State														
c. Local														
NET PROFIT (LOSS) AFTER TAXES														

Profit & Loss (Income) Statement

Business Name: _____

Beginning: _____ ___, _____   **Ending:** _____ ___, _____

INCOME		
1. Sales revenues		$
2. Cost of goods sold (c – d)		
a. Beginning inventory (1/01)		
b. Purchases		
c. C.O.G. avail. sale (a + b)		
d. Less ending inventory (12/31)		
3. Gross profit on sales (1 – 2)		$
EXPENSES		
1. Variable (selling) (a thru h)		
a.		
b.		
c.		
d.		
e.		
f.		
g. Misc. variable (selling) expense		
h. Depreciation (prod/serv. assets)		
2. Fixed (administrative) (a thru h)		
a.		
b.		
c.		
d.		
e.		
f.		
g. Misc. fixed (administrative) expense		
h. Depreciation (office equipment)		
Total operating expenses (1 + 2)		
Net income from operations (GP – Exp)		$
Other income (interest income)		
Other expense (interest expense)		
Net profit (loss) before taxes		$
Taxes		
a. Federal		
b. State		
c. Local		
NET PROFIT (LOSS) AFTER TAXES		$

Financial Statement Analysis
Ratio Table

Business Name: _____   **For the Year:** _____

Type of Analysis	Formula	Projected: Year 1	Historical: Year 1
1. Liquidity analysis a. Net working capital	**Balance Sheet** Current Assets — Current Liabilities	Current Assets _____ Current Liabilities _____ **Net Working Capital** $ _____	Current Assets _____ Current Liabilities _____ **Net Working Capital** $ _____
b. Current ratio	**Balance Sheet** Current Assets Current Liabilities	Current Assets _____ Current Liabilities _____ **Current Ratio** ____ . ____	Current Assets _____ Current Liabilities _____ **Current Ratio** ____ . ____
c. Quick ratio	**Balance Sheet** Current Assets minus Inventory Current Liabilities	Current Assets _____ Inventory _____ Current Liabilities _____ **Quick Ratio** ____ . ____	Current Assets _____ Inventory _____ Current Liabilities _____ **Quick Ratio** ____ . ____
2. Profitability analysis a. Gross profit margin	**Income Statement** Gross Profits Sales	Gross Profits _____ Sales _____ **Gross Profit Margin** _____ %	Gross Profits _____ Sales _____ **Gross Profit Margin** _____ %
b. Operating profit margin	Income From Operations Sales	Income From Ops. _____ Sales _____ **Operating Profit Margin** _____ %	Income From Ops. _____ Sales _____ **Operating Profit Margin** _____ %
c. Net profit margin	Net Profits Sales	Net Profits _____ Sales _____ **Net Profit Margin** _____ %	Net Profits _____ Sales _____ **Net Profit Margin** _____ %
3. Debt ratios a. Debt to assets	**Balance Sheet** Total Liabilities Total Assets	Total Liabilities _____ Total Assets _____ **Debt to Assets Ratio** _____ %	Total Liabilities _____ Total Assets _____ **Debt to Assets Ratio** _____ %
b. Debt to equity	Total Liabilities Total Owners' Equity	Total Liabilities _____ Total Owners' Equity _____ **Debt to Equity Ratio** _____ %	Total Liabilities _____ Total Owners' Equity _____ **Debt to Equity Ratio** _____ %
4. Measures of investment a. ROI *(Return on Investment)*	**Balance Sheet** Net Profits Total Assets	Net Profits _____ Total Assets _____ **ROI (Return on Invest.)** _____ %	Net Profits _____ Total Assets _____ **ROI (Return on Invest.)** _____ %
5. Vertical financial statement analysis	**Balance Sheet** 1. Each asset % of Total Assets 2. Liability & Equity % of Total L&E **Income Statement** 3. All items % of Total Revenues	**NOTE:** *See Attached* **Balance Sheet &** **Income Statement**	**NOTE:** *See Attached* **Balance Sheet &** **Income Statement**
6. Horizontal financial statement analysis	**Balance Sheet** 1. Assets, Liab & Equity measured against 2nd year. Increases and decreases stated as amount & % **Income Statement** 2. Revenues & Expenses measured against 2nd year. Increases and decreases stated as amount & %	**NOTE:** *See Attached* **Balance Sheet** **&** **Income Statement**	**NOTE:** *See Attached* **Balance Sheet** **&** **Income Statement**

Competition Evaluation Worksheet

1. COMPETITOR: _____

    _____

2. LOCATION: _____

    _____

3. PRODUCTS OR SERVICES OFFERED: _____

    _____

4. METHODS OF DISTRIBUTION: _____

    _____

5. IMAGE: _____

    a. Packaging: _____

    b. Promotional materials: _____

    c. Methods of advertising: _____

    d. Quality of product or service: _____

6. PRICING STRUCTURE: _____

    _____

7. BUSINESS HISTORY & CURRENT PERFORMANCE: _____

    _____

8. MARKET SHARE (number, types, and location of customers): _____

    _____

9. STRENGTHS (the strengths of the competition can become your strengths): _____

    _____

10. WEAKNESSES (looking at the weaknesses of the competition can help you find ways of being unique and of benefiting the customer):

    _____

    _____

Note: A Competition Evaluation Worksheet should be made for each competitor. Keep these records and update them. It pays to continue to rate your competition throughout the lifetime of your business.

GLOSSARY OF BUSINESS AND FINANCIAL TERMS

The following glossary will define business and financial terms with which you may not be familiar. Use of these terms will help you to speak and write in a language that will be understood by potential lenders and investors as well as business associates with whom you may be dealing.

account A record of a business transaction.

accountant One who is skilled at keeping business records. Usually, a highly trained professional rather than one who keeps books. An accountant can set up the books needed for a business to operate and help the owner understand them.

accounts receivable A record of what is owed to you. All of the credit accounts taken together are your "accounts receivable."

amortization To liquidate on an installment basis: the process of gradually paying off a liability over a period of time.

analysis Breaking an idea or problem down into its parts: a thorough examination of the parts of anything.

articles of incorporation A legal document filed with the state which sets forth the purposes and regulations for a corporation. Each state has different regulations.

asset Anything of worth that is owned. Accounts receivable are an asset.

bad debts Money owed to you that you cannot collect.

balance The amount of money remaining in an account.

balance sheet An itemized statement which lists the total assets and the total liabilities of a given business to portray its net worth at a given moment in time.

bookkeeping The process of recording business transactions into the accounting records.

breakeven analysis A method used to determine the point at which the business will neither make a profit nor incur a loss. That point is expressed in either the total dollars of revenue exactly offset by total expenses or in total units of production, the cost of which exactly equals the income derived by their sale.

budget A plan expressed in financial terms.

business venture Taking financial risks in a commercial enterprise.

capital Money available to invest or the total of accumulated assets available for production.

capital equipment Equipment that you use to manufacture a product, provide a service, or use to sell, store, and deliver merchandise. Such equipment will not be sold in the normal course of business, but will be used and worn out or consumed in the course of business.

cash Money in hand or readily available.

cash discount A deduction that is given for prompt payment of a bill.

cash flow The actual movement of cash into and out of a business: cash inflow and cash outflow.

cash receipts The money received by a business from customers.

collateral Something of value given or held as a pledge that a debt or obligation will be fulfilled.

contract An agreement regarding mutual responsibilities between two or more parties.

controllable expenses Those expenses which can be controlled or restrained by the business person.

corporation A voluntary organization of persons, either actual individuals or legal entities, legally bound together to form a business enterprise; an artificial legal entity created by government grant and treated by law as an individual.

co-signers Joint signers of a loan agreement, pledging to meet the obligations in case of default.

customs broker Licensed individual, who for a fee, handles the necessary papers and steps in obtaining clearance of goods through the customs.

customs duty Tax levied on goods imported into the United States. In some nations it may also refer to the tax on goods exported from that country.

debit Monies paid out.

debt That which is owed.

debt capital The part of the investment capital which must be borrowed.

depreciation A decrease in value through age, wear, or deterioration. Depreciation is a normal expense of doing business which must be taken into account. There are laws and regulations governing the manner and time periods that may be used for depreciation.

entrepreneur An innovator of business enterprise who recognizes opportunities to introduce a new product, a new process, or an improved organization, and who raises the necessary money, assembles the factors for production, and organizes an operation to exploit the opportunity.

equity The monetary value of a property or business that exceeds the claims and/or liens against it by others.

financial statements Documents that show your financial situation.

fixed expenses Those costs that don't vary from one period to the next. Generally, these expenses are not affected by the volume of business. Fixed expenses are the basic costs that every business will have each month.

freight forwarder Company responsible for handling transport of imported and exported goods; deals with documentation, permits, and transport.

gross Overall total before deductions.

income statement A financial document that shows how much money (revenue) came in and how much money (expense) was paid out. See also profit & loss statement.

interest The cost of borrowing money.

inventory A list of assets being held for sale.

lease A long-term rental agreement.

letter of credit Instrument issued by a bank to an individual or business by which the bank substitutes its own credit for that of the individual or business.

liability insurance Risk protection for actions for which a business is liable.

limited partnership A legal partnership where some owners are allowed to assume responsibility only up to the amount invested.

liquidate To settle a debt or to convert to cash.

loan Money lent at interest.

management The art of conducting and supervising a business.

marketing All the activities involved in the buying and selling of a product or service.

merchandise Goods bought and sold in a business. "Merchandise" or stock is a part of inventory.

net What is left after deducting all expenses from the gross.

net worth The owner's equity in a given business represented by the excess of the total assets over the total amounts owing to outside creditors (total liabilities) at a given moment in time. The net worth of an individual is determined by deducting the amount of all personal liabilities from the total of all personal assets.

nonrecurring One time, not repeating. "Nonrecurring" expenses are those involved in starting a business, which only have to be paid once and will not occur again.

operating costs Expenditures arising out of current business activities. The costs incurred to do business: salaries, electricity, rental, deliveries, etc.

partnership A legal business relationship of two or more people who share responsibilities, resources, profits, and liabilities.

payable Ready to be paid. One of the standard accounts kept by a bookkeeper is "accounts payable." This is a list of those bills that are current and due to be paid.

profit Financial gain; returns over expenditures.

profit & loss statement A list of the total amount of sales (revenues) and total costs (expenses). The difference between revenues and expenses is your profit or loss. Same as income statement.

profit margin The difference between your selling price and all of your costs.

pro forma A projection or estimate of what may result in the future from actions in the present. A pro forma financial statement is one that shows how the actual operations of the business will turn out if certain assumptions are achieved.

ratio The relationship of one thing to another. A "ratio" is a shortcut way of comparing things that can be expressed as numbers or degrees.

receivable Ready for payment. When you sell on credit, you keep an "accounts receivable" as a record of what is owed to you and who owes it. In accounting, a "receivable" is an asset.

retail Selling directly to the consumer.

service business A retail business that deals in activities for the benefit of others.

share One of the equal parts into which the ownership of a corporation is divided. A "share" represents a part ownership in a corporation.

stock An ownership share in a corporation; another name for a share. Another definition would be accumulated merchandise.

takeover The acquisition of one company by another.

target market The specific individuals, distinguished by socio-economic, demographic, and interest characteristics, who are the most likely potential customers for the goods and services of a business.

tariff Duties imposed on exports and imports.

terms of sale The conditions concerning payment for a purchase.

trade credit Permission to buy from suppliers on open account.

volume An amount or quantity of business; the "volume" of a business is the total it sells over a period of time.

wholesale Selling for resale.

working capital, net The excess of current assets over current liabilities.

INDEX